Eliakum Zunser

Eliakum Zunser

POET OF HIS PEOPLE

By Sol Liptzin

BEHRMAN HOUSE, INC. · PUBLISHERS

CONTENTS

INTRODUCTION

ELIAKUM ZUNSER is a legend. He achieved this distinction during his lifetime, and for almost a century the Yiddish-speaking millions have revered him as Eliakum the Bard or even more simply as Eliakum. He has become a fruitful subject for storytellers and weavers of anecdotes. In this process the real man has been obscured and the need has arisen to restore the true contours of this unique personality and his genuine contributions as poetic pioneer of modern Zionism, as the voice of the inarticulate denizen of the Russian Pale, as the singer of the Jewish immigrant generation in America.

Zunser's creative life spanned the decades from the Crimean War to the eve of World War I, the decades when Jewish life was in constant ferment, when ideas were sown that are only now attaining fruition, and movements arose that are only now being crowned with success or finally discarded. Zunser was the sensitive seismograph that faithfully recorded the reactions of the common man to the counsels of despair and to the messianic panaceas, as well as to the less sensational but more practical wisdom of original Jewish thinkers.

When Zunser appeared upon the scene, medievalism was still shrouding Jewish life in Eastern Europe and rabbinism was holding sway over the minds of his coreligionists. Even rebellious spirits, influenced by Western rationalism, wrote solely for the fraternity of the learned in the sacred Hebrew tongue. Zunser dared, at the risk of calumny and ostracism, to bring the fruits of Enlightenment or *Haskalah* to the superstition-ridden masses in their own tongue, the Yiddish of the market place and the home.

In Zunser's youth Czar Nicholas I was heaping harsh decree

7

upon harsh decree on his Jewish subjects in order to breed despair among them and thus break their will to live on as Jews. The worst of these decrees tore children from the arms of mothers and removed them to remote Siberia, far from Jewish settlements. It condemned them to drag out a hopeless existence in military entombment for twenty-five years and more. Zunser, trapped by this decree but miraculously saved, devoted his talents to building up the hope, courage, and integrity of his people. As wedding bard and at public festivities, he brought cheer and merriment to ever-widening audiences and helped to lighten, with his heart-warming verses and catchy tunes, burdensome days and sorrow-laden nights in ghetto communities.

Zunser's most creative period coincided with the reign of Alexander II, the so-called Golden Age of Russian Jewry. The spirit of liberalism, which brought about the emancipation of the serfs, opened up to the Jews wider economic opportunities, equality of education, freer participation in the arts, sciences, and professions. At the same time, however, it also gave rise to certain unhealthy phenomena and unleashed various dangerous forces. Enlightenment led to assimilation and Russification at an ever-increasing tempo. The final results included, on the one hand, a weakening of Jewish internal cohesion, as the financial and intellectual elite strove for a complete break with the Jewish past, even to the point of conversion. On the other hand, there was an intensification of anti-Jewish sentiment among the majority population, which resented the intrusion of too many representatives of a strange ethnic group into the Slavic cultural domain. Zunser foresaw these developments. He warned of the poison that lurked in an overdosage of alien manna. He foretold the price in suffering that would have to be paid by the entire Jewish population for the sins of those who strayed too far from the ways ordained for this unique group by God or destiny. The present generation, experiencing the Golden Age of American Jewry, might well profit from a better acquaintance with these historic developments that led in Eastern Europe, no less than later on in Central Europe, from Enlightenment and Assimilation to pogroms and efforts at utter annihilation. Zunser's poems, satires, and essays of the 1860's and 1870's reflect attitudes, both fruitful and erroneous, that still deserve careful pondering in our day.

Zunser's influence reached its peak during the reign of Alexander III. When catastrophe broke upon Russian Jewry in the 1880's, he directed his people's gaze to a fairer goal than the inhospitable Czarist realm. He became the singer of Zion, the inspirer of the hardy, pre-Herzlian pioneers who set out to reclaim the ancient soil of Israel with plow and shovel and who sought, in the process of colonization, to restore their own souls to health and happiness.

When fate prevented Zunser from joining these pioneers, who sang his songs in fields and orange groves, he migrated westward along with hundreds of thousands of his coreligionists, and became the lyricist of social justice in the New World. He became the preacher of the dignity of labor at a time when sweatshops and peddling were undermining Jewish morale. He became the eloquent advocate of a creative integration of Jewish and American ideals, an integration not of the melting-pot variety but one in which Jew and Gentile might live in an harmonious interchange of cultural values.

Two World Wars have swept over the earth since Zunser's death and still the nations who inhabit it are seething with turmoil and unrest. Amidst the present clash of ideologies embracing vast continents, Zunser's people, more grievously wounded than all others by the recent cataclysm, is groping its way past confusion and beyond despair to new clarity and to an intense reaffirmation of its own historic way of life. It seeks inspiration for the long, arduous, heroic road ahead in its seers and singers of the many, many generations since Abraham first set forth from Ur of the Chaldees in pursuit of an unearthly vision, and David of Bethlehem first sang psalms of the Lord whose spirit dwells in Zion. As a faithful interpreter of Israel's pain and Israel's role on this terrestrial planet, Elia-kum Zunser, who in the night of Jewish affliction comforted his coreligionists with his songs of a new dawn, must ever be counted among the pioneers of the contemporary Jewish renascence.

BIBLIOGRAPHIC NOTE

A BIBLIOGRAPHY of Eliakum Zunser's publications is available in Zalman Reisen's *Lexikon fun der yiddisher Literatur, Presse, un Filologye*, Vilna, 1929, III, 267–271. This bibliography supersedes the earlier one included in S. M. Ginsburg and P. S. Marek's *Ievreyskia Narodnia Piesni V Rossii*, St. Petersburg, 1901, pp. IX–XIII.

Zunser's *Ale Verk*, New York, 1920, contains, in three volumes, almost all his printed poems, his drama *Mekhiras Yosef*, his autobiography *Geshikhte fun mein Leben*, a few prose selections, two riddles, and several aphorisms. This is the basic text and the main source for our knowledge of Zunser. The wording does not, however, always correspond with that in the earlier editions, probably because several variants were available to the editors and the last rather than the first wording seemed to have been generally preferred as closer to the bard's final intentions. The contemporary Yiddish poet B. Bialostotsky appended to each volume explanatory notes for obsolete expressions that are no longer easily understandable and for customs, folkways, and historic events with which readers nowadays are not as well acquainted as were Zunser's audiences.

Zunser's *feuilletons* of the 1870's in *Kol L'Am* have hitherto escaped notice, probably because they generally appeared under a pseudonym.

Zunser's melodies are available in *Selected Songs*, arranged for voice with piano accompaniment by William Fichandler, based on notes by Joseph Rumshinsky, New York, 1928. This volume also contains English paraphrases of the Yiddish songs by Maximilian Hurwitz. The musical illustrations used in the present volume are taken from the transcriptions by Joseph

Rumshinsky, who made the notations as Zunser sang the melodies to him shortly before the poet's death. The melodies to several songs in *Mekhiras Yosef* are included in the text of the drama, reprinted in *Ale Verk*.

Zunser frequently contributed to Yiddish periodicals, annuals, and anthologies. These isolated poems were afterwards reprinted in his various collections.

The literature on Zunser is enormous and almost entirely in Yiddish. The many articles in newspapers and periodicals testify to his great vogue, but only a few are of importance for literary scholarship and these have been mentioned in the present study.

This study could not have appeared but for the cooperation of the Zunser family. Mr. Charles Zunser, the bard's son, placed at my disposal not only published material gathered during a lifetime by himself and by his older brother Philip, but he also recorded his personal recollections of the Zunser Circle in New York. His vivid narrative of his father's last days is available in Yiddish in *Ale Verk*. He has, moreover, been most generous with his time and comments during the various stages of the present work. Mrs. Sadie Hyman, the bard's daughter, was helpful with her recorded notes on the last years of her father and mother. It is a pleasant duty to acknowledge my indebtedness.

SOL LIPTZIN

Eliakum Zunser

CHAPTER I

Ancestry

AMERICAN Jews are numbered in the millions.
Some of them are descendants of the Sephardic merchants who
came in the seventeenth and eighteenth centuries from Western
Europe to the newly established colonies in order to trade and
to worship in freedom. A larger group traces its ancestry back
to the Central European idealists and realists who, throughout
the nineteenth century, sought a wider field for their industrial
and commercial talents, unhindered by political disabilities and
religious discrimination. But the largest group stems from the
immigrant generation that left Eastern Europe in the third of a
century between the Russian pogroms of 1881 and the outbreak
of the First World War in 1914. This immigrant generation
found in Eliakum Zunser the lyric voice that gave utterance to
its simple joys and sorrows, thoughts and dreams, both in the
Old World and the New.

Zunser was affectionately known as the People's Bard. His
songs lulled to sleep the child in its cradle, and blessed the bride
on her wedding day. His verses accompanied venturesome
youth as it set forth across the Atlantic in search of a brighter
future, and his melodies seeped into the hearts of aging fathers
and mothers left behind in pogrom-ridden provinces. He was
the sensitive interpreter of Jewish martyrdom and Jewish glory
in an era not unlike our own, an era when martyrdom and glory
were the usual experiences of the average denizen of the
ghetto.

Zunser gave his heart to his people and they returned his love. They did not venerate him as a unique genius. They felt akin to him and they shared with him their pain-laden sighs, their gifts of tears, their cries of exultation.

Zunser was born in Vilna on October 13, 1836, and died in New York on September 22, 1913. The seventy-seven years of his life witnessed momentous transformations in habitual Jewish ways of thinking and feeling. At his birth, events set in motion by French revolutionary ideas and by the Napoleonic invasion of Russia were still fresh in the minds of his townsmen, and at his death, the First World War was imminent, a mere matter of months.

Zunser was able to trace his ancestry back to his great-grandfather, Eliahu Zunser, a pupil of Vilna's brightest luminary, the Gaon Rabbi Eliahu. The name Zunser was probably derived from Zunse, a little village near Vilna where the family may have dwelt for generations before moving to the larger town. Long before the intellectual center of Lithuania was incorporated into the Russian Empire, the Zunsers were participating in the activities of the Jewish community, which enjoyed considerable autonomy.

This autonomy was not limited to religious matters. It embraced a wide variety of cultural, financial, and political functions. The Jews formed a town within a town, a state within the state. They had their own courts, which adjudicated disputes between Jew and Jew and handed down binding decisions based on Jewish law. They paid taxes to their own fiscal officers, who were required to turn over only specific funds to the general treasury and who could use other funds for distinct Jewish purposes. The rabbi was the uncrowned ruler of this enclave and the greater his learning, the more absolute was the power he wielded over his willing subjects.

Learning was the magic wand sought by all. To be a pupil of the eminent Gaon meant to join the circle of the elite, and though this did not assure a person adequate bread, it normally did lead him to a marriage into a well-to-do family. He could then continue to study throughout his entire life, unperturbed by mundane matters.

The Gaon Eliahu, who was born in 1720 and died in 1797, left an indelible impress not only upon his immediate disciples but upon all Lithuania, and not merely upon his own century but also far into the nineteenth. Eliakum Zunser still bore in his psychic configuration traits that stemmed from the seed implanted in the days of his great-grandfather by this profoundest theologian of Eastern Jewry.

The Vilna Gaon was a scholar who scorned material wealth and physical comforts. Day and night, year after year, he sat in his study, bent over holy books, seeking to discover the true meaning of the Talmudic sages. He refused to occupy an official rabbinical position, since this might involve him in details of administration and distract him from the pursuit of knowledge for its own sake. There is a legend that once when he was explaining a difficult passage to his disciples, a thunderstorm broke loose. One of his pupils commented on the violence of the thunder and lightning. The Gaon rebuked him for his lack of attention; a person engaged in studying had no right to hear the crash of thunder or to notice the flash of lightning.*

The Gaon has been called the last great theologian of classical Rabbinism. His authority was unquestioned by his townsmen. Though not a single one of his seventy books and tracts was published during his lifetime, his well-reasoned interpretations of divine law and orthodox conduct were transmitted from mouth to mouth by his zealous disciples, and found instant acceptance among rabbis and laymen.

Eliahu Zunser must have led a blameless life in accordance with the severe rules of conduct laid down by the Gaon, because he was honored in death by burial near his revered teacher.

Mordecai Herz Zunser, one of his sons, continued the family tradition of pure scholarship. He settled in Antokol, a suburb of Vilna, and here he was often called upon to settle disputed

*Mendel Silver, *The Gaon of Vilna*, New York, 1905, p. 24.

matters of rabbinical law. His wife was the main support of the family. This was not unusual, since a wife who relieved her husband of domestic cares and freed him for a life of learning might expect to obtain an eternal reward in the world-to-come. Vilna long remembered her as "Sorele, di Zunserke."

Another son was Akiba, the grandfather of the poet. Although Akiba was both tradesman and scholar, he was more interested in the elucidation of Talmudic passages than in the buying and selling of spices. He never sought to get rich through speculative ventures of his own but contented himself with remaining all his years in the service of Isaac Danziger, a prominent Jew of Vilna and the owner of a spice shop.

Isaac Danziger was the son of a noted scholar who had left his native city of Danzig for the Lithuanian metropolis, and who had risen to a high judicial office in the local Jewish community. This scholar, Abraham ben Yekhiel Mikhel Danziger, is generally referred to as the *Khayye Adam*, or *Life of Man*, a title derived from the more popular of his two ethical treatises. This custom of calling an author by the title of his work was prevalent in rabbinical circles. The books of Abraham Danziger explained, in accordance with traditional codes and in the spirit of the Gaon, the proper behavior for a righteous person who wished to walk in the ways of the Lord.

In such a learned, pious environment, Akiba Zunser was unlikely to permit his children to be exposed to the new breezes of Enlightenment and scepticism which were being wafted eastward from the Berlin circle about Moses Mendelssohn. On the contrary, he was very proud of his son Eliahu Mordecai Zunser, who from boyhood on displayed a keenness of mind admirably suited for Talmudic argumentation. This son managed to complete thirteen times over every line of the immense volumes of the Talmud and the numerous commentaries before he was suddenly overtaken, while still in his thirties, by the Angel of Death.

Akiba Zunser was less proud of his other son, Feive Zunser, the father of the poet. No amount of stimulus and no parental pressure could make him a sage in Israel. His talent lay in his skilled hands. He preferred concrete doing to abstract thinking, the handling of materials to the juggling of concepts. This fondness for craftsmanship was looked at askance.

The Jews of Vilna, as of other communities in Russia, Galicia, and Rumania, were divided into two classes: the intellectual aristocrats and the less learned plebeians. The former consisted of rabbis, petty magistrates, heads of academies, cantors, teachers, and students. They spent their lives in houses of prayer, poring over large tomes whose covers were worm-eaten and whose creased pages were worn with age and constant use. They exercised their minds on problems that had been posed by Babylonian sages more than a thousand years before. They despised the pleasures of the senses and sought the purification of their souls by fasting, praying, and following meticulously every precept laid down in holy texts. They regarded manual labor as degrading; it was always a sad decision for a father to have to sanction his son's learning a trade. Akiba Zunser, however, remembered the admonition of the Gaon that whosoever was unfit for pure scholarship should be taught a trade and thus be enabled to support his more gifted coreligionists. Besides, the Napoleonic Wars increased the demand for manual laborers just when Feive was completing his schooling. Lithuania was a principal theatre of conflict in the campaign of 1812, and competent workmen were needed to rebuild towns and villages ravaged by the French and the Russian armies.

Feive Zunser became a carpenter well known for his skill. Yet so poor were the rewards of honest labor that, after the flurry of reconstruction had subsided, he could barely provide for himself and his growing family. When Saturday or a holiday came, he was often at a loss to assure his wife and children the prescribed festive meal.

It was not unusual for a Jew of Vilna to live all week on a diet of herring, potatoes, and bread, and, if necessary, to skip a meal now and then. But a Sabbath without wine or meat or fish was a real tragedy. There is a Yiddish proverb that on Friday evening every Jew is a king. The worries of the week are put aside. The ragged, mud-stained clothes are shed. The ritual bath and the raiments of the Sabbath usher in a new life. The bedraggled, harassed housewife is transformed into a queen and the straw-thatched hovel into a resplendent palace. Every utensil has been cleaned, the lit candles shed a holy glow on the newly burnished candlesticks and the freshly laundered table-cloth. Forgotten are the nervous strains of the morning and afternoon and the fear of the day after the morrow. The struggle for existence that rages all week in the market place, the envy and hatred that lurk in every street, the dreariness of the material world—everything gray and gloomy and defiling yields to sweet enchantment and peaceful sanctity in the fairy realm of the Sabbath. The soul takes on a dazzling brightness. It sings melodies about the angelic hosts and ascends on wings of faith to the seat of the King of Kings. This mood of sacred elevation is heightened by perhaps the first hot meal of the week: fish and fowl and steaming golden soup brought to the gaily decked table in a festive bowl, the heirloom of generations.*

Feive Zunser's anxiety lest his family's Sabbath be ruined must have moved the Angel of the Sabbath to intercede for him at the throne of heaven. In the darkest hours a miracle would repeatedly occur. A landowner would send for him and place an order for work. Perhaps these miracles took place also because of his reputation as an expert carpenter, for other, less skilled craftsmen fared much worse.

To the poet, the years when his father provided for the household, no matter how poorly, seemed Elysian in compari-son with the years of starvation and degradation that followed Feive Zunser's sudden death. Eliakum was barely eleven when this catastrophe overtook the family.

A new military hospital was then being built in Antokol. Feive had been engaged to do carpentry work. Every evening he walked home to see his wife and children, shared a frugal

* See A. S. Sachs, *Khoreve Velten*, New York, 1917, p. 74.

meal with them, and returned to the hospital, where he was
expected to stay overnight. On a December evening in 1847, he
came into the house, recited his evening prayers and a special
prayer commemorating the lighting of the candles. It was the
second night of Hanukkah, the festival recalling the liberation
of the Jews from Greco-Syrian tyranny, a most happy occasion in Jewish homes. After eating and offering thanks to God,
who had bestowed upon him a share in the bounties of this
earth, he examined his oldest son Eliakum on the Bible lesson of
the week. He then took his few pieces of bread and a couple of
potatoes, the food that was to last him until the following
evening, and left the house.

The next morning Feive's wife, Etta Kayle, was horrified
when she got a message from the hospital, inquiring why her
husband had not turned up for the night as usual. Obviously,
something terrible must have happened. A search was immediately begun. Soon Feive's body was discovered in a pile of snow
near the hospital. An autopsy revealed that he had taken ill
suddenly. His cries for help had been unheard—he had collapsed in the snow and died alone.

Feive Zunser was forty-five in December 1847, at the time of
his unexpected end. He had been married for twenty-one years.
He left three children, of whom Eliakum was the oldest. Akiba,
the younger son, was seven. The youngest child was a girl of
about eighteen months.

With the breadwinner gone, the survivors faced starvation.
On the very day of the funeral, when the widow and the
orphaned children came home from the cemetery, they found
the house without a crumb of bread or a peel of potato. The
following morning Etta Kayle's sister arrived, and took the
four famished mourners to her home. Despite her own poverty,
she shared with the bereaved family the little that she had. More
important still, she provided work for the widow. This consisted of delivering milk to those affluent customers who could
afford milk every day. Eliakum's mother had to be up each
morning at five and had to complete her route before she could

think of feeding her children. At first her work did not bring
her sufficient money to provide adequately for four hungry
mouths. But soon the little girl died. Then there was one mouth
less to feed, and each got a more satisfying share of the bread.

It was not by bread alone, however, that Jewish children
lived. From the age of three, food for the soul was also imparted
to them, generally in bigger portions than they could well
digest. Little children, who should have been outdoors in the
fresh air and life-giving sunlight, were shut from dawn to dusk
in a narrow, filthy room, where the air was close and stale, the
floor damp and cold, and the walls dark from the smoky fire-
place in winter and from the hosts of flies in summer. An autocrat, with a cat-o'-nine-tails as scepter, enforced strict attention
and kept young eyes glued to vaguely decipherable hieroglyphs.

Eliakum Zunser was spared from attending this children's
purgatory, known as the *Kheder*, until he was five. During these
early years, in which he was permitted more contact with the
outdoors than were other Jewish children, he learned to observe
details of nature in forest, brook, and ravine. He learned to listen
to the song of birds and to the ripple of waters, and thus to
become more sensitive to sound. He watched the change in the
color of earth from the green of April to the gold of October.
He came to love the soil that responded so richly to the stimu-
lating touch of the plowman and the caressing hand of the
sower of seeds. This early love never left him. It later found
expression in the most famous of his songs, which begins: "In
the plow lies our bliss and blessedness." The precious freedom,
the absence of restraint, the communion with nature, made it
impossible for him to be broken by later adversity or to submit
in his inner soul to the authority of the brutal knout as did
others who were thrust even sooner out of golden childhood.
The poet and wanderer, the dreamer and lover of nature, were
shaped in this pre-school period. It was with his school years,
however, that Zunser's remembered and recorded experiences
began.

CHAPTER II

Boyhood

LITTLE is known of Eliakum Zunser's first school or *Kheder*. Although he began somewhat later than other children, he made such rapid progress that within a year he learned not only to read the entire prayers for weekdays and Sabbath, but also to translate the Pentateuch from the original Hebrew into an archaic Yiddish. This Yiddish was not the vernacular that the boy used in his home but an older form, more properly called *Khumesh-Taytsh*. Its obsolescent vocabulary had survived only in classrooms, where teachers continued to drill, with every new generation, traditional renderings of earlier centuries. Often, therefore, a pupil would translate from the unknown Semitic tongue abstract material far beyond the grasp of a six-year-old into a Judeo-German considerably removed from his own Lithuanian Yiddish. The school never dared to question the holiness of every Hebrew word handed down to Moses at Sinai. It even regarded as semi-sacred the translations into other languages used by the Jews in earlier days, from Aramaic to Old Yiddish, and the individual teacher did not feel free to modernize a vocabulary which was becoming ever more obsolete. Its archaic flavor, which differentiated it from the common speech of the market place, gave added dignity and solemnity to the mental acrobatics.

In his second year at school, Zunser was sufficiently advanced in his studies to be introduced to the legal problems discussed with great subtlety in the Talmudic-Aramaic texts. These codified both the ancient laws of Palestine and the interpretations of jurisprudence by Jewish masters in late Roman antiquity and in Babylonian academies.

From Zunser's references to the *Kheder* in his poems, we can reconstruct to some extent his educational experiences in this primary school. There were three authorities he had to obey: the teacher, the teacher's wife, and the teacher's assistant. He retained vivid memories not of the teacher's face but of his sharp tongue, which scolded and threatened at all hours, and of his restless hand, which was expert at slapping, spanking, and beating. Zunser associated the *Rebitsin,* or teacher's wife, with kitchen tasks. She always wore an apron. When she sent a child on an errand such as fetching water from the well, what a relief from the interminable repetition of incantations and prayers those precious few moments afforded! What a joy to prance with pails and buckets along the streets and to exercise muscles that were becoming flabby from disuse! Zunser also recalled the *Behelfer,* or teacher's assistant, as a glutton. It was the assistant's duty to bring the children to school in the morning and take them home in the dark of night. If the children were too small and if they tired too easily, he had to carry them on his back. Unable to satisfy his hunger with the meager food which the *Rebitsin* left over for him, he helped himself as an uninvited partner to the lunches which the children brought along from home.

The daily lesson was drilled into none-too-attentive boys by teacher and assistant with the aid of a cat-o'-nine-tails, an indispensable educational tool of the *Kheder.* The weekly assignment was begun on Sunday morning. Pupils were expected to master it by Thursday evening. Harsh, indeed, was the fate of a youngster who failed when tested by his father before the Sabbath, or by fathers of prospective pupils in the course of the Sabbath, since failure might result in an economic loss for his teacher. A child learned soon enough to be most cooperative at school. A teacher was more to be feared than mother or father.

An early song of Zunser's, popular during the reign of Alexander II, bore the refrain: "One doesn't tell tales out of school."

In another poem *The Godfather* (*Der Sandek*), Zunser described, probably on the basis of personal observation, a teacher-entrepreneur who made use of the festive ceremony of circumcision, when the boy was but eight days old, to elicit a promise from the parents that their son would be sent to his school. When the parents, a few years later, changed their mind, the teacher threatened to drag them to court and to rain curses upon the head of the child, unless given reparations in cash. The competition between teachers for a new pupil was depicted with venomous skill by Zunser. The first teacher to arrive warns against registering the boy with his colleagues, each of whom is supposedly riddled with faults. One has an overcrowded classroom, smelly, smoky, damp; another is too highbrow, tainted with Moses Mendelssohn's ideas of reform; a third is a glutton and ignoramus, who pinches his wards; a fourth is a wag, who married a shrew. While the first teacher is still talking, a competitor comes upon the scene. The two moral preceptors then begin to fight like vicious roosters. They proceed from shouts and abuses to blows, pulling of beards, tearing of coats. Father and mother look on completely bewildered. The youngster has made up his mind, however; he wants to go with the teacher who gave him a piece of candy.

Zunser must have been a witness to similar scenes in his boyhood, for he afterwards warned prospective teachers: "May God give you a better profession than teaching; but if, alas, you are doomed to teach, conduct yourselves differently. Little creatures need character training above all. So don't let a child hear oaths and curses, because these will burrow into its head like worms into a young apple. Children are wards entrusted to you, and you are paid by fathers and mothers to guard these wards against harm and to implant into them good habits. If a child sees you behaving badly, if it hears falsehood and deception within your walls, the seeds of corruption enter its soul and the beautiful flower will become a prickly thorn."

After two years in the *Kheder* or primary school, Zunser gained admittance to *Ramaila's Yeshiva*. His father was proud that his older son was accepted in this most famous educational institution of Vilna, especially since the satisfactory pursuit of Talmudic studies under teachers of standing meant not only thorough orthodox training but also probable exemption from military service. Four teachers supervised the studies of several hundred pupils of varying ages. The most authoritative of the four was the rector, Rabbi Mordecai Meltzer, who had helped to found the school in 1831, five years before Zunser's birth, and who presided over its destiny during the following two decades.

The students at the Yeshiva, with rare exceptions, had no funds of their own. Since the study of the Torah called for total concentration, it was felt that they were entitled to public support.* This took the form of taxing each householder who could carry the burden with a day's support of a student. Great skill was required on the part of the school authorities to see that each youth was provided for every day of the week, and there were times when even their most strenuous efforts left some students without food for one or two days out of seven. Even those who missed no meals were not too happy with this custom of eating a day here and a day there. Zunser remarked that the most fortunate pupils still had to reckon with seven masters, seven housewives, and seven maids. Yet, all twenty-one together could not satisfy the appetite of a single growing boy. Furthermore, it was most degrading to have to go to a strange house for meals three times a day and to have to knock at seven different doors each week. It was an insult to a young man's dignity. It had a demoralizing effect upon his character. It trained him in flattery, hypocrisy, and servility.

Rabbi Israel Salanter, who presided over *Ramaila's Yeshiva* for a year before founding his own school, tried to abolish the

* C. W. Rhines, "Public Support for Students in the Past," *Yivo Bleter*, 1946, XXVIII, 291–316.

custom of day-eating. He ordained that all who contributed days were to bring the food to the House of Learning rather than to require the student of Torah to interrupt his studies and go to the patron's house. His efforts were not too successful, however, and the custom continued with but slight modifications until the present century.

Zunser described a picturesque personality whom the youth of Vilna venerated as their patron saint because he had developed a unique scheme for providing food for those students who were now and then without a day's board. He was called Simeon *Kaftan* because of his long robe of gray linen which reached to the ground, and he was the most distinguished representative of a special class of mendicants that could flourish nowhere but in the learned town of Vilna. These were the beggars for beggars, pious, good-hearted individuals who collected alms in order to support others and who hoped thereby to earn a special seat in Paradise. They contented themselves with little—a bit of stale bread as a meal, a wooden bench in the synagogue as a couch. They exposed themselves to the jeering of the street urchins and to the vagaries of wind and weather. They turned up at every public function and at every private celebration, reminding the participants that "charity brings salvation from death."

Simeon Kaftan made a living by working during the night for a manufacturer of snuff tobacco. Coming from work, he would take up his position in the main Jewish street every morning, with a large collection box in his hand, and solicit hour after hour contributions for his protégés, the pupils of Vilna's Jewish schools. His background was not known to anyone in town, and he never engaged in lengthy conversations with grown-ups, but all Jews and Christians of the community respected him because of his selfless, untiring devotion to his humane project.

Simeon had unlimited credit with the bakers of Vilna. They supplied him with large loaves of bread, which he distributed in Houses of Learning to famished pupils who were without a day's board. He was most concerned about his wards when the Sabbath came, for it seemed intolerable to him that a young man who devoted his heart and soul to Torah, or learning for its own sake, should go hungry on the holiest day of the week. Simeon would, therefore, spend Saturday afternoons in the courtyard of Vilna's largest synagogue. In front of him was a big pot and in his pockets were large wooden spoons. Vilna's families would send him whatever was left over from the festive meal and he would immediately distribute these delicacies among his studious, unworldly youths.

When Simeon, the beggars' beggar, died, twenty thousand Jews attended his funeral, the pulpits of the town resounded with eulogies, and scoffers who had ridiculed him because of his strange garb were filled with remorse and proposed the continuation of his charitable activities. Count Muraviev, Governor-General of Vilna, was so impressed by his saintliness that he had a portrait of this strange mendicant hung in his official reception hall.

Zunser himself did not resort to day-boarding. Since his mother was well known in Vilna, she would have felt disgraced if her son had had to depend upon the generosity of others. As a result, Zunser probably went hungry more often than the average day-boarder. Each Sunday he left his mother's home in suburban Antokol and made his way on foot to Vilna, where he stayed at the Yeshiva until Friday morning. His mother gave him a loaf of bread and a few kopecks for the week. With this small sum he could barely afford to buy some cooked chick peas twice a day. The inadequate, monotonous diet of bread and peas did not worry him overmuch, however, for his undernourished body found compensation in a feverishly stimulated mind. In his imagination, the emaciated lad saw himself enjoying in another world luscious rewards for his temporary abstinence in this terrestrial vale of tears: a slice of the Leviathan, a cutlet of the Messianic Ox, and wine served only to the elect.

These visions delighted him with special vividness on Thursdays when he, along with his schoolmates, had to stay up all night reviewing the Talmudic passages studied during the entire week.

Zunser was more troubled when he realized that every Friday and every holiday eve when he came home to his family, his mother gave him and his younger brother Akiba whatever food was in the house, while she herself went hungry. He, therefore, decided not to come to Antokol on weekends but rather to depend on the generosity of Simeon Kaftan. Zunser idealized his benefactor: "I cannot recall this holy man without tears in my eyes, and the question often comes to my mind: shall we Jews ever have another saint, another immaculate soul, like Reb Simeon Kaftan of Blessed Memory?"

Chronic undernourishment could not long remain unnoticed. One of his teachers feared that Zunser might be forced to give up further schooling. He therefore appealed to Sarah Gordon, a well-to-do matron of Vilna and a distant relative of the promising youngster, to provide a scholarship for him. She did so and for the next two years Zunser could devote himself wholly to his studies, assured of three meals a day.

The most important event that occurred in *Ramaila's Yeshiva* while Zunser was a pupil was the visit of the Anglo-Jewish aristocrat, Sir Moses Montefiore, in 1846. This philanthropist and humanitarian, who had intervened so successfully in the Damascus Affair of 1840 and had obtained the release of the Turkish Jews libelously accused of ritual murder, was urged to take up the cause of the Russian Jews, who were being subjected to increasingly repressive laws. He was unsuccessful in his efforts to obtain an audience with Czar Nicholas I during the Russian monarch's state visit at the Court of Queen Victoria. He thereupon set out for St. Petersburg to make his plea for his oppressed coreligionists. There he was received by the Czar and the ministers of the government with official courtesy. His remarks were listened to most politely. The Czar suggested that the English nobleman tour some of the Jewish communities and get to know these strange subjects at first hand. Vilna was put on the itinerary.

The city welcomed the eminent guest with tremendous enthusiasm. The entire Jewish population of about 25,000 surged to the streets to catch a glimpse of him. The eleven days of his stay formed one continuous holiday. At *Ramaila's Yeshiva*, Zunser's teacher, Rabbi Mordecai Meltzer, delivered an address in honor of the new Moses who was coming as another deliverer in Jewry's hour of distress. The assembled students listened reverently to the reply made in Hebrew by Montefiore's secretary, the Orientalist L. Loewe. They crowded about the magnificent carriage bearing the aristocrat's coat-of-arms, which included the word Jerusalem in Hebrew characters. This visit did much to raise the spirit of the Jewish community, but except for this betterment of morale, there were no practical, tangible results. The government made no commitments and removed none of the legal hardships from which the Jews suffered.

The Czarist regime justified its anti-Jewish measures on the ground that the Jews were an unproductive sector of the population. They were ashamed of manual labor and they shunned all contact with the soil. Enlightened Jews recognized the desirability of counteracting this deep-rooted prejudice against physical work. Isaac Baer Levinsohn, who has often been called the Moses Mendelssohn of Russian Jewry, advocated that Jewish youth be taught modern languages and the achievements of contemporary culture, and especially that they be trained in new vocations and practical trades. He pointed out, in his Hebrew essays addressed to his coreligionists and endorsed by the government, that the Jews in their early history were preeminently an agricultural people, that only with the loss of their national territory was their economic condition altered. If they subsequently engaged in moneylending and commercial transactions of all kinds, it was because they were not admitted to Christian guilds and were excluded from the ownership of land.

By returning to more productive trades, they would become better citizens and would find their lot under the Czar much improved.*

Similar proposals were submitted by the Hebrew poet Abraham Baer Lebensohn in a memorandum prepared for Moses Montefiore during his stay in Vilna. Lebensohn too attributed the worsening plight of the Jews to their overemphasis of Talmudic education and to their lack of skill in handicrafts.

Young Zunser could not remain unaffected by these new currents of thought, discussed by his classmates vigorously and with considerable sympathy despite the fact that the elders regarded these heresies with utmost contempt. The realization dawned upon him that the wisdom of the rabbinical sages was not the sole wisdom available to man. He was growing up, and he was becoming more and more dissatisfied with the answers offered by his teachers to the questions that concerned him most deeply. What goal could he discern at the end of the long and arduous road he was following through the mazes of the Talmud? Would he too ultimately join the ranks of the intellectually unemployed, the lean and hungry scholars, the useless purveyors of sterile knowledge? There was, of course, the possibility of an appointment as rabbi at some time in the remote future. But it became increasingly clear to him that a trade in hand was of greater value than any such remote possibility. Besides, he did not relish the prospect of being dependent upon his mother's hard-earned pennies or upon the generosity of distant relatives and strangers for many additional years. He therefore decided to face social disapproval and learn a trade. At the same time, he also planned to keep up his Hebrew studies during his free hours.

This decision was not easy for him, but he never regretted it. In his poem *Der Sandek*, he wrote years afterwards:

> We Jews fail to prosper because we are ashamed of manual labor. If people of the better class were to give their children a trade in hand and at the same time an education

* Louis S. Greenberg, *Isaac Baer Levinsohn*, New York, 1930, p. 23.

and good manners, then craftsmanship would revive and the country would have educated Jewish cobblers, tailors, and blacksmiths.

Zunser was attracted to a specialized handicraft, in which he could assume fairly steady employment and which did not require too much physical strength. This was the profession of braiding, the skillful sewing of golden threads on the collars and cuffs of military and civilian officials of all ranks. He was initiated into the braiders' guild and signed a six-year contract as apprentice to a local master-artisan. The latter undertook to teach him the trade and to pay him twenty rubles at the expiration of the contract.

Within a single year Zunser managed to learn the art of braiding to such perfection that his fellow apprentices looked up to him as an expert. Nevertheless, he still faced the prospect of serving for five more years at only nominal pay.

The longer he was away from the Yeshiva, the more practical became his outlook upon life. Since his studies were unsupervised, he could adventure among books of his own choosing. He learned to trust his own insight and to profit by his own experience. He began to view the world realistically, not through the eyes of Talmudic sages. Whereas he had previously sought beauty in yellowed scripts and had dwelt in the dim past, he now turned to the immediate present. He rediscovered the beautiful in nature and in man, unseen by him since childhood. He was stimulated to probe ever deeper with his questions and to seek out ever-new avenues of information. He wondered why he had studied the Pentateuch again and again but had never been permitted to delve into the other books of the Bible, which were also composed in the sacred tongue. He found it illogical that the study of Hebrew grammar and usage, apart from the holy texts, should be frowned upon by his religious instructors.

In his leisure hours, he discovered the sublime poetry of the Psalms, the social idealism of the Prophets, the mature wisdom of Job, and the gentle pessimism of Ecclesiastes. He also taught himself such useful subjects as arithmetic and algebra. He then ventured into modern literature. He obtained the precious works of contemporary Hebrew writers who had been branded as heretics by his former teachers, and he even practiced writing in their style. He was most profoundly influenced by the prose and verse of Hartwig Wessely (Naphtali Herz Weisel), whose popularity in Eastern Europe far exceeded that in his own native Germany.

Wessely was a follower of Moses Mendelssohn, but unlike so many disciples of the great reformer, he was not completely dazzled by the light that suddenly streamed into Jewish life from Germany, France, and England. He did not echo the mocking laughter of Voltaire and he did not lose his faith in God under the blows of Diderot and the Encyclopedists. He did not advocate complete assimilation to European ways. He rather sought to effect a synthesis between Orthodox Judaism and the new spirit of Enlightenment.

Zunser read Wessely's philosophical and political tracts with the same devotion he had formerly given to the Talmud, but these pamphlets spoke solely to his mind and not to his heart. It was Wessely's poetic epic on the life of Moses, *Shire Tifereth,* which warmed his heart and which roused his slumbering poetic talent. This epic in eighteen cantos, publication of which was begun in 1789 and completed in 1829, was regarded in the mid-nineteenth century as the finest poetic achievement of the neo-Hebraic revival, but it is rarely read today. It was modeled after Klopstock's *Messias,* an epic of man's redemption, which, in turn, was based upon Milton's *Paradise Lost* and *Paradise Regained.* When young Zunser in his fourteenth or fifteenth year composed his first song in Hebrew, *Zion, Most Beautiful,* under the spell of Wessely's rhetorical verses, he was probably unaware that the shade of the English poet John Milton was at his elbow directing the flow of his thoughts.

Zunser was gradually arriving at the same conclusions as

Wessely. The more he read, the more he was convinced that faith and reason, Torah and Enlightenment, could go hand in hand without detriment to each other. He came to feel that reason would cleanse faith of the accumulated weeds of superstition, and Enlightenment would restore to the Torah its original purity by brushing away all the absurd interpretations with which the centuries had befogged it.

This approach was shared by a growing minority of Jewish intellectuals in Vilna. These young men had to reckon with the violent hostility of their parents, who feared, not entirely without justification, that the first breach in the protecting wall erected about the ancient religion might lead to ultimate collapse of the entire venerated structure. They therefore insisted on unswerving adherence to every belief, custom, and ritual sanctioned by age. The young rationalists were known as *Maskilim*, but their opponents dubbed them *Berliners* or *Berlincheks*, because the new wisdom they imbibed stemmed from Berlin, from the philosophic circle about Moses Mendelssohn. *Berliner* was a term of scorn and hatred in the mouths of the fathers. But to the sons, it designated membership in an international brotherhood of clearheaded thinkers. They smuggled into their attics the new Hebrew periodicals published abroad, and risked real danger in exploring this contraband wisdom by candlelight in the dead of night.

In his *Autobiography*, Zunser paid tribute to these courageous souls:

> The small group of Jewish pioneers of Enlightenment in Russia was surrounded on all sides by a powerful foe. Curses and bans rained down upon them. Communities ostracized them and turned them over to the military. The schism between parents and children grew wider and deeper from day to day. Jewish youths suffered terrible persecution but they did not retreat from the battlefield. They waged war for a holy ideal: for a purified faith and for liberating Enlightenment. They were the modern Mac-

cabees. They unfurled the banner of Jewish nationalism and they carried it from town to town, from village to village. Every city and hamlet contained a few of these heroes, who exercised great influence over their fellows and who recruited ever new adherents until a tremendous army was formed.

The great-grandson of Eliahu Zunser, who in the eighteenth century sat at the feet of the Vilna Gaon, was drifting ever further into the camp of the radicals, the innovators, the heretics.

CHAPTER III

Youth

IN HIS adolescent years, Eliakum Zunser was making rapid strides not only in his thinking but also in his ability to feel and observe. Now that his eyes were no longer glued to the Talmud from dawn to dusk, he could become intensely aware of the physical world about him. He could recapture the sense of freedom that had eluded him since his fifth year—the joy in being alive, the light-heartedness which comes with healthy exercise in play and fun. He could associate with companions whose talk was not of books but of things fashioned by trained eyes and skillful hands. Among his playmates in Kochel's Hoif, a Vilna courtyard, the youngest and brightest was Motke, the innkeeper's son, who was later to win renown as Mark Antokolsky, the favorite sculptor of Czar Alexander II.

Zunser tells in his memoirs of some of the humiliations that his playmate Motke had to endure because he would not sit quietly on the Talmudic bench. He would steal away from the class-room, climb stealthily to the attic of the inn, and there carve out of wood or mold out of clay various figures which were derided as idols by those who saw them. Often the boy's father found him at this unholy task and beat him savagely. Once he dragged him down from the attic and placed him at the water pump in the courtyard in freezing weather. He kept him pumping for a long time as punishment for breaking the divine commandment which forbade the making of graven images. The young genius nearly froze to death. Still he would not stop his woodcarving. The father then threatened to make him a chimney sweep. But the boy proved incorrigible in his passion for the plastic arts. Finally, he won his battle. He was taken out of school and apprenticed to a woodcarver. Year after year, he worked in the Vilna ghetto, not understood by his neighbors, eating the bitter bread of poverty, and creating artistic objects for which there was little demand. Zunser, the braider's apprentice, sympathized with the struggling sculptor, who was later to rise from poverty and disgrace to wealth and honor, but he could be of no practical help.

The years of suffering left their mark upon Antokolsky's masterpieces of bronze and marble. He became the sculptor of man's sorrow and of man's inhumanity to man. He was twenty years old when a stroke of fortune rescued him from neglect and hunger. The wife of Governor-General Nazimov saw his woodcarvings, recognized his genius, and had him sent to the Imperial Academy of Art at St. Petersburg. Before long, the report reached his former classmates in Vilna that the woodcarver had become an eminent sculptor. Czar Alexander II had climbed up to Motke's fourth-floor studio and acquired the statue "Ivan the Terrible" for the Hermitage Museum. Ten years after Antokolsky left his native city, he returned to wed the daughter of one of its richest merchants. Then he went abroad and spent most of his remaining years in Paris and Rome. Vilna remembered, however, that the venerated sculptor and the people's bard had played together in Kochel's Hoif in their young years, and erected a tablet on this spot in honor of Mark Antokolsky and Eliakum Zunser.

Not too many of Zunser's hours were devoted to play, for the master-braider insisted that all tasks be done on time. Nevertheless, while his hands were at work braiding golden threads, Zunser's imagination was free to roam far and wide. It transported him to groves of Eden and to palaces in exotic lands. It revivified for him legendary heroes and heroines of the Jewish past. The verses of the *Song of Songs*, which he had so often chanted on Friday evenings and in which he had found expressed the longing of Israel for its God, he now reinterpreted in his daydreams more literally as love lyrics of the ardent King Solomon for the swarthy Sulamith.

Zunser had associated at *Kheder* and Yeshiva with boys only, and had shared their attitude of superiority and apparent indifference toward the less educated sex. Now for the first time he was brought into constant contact with a girl of about his own age, his master's daughter. The youth had until then been unaware of the irrational forces that motivated human beings in their relations toward each other. Now he found himself sympathizing with a strange creature, a timid girl who had grown up, pure and modest and pious, under her mother's tutelage, and who was being discussed by marriage brokers as a prospective bride. Only after negotiations between the girl's parents and the parents of a marriageable young man were successfully completed did Zunser reflect that there was something wrong in the failure of elders to consult the wishes of the young people involved. His reflections found vent in a sad song entitled *Jewish Marriages* (*Yiddishe Shidukhim*), whose words and melody immediately spread throughout the entire town.

Only one of the original four stanzas has been preserved. In this the youth voiced the protest of his age group against the tendency of elders to lead children to marriage as to the slaughter pen. Whosoever knows how girls are married off, he exclaimed, also knows that such marriages rarely make for happiness. The brokers come with false faces and glib tongues and sing the praises of a young man. Parents are induced to give their consent without consulting their daughter. They then lead the bride to the wedding as to a sacrificial altar. Her eyes are covered with a veil. Her heart is full of wounds. But father and mother walk gleefully beside her, unaware of the years of regret that are to follow.

Unlike Zunser's first philosophic poem, for which Wessely served as model, *Jewish Marriages* was meant to be sung. It gained instant popularity because it was composed in Yiddish, the language of the common people. Hebrew was the normal medium for dignified abstract poetry, appealing to reason and the imagination. Yiddish was the language of the heart. Neither orthodox rabbis nor enlightened scholars, however, deigned to use it. They thus cut themselves off from direct contact with the masses. The joys and sorrows of the ordinary Yiddish-speaking man and woman were reflected principally in anonymous folksongs and folktales. It was, therefore, a bold innovation for Zunser, who had mastered Hebrew as well as had any of his contemporaries, to turn to the despised Yiddish as his poetic vehicle.

The uniqueness of Zunser's achievement cannot be overemphasized. By the end of the nineteenth century Yiddish could boast of a rich literature in prose, verse, and drama. But when Zunser began to write in Yiddish in the 1850's, its very existence as a language was under severe attack. It was referred to not as Yiddish but as a "jargon." The few pamphleteers who resorted to it apologized for its use on the ground of necessity, since they wished to reach ignorant women and uneducated men.

Isaac Baer Levinsohn, who wrote *Di Hefker-Velt*, the first original work of the Russian Enlightenment in Yiddish, circulated it in manuscript form and would not allow it to be published during his lifetime. He looked upon the use of Yiddish as a temporary evil and wished to hasten the day of its disappearance. He called it a corrupt mixture of Hebrew, Russian, French, Polish, and German, a crippled organism in which there was not a sound limb, a language which barely sufficed for simple objects and elementary concepts but which was utterly worthless for elevated discourse. He wondered why Russian Jews clung to this hybrid dialect when they could use either pure German, with its rich and charming vocabulary, or else the speech of their Slavic neighbors. He evolved a theory of the Slavic origin of the Russian Jews, upon whom a corrupt "Judeo-German" was later imposed by immigrants from the West.

Levinsohn's approach was shared by Jewish intellectuals throughout Russia. Not even Mendele Mokher Sforim, who is today revered as the grandfather of modern Yiddish literature and who was born in the same year as Eliakum Zunser, thought of making use of the despised tongue in his early songs and writings composed in the 1850's. Mendele too was an impoverished student, who spent several months at *Ramaila's Yeshiva* under the same teachers as Zunser. He too was struggling valiantly to emancipate himself from his stifling rabbinical environment. But Mendele's first literary ventures were all in Hebrew. Not until about a decade after Zunser's first Yiddish songs did Mendele risk his own barely won reputation as a Hebrew scholar by attempting his first Yiddish story. In his memoirs, he recounted the reasons that induced him to change from Hebrew to Yiddish in 1863. They were the same reasons that led Zunser to this conclusion much earlier.

The following thought came to me [wrote Mendele]. I looked at the life of my people and I wanted to give them stories from the Jewish fountain in the sacred tongue. Most of them, however, didn't understand this tongue. They talked Yiddish. . . . The Yiddish of my time was an empty vessel which contained nothing of beauty, nothing save foolish jokes and gossip. . . . Women and ignorant folk read the stuff and did not really grasp it. The rest of the people were ashamed to read Yiddish, even though they did not know any other language, because they did not want to reveal their backwardness. If a person could not resist temptation and did peep into a Yiddish book, he laughed at himself and explained: I am just having fun looking at what our foolish women are reading. Our intellectuals thought only of writing in our holy tongue and had no interest in the common man. They looked down upon Yiddish with supreme scorn. If in an odd moment one writer out of ten made use of the accursed jargon, he kept his manuscript out of sight, locked and bolted, so that this disgrace would not come to light and harm his good standing. My embarrassment was great indeed when I realized that association with the lowly maid Yiddish would cover me with shame. I listened to the admonitions of my admirers, the lovers of Hebrew, not to drag my name in the gutter and not to squander my talent on the unworthy hussy. But my desire to be useful to my people was stronger than my vanity and I decided: come what may, I shall have pity on Yiddish, the outcast daughter of my people.*

Mendele won over the editor of the influential Hebrew periodical *Hamelitz* to the idea of publishing a Yiddish sheet for the ordinary man. Thus the first Yiddish newspaper on Russian soil, *Kol Mvaser*, was born in 1863. By that time, however, Zunser's Yiddish songs were circulating as penny booklets throughout the land, and were moving the hearts of men, women, and children to laughter and to tears. Zunser's verses were recalling past tragedies, painting present suffering, and inspiring hope of better days to come. If, therefore, Mendele is rightfully called the grandfather of Yiddish literature, Eliakum Zunser, who preceded him, may well lay claim to the title of great-grandfather of this literature. The foundation for Zunser's literary personality as the people's bard was laid in the 1850's, in the years of wandering, in the harsh misfortunes that befell him, and in his discovery that Jews of all social levels responded with weeping and applause to his simple chants and rhymed observations.

After his first year as braider's apprentice, Zunser was anxious to leave his master's home, but found himself bound by a contract. Five more years of servitude loomed ahead under an employer who was becoming ever more hated. If he were to tear himself free, the rules of the guild would make it impossible for him to practice in Vilna the handicraft which he had just learned so well. But how could he stay on and submit to daily abuse by his employer and the latter's wife, daughter, son-in-law, and bawling grandchild? In accordance with the prevailing custom, the bride's family was required to support their new son-in-law in their own home for a year or two or three. Zunser

* Mendele Mokher Sforim, *Ale Verk*, Warsaw, 1928, XIX, 164-5.

could not help but make constant comparisons between himself, the abused apprentice, and the pampered additional member of the household whose infant he was called upon to cradle in spare moments. Escape to a distant community offered the only prospect of relief from his intolerable situation. Undaunted by possible perils, perhaps even lured by a love for adventure, the restless youth set out on foot, traversed all of Lithuania, and crossed over into the Latvian province of Kurland. At Bauska, a town near Riga with a considerable Jewish population, he found a new employer at whose house he could stay. For two years he remained there, working by day as braider and studying at night under the direction of the town's rabbi, Yankele Boisker.

At the same time Zunser continued to keep in touch with the newest tendencies among the *Maskilim*, or enlightened Hebraists. He was especially fond of three secular writers who opened up new horizons for the generation maturing in the mid-century decades. These creators of the neo-Hebraic literature were Mordecai Aaron Guenzburg, Kalman Schulman, and Abraham Mapu.

Although Guenzburg, who has been called the father of modern Hebrew prose, was not a native of Vilna, he worked for a publisher and taught in this city from 1829 until his death in 1846. He opposed the extremes of Assimilation and uncritical Orthodoxy. He did not wish to alter the basic articles of the Jewish faith since he held that these were rooted in Jewish national experience. But he had no objection to their being tested by the laws of logic. He was convinced that Judaism could survive scepticism and honest criticism. Freedom of thought and inquiry was, in his opinion, compatible with true belief. Philosophy was a valuable tool. It could be made to serve religion. It could help to free religion from undesirable parasitical growths. Guenzburg also recommended the study of history in order to better evaluate customs of the past and the present. He translated and adapted several standard historical texts for his Hebrew audience. Among these was *The Discov-*

ery of America by the German author J. H. Campe, a booklet
which helped to shape the legend of America for large sectors
of Eastern Jewry. It was probably Guenzburg's adaptation of
Campe that aroused in Zunser his earliest interest in America as
a land of marvels.

Like Guenzburg, Kalman Schulman was a facile Vilna publicist who sought to bring secular knowledge to Hebrew readers.
It is not certain whether young Zunser ever pored over Schulman's nine-volume history of the world or ten-volume geography of the globe. But there is hardly any doubt that he read and
was fascinated by Schulman's translation of Eugène Sue's
Mysteries of Paris. This bulky novel was then at the crest of
its European vogue. It had been rendered into German from
the original French in 1844, and Schulman's version in Hebrew
was probably taken from the German. When the novel appeared in 1847, it inaugurated a new literary genre in the revived
ancient tongue. The young men who could escape from the
argumentative Talmudic folios found emotional release in this
work of fiction. They shuddered at the breathtaking adven-
tures of virtuous harlots and honest criminals, and last-minute
rescues by a noble prince who moved incognito through the
slums and hideouts of Paris.

Under the influence of Eugène Sue, Abraham Mapu completed the first original novel of Jewish life in the Hebrew
tongue. This historical romance, entitled *Love of Zion,* appeared in 1852, and Zunser was among its earliest readers. It
told of the love of Amnon and Tamar in the days of King
Hezekiah and the prophet Isaiah. It depicted in vivid colors
idyllic scenes of harvest time in the hills and valleys of Judea,
the joyous gathering of the vines, the healthy labor of Jewish
villagers followed by the relaxation of song and dance and
exhilarating laughter. The novel roused in ghetto quarters a
longing for the neglected motherland, an urge to return to the
Palestinian earth. Mapu's impression upon Zunser was enduring.
If the latter afterwards became the singer of the *Khoveve Zion,*
or Lovers of Zion, and if his lyric with the refrain "In the plow

lies our bliss and blessedness" later found an instantaneous echo in the hearts of millions, it was in no small measure because of the emotional conversion to Zion effected among the Russian Jews by Mapu's sentimental, idealizing romance. Zunser expressed in melody and rhyme what Mapu had painted earlier in entrancing prose. The message of Herzl at the close of the century fell on fruitful soil in Eastern Europe because this soil had been thoroughly prepared by the novelist of the people and the bard of the people.

Before Zunser matured into the singer of Zion, however, he had to survive severe blows at the hands of a cruel fate. His all too brief youth came to a sudden end. When his brother was seized for military service and driven on foot to Siberia and when he himself was sold into military servitude, he experienced in his own flesh the horror and the helplessness of Jewish life in the Diaspora.

CHAPTER IV

Cantonist

Zunser's account of his impressment into military service, along with thousands of Jewish children from the ages of eight and nine, reads like a nightmare. Yet his observations are corroborated by official documents and memoirs of his contemporaries who survived similar experiences. The opening of the Czarist archives, after the Revolution of 1917, enabled scholars to confirm almost incredible acts of cruelty and savagery directed against Jews under the guise of military regulations.

In his *Autobiography*, Zunser referred to Jewish history as a book in which every page had a bloodstain. He reviewed the horrors endured by his forefathers in Egypt, Babylon, Rome, and Spain. He then asserted that the largest bloodstain in Jewish history stood for that terrible period in the reign of Czar Nicholas I, when young Jewish children were torn brutally from the arms of their parents and sent off as soldiers.

In reviewing the details of this savagery, unparalleled in all history, the blood in our veins freezes with terror. The mothers whose children were seized by the Egyptians, Chaldeans, Romans, and Spanish priests could at least comfort themselves with the thought that their children escaped long and dire suffering by a quick death. Jewish mothers, during the reign of Nicholas I, did not have even this consolation. Their little ones were grabbed by force, driven to

the remote tundras of Siberia or to the steppes of the
Caucasus, and handed over to savage peasants or to wild
Cossacks to be raised as soldiers. Never again did mothers
see them. Some of these young Jewish victims were forcibly
baptized and remained forever in those remote regions,
while others, who refused to submit to baptism, were beaten
to death or drowned in the rivers.

How was such inhumanity possible only a century ago? The
answer is not difficult today. It can be supplied by the survivors
of Maidanek, Oswiecim, Treblinka, and other extermination
camps of our generation. It can be read in the boastful reports
of Nazi officials and their henchmen throughout Europe. It can
be heard from the lips of Jewish refugees now scattered on all
continents. If a cultured people in the heart of Europe resorted
so recently to genocide as part of a political philosophy, spar-
ing neither graybeards nor women nor suckling babes, what
wonder that the rulers of a more primitive people on the
periphery of the Occident should have yielded a century ago
to the appeal of religious fanaticism, and sought the decimation
of Jewry by the compulsory conversion of its young?

The Jews were a strange and uncanny group in the eyes of
their Russian neighbors. They were not only restricted by law
to the Pale, a few provinces along the western border, but they
also shut themselves off voluntarily from too intimate contact
with non-Jews. As a result, the legend of the Jew bore little
resemblance to reality, even among the most educated Russians
and the highest government officials. The Jew was portrayed in
fiction and drama as a dirty, vile creature, a dishonest wretch
who would do anything for money, a spy who would not
scruple to betray all sides for his own advantage, an inferior
being to whom nothing was sacred and who, therefore, deserved
only contempt and the worst possible treatment. Pushkin,
Gogol, Dostoevsky—the most sensitive Russian men of letters
lost their usual keen insight into human souls when they presented Jewish characters, because to them such characters were
subhuman, abominable, immoral, and money-mad.

The military profession, as an honorable and dignified calling, was, therefore, at first closed to Jews. In return for their exemption from the army, they were required to pay a special tax into the imperial treasury. In 1800 the poet Derzhavin suggested to Czar Paul the desirability of recruiting Jews. But the scorn in which they were held in aristocratic circles militated against the acceptance of this proposal. Alexander I received a suggestion in 1807 to draft Jews for menial tasks behind the front, but did not act on it.

Czar Nicholas I, however, determined to introduce military service among the Jews as soon as he ascended the throne. His main purpose was not the strengthening of his army but rather the winning of new converts to the Greek Orthodox Church, as well as the weakening of the Jewish population by reducing the numbers of young Jews. As crown prince, he had already stigmatized these subjects as unhealthy parasites, as Russia's leeches. No sooner was he in absolute control of his country's destiny than he directed that immediate steps be taken to make Jews more useful to the Empire by converting them to the Christian faith. His ministers prepared a memorandum for him, outlining the most practical procedure. They reported that the Jews were a criminal and evil group, that they hated all other peoples, and that they had always formed a harmful enclave in the lands they inhabited. They were sunk in superstition. They refused to work on the soil—they preferred to trade and to swindle. They increased disproportionately because of early marriages. The most effective means of combating their growth would be to recruit them for the army at a rate double that of the Christian population. It was perfectly just to require of them twice the normal number of recruits, since they were also taxed doubly in other respects. If they attempted to avoid service they should be punished harshly. Furthermore, in order to get them to change their religion, it would be advisable to take them at as early an age as possible.*

In August 1827, Nicholas I promulgated his infamous decree

* Saul M. Ginsburg, *Historishe Verk*, New York, 1937, II, 8.

on the recruiting of Jews. It authorized the drafting of Jewish boys from the age of twelve. During the years between twelve and eighteen, they were to be farmed out to Russians in provinces where they would not come into contact with their coreligionists. There the future recruits were to work the soil and to undergo training in the proper faith. At eighteen they were to enter the army and serve for twenty-five years.

These children were known as cantonists, a designation for selectees for different cantons or training centers. Vilna, which had a Jewish population of 25,000 when Zunser was a boy, was expected to supply 250 cantonists annually. Since the Jews enjoyed autonomy in fiscal matters—the government having found it easier to deal with a single responsible body of deputies than with numerous individuals—they were also granted autonomy in the selection of recruits. The presiding officer, known as *Izborshtchik*, and the deputies were charged with carrying out the decree. Since their positions depended to some extent upon their maintaining the good will of the rich taxpayers, the full weight of the recruiting law fell upon the poorer Jews. Eliakum Zunser and his young brother Akiba were directly threatened.

When the season for recruiting approached, terror prevailed in the Jewish communities. All who could escape fled to the forests or crossed the border or hid in distant settlements. Some even mutilated themselves by cutting off a thumb or a toe. As a result, some towns had difficulty in meeting the quotas. The Czar was implacable, however, and decreed that for every missing Jew, three others were to be seized. Furthermore, anyone convicted of hiding or of abetting the escape of a prospective recruit was himself to be punished by military service. In addition, his community was to pay a huge fine. If the Jewish deputies or elders still failed to meet the prescribed quotas, they themselves were to be inducted. The deputies were, therefore, forced to resort to draconic measures in their search for sufficient recruits. They engaged *Khapers*, official "catchers" or kidnapers, to track down young men and to drag them to the

recruiting pen of the Jewish community. These victims were
to be kept under strict surveillance until the day of induction.
They were then to be turned over to the Russian authorities as
a group for transportation to Siberia or the Arctic. Since the
quotas were constantly increasing and the available recruits of
military age were quickly exhausted, children of eight and nine
were certified as twelve and carried off. Parents who were
required to supply a recruit could meet their legal obligation
by handing over a substitute for their own son. This possibility
opened up a lucrative market for gangsters, blackmailers, and
private kidnapers. A later provision permitted the turning in
as a recruit of any Jew who was caught away from home without a passport. Traveling from town to town was thus most
unsafe, since gangs of brigands would fall upon any person in
an inn or on the highway, tear up his documents, and deliver
him to the local Jewish community in return for a receipt
which could then be sold to the highest bidder.

One day, while Eliakum Zunser was in Bauska, working and
studying, the news reached him that his younger brother Akiba
had been seized for military service. This blow completely
overwhelmed him. He pictured his poor mother in her loneliness and agony. He felt that in this hour of tragedy his place
was at her side and so, without a kopeck in his pocket, he made
his way on foot back to his native Vilna.

His mother greeted him with an outburst of tears.

"Now you are my only child, I have nobody else in this
world," she wailed.

Then she told him the entire story.

It was in the evening. She had just recited the bedtime prayer
with her child and was preparing for sleep when suddenly the
door opened. In rushed the official kidnapers. She begged,
pleaded, and wept—all to no avail. She called attention to the law
which specifically stated that only families with three or more
children were required to furnish a recruit. She had only two
children. This legalistic argument merely roused laughter. She
resisted and fought like a tigress, but she was hurled to the

ground and the child torn from her arms. As she lay on the
floor, injured and unconscious, Akiba was carried out of the
house. Shortly thereafter, he was put into a uniform and, together with other children, loaded on a vehicle for Siberia.

In recounting his brother's ordeal, Eliakum passed over in
silence the final scene, when the parents were permitted to bid
a last farewell to their children, assembled for the transport.
But the Hebrew writer I. L. Levin was an eyewitness to a
similar transport in the very same year.

> Near a house stood a large and high wagon, to which a
> pair of horses were harnessed. Soldiers brought out children
> from the house, one after another, and deposited them into
> the truck. Soon it was packed to capacity. Children were
> sitting or lying on top of each other like herring in a
> barrel. Fathers, mothers, and relatives stood around. A per-
> son who has not seen the agonized parting of parents from
> their little children and who has not heard their helpless
> lamentations that penetrate to heaven does not know real
> tragedy. One father gives his boy a little book of Psalms.
> Another hands his son phylacteries. From all sides are
> heard admonitions: "Remain a Jew; no matter what happens,
> hold fast to Jewishness!" Mothers wring their hands, the
> hopeless tears never stop, moans of agony and cries of de-
> spair resound. I was then nine. I kept looking at the sky. I
> felt that now, at any moment, God must perform a miracle.
> He must rain down pitch and tar upon the murderers. He
> must scatter them, so that the imprisoned children could
> return to their mothers, who were bathed in tears. But the
> sky remained calm and the wagon began to move to the
> accompaniment of piercing cries and shouts.*

The law required that the children be transported by wagon,
but the officer in charge of Akiba's group preferred to pocket
the money provided for this purpose. So, after a short ride, he
drove the children on foot for the remainder of the distance.
After eight weeks they reached the Yenisei Province in north-

* Saul M. Ginsburg, *Yiddishe Leiden in Zarishen Russland*, New York,
1938, p. 38.

western Siberia. Akiba was fortunate in surviving this trip. Not all of his companions did.

There are records of transports of children who were driven on foot for a full year before they covered the distance from the Polish provinces to Eastern Siberia. They marched in the mud month after month. They were hungry and ill. Their underclothes were teeming with lice. They were beaten with the knout for the slightest infraction of arbitrary commands. They died along the road like flies, and their death was a merciful release from suffering.

The revolutionist and writer Alexander Herzen once passed a party of Jewish cantonists resting along a road. A moment later, at an officer's command, the children were lined up to continue the march.

> This was one of the most terrible scenes I have ever witnessed. Poor, poor children! The boys of twelve and thirteen did look somehow presentable. But the little ones of eight and nine! The blackest brush cannot paint the horror. Pale, exhausted, frightened, they stood in their ill-fitting coarse military coats. Their helpless, pleading glances followed the soldiers who were placing them in files. Their wan lips and the blue marks under their eyes plainly indicated that they were feverish, suffering from colds. A strong wind was blowing and the sick children, without care or help, were marching on—on toward their grave.*

Akiba Zunser was turned over to a peasant in a Siberian village along the Yenisei River. He was made to feed the swine and to fell trees in the forest. He had no furskin coat to protect him against the Siberian cold. Yet he survived. He was even able to retain his Jewishness unmolested by Greek Orthodox missionaries because the peasant, who had a large family to support, did not concern himself overmuch with the religious practices of his new worker.

It was not until his seventeenth year, therefore, that Akiba's battling for his Jewish faith assumed heroic proportions. He

* *Ibid.*, p. 40.

was then certified as eighteen by the military authorities and
transferred to the barracks of Tobolsk.

Normal life in the barracks was difficult enough, but special
cruelties awaited a Jewish cantonist who would not abjure his
religion. Recruits were organized in groups of ten under the
immediate supervision of a veteran soldier, whose duty it was
to drill the newcomers and to teach them rigorous army dis-
cipline. Such a group leader had a right to do with his underlings whatever his heart desired. He could display his prowess
by knocking out five teeth of a recruit with a single blow. No
appeal to a higher officer would get a hearing, and there was no
judge to listen to complaints. The mere attempt to go above
the head of the immediate superior would result in fifty, a
hundred, or even two hundred savage lashes with efficiently
fashioned reeds, which were always kept in readiness in large
quantities. A recruit was always streaked with black and blue
marks and often covered with gashes and wounds. From the
pettiest officer to the commander in charge, everybody wielded
the rod. The food was so bad that dogs disdained to touch it.
A Jewish recruit was of less value than a worm that crawled on
the ground. He rarely caught sight of a fellow Jew. He had no
Sabbaths and no holidays. Upon the slightest pretext, he was
hurled into a dark dungeon. He could alleviate his lot only by
accepting baptism—and yet many a Jewish recruit refused.
Many a child endured twenty-five years and more of physical
and spiritual agony for the sake of his God.

Among these heroes was Akiba Zunser. At Tobolsk every
form of diabolic torture was tried in order to bring about his
conversion. Still he remained steadfast. Finally, when his stub-
bornnness could not be broken, a priest came into his room,
where he was sleeping with fifty other recruits, and sprinkled
him with holy water during the night. When he woke up the
next morning, he was told that he was a Christian. He still
refused to abjure his religion and was subjected to further tortures. Beatings, starvation, semi-naked exposure in the frost,
repeated ducking in the river—nothing could budge him. He

even managed to get word to his brother Eliakum, who sent him phylacteries. The young hero would put these *Tefilin* on his forehead and on his left arm, and say his Hebrew prayers in the barracks in the presence of others. His torturers ultimately tired of the ineffective whippings and lashings. Since he performed his other tasks meticulously and was an excellent player in the regimental band, they let him alone. His corporal pretended not to notice his religious aberrations and ceased to report him to the church authorities and military commanders.

Not until 1877, almost a quarter of a century after "catchers" had snatched him from the arms of his weeping mother, was Akiba released under the law of Nicholas I's successor. It permitted a reduction in the term of compulsory service in certain cases. Eliakum, who by that time had reached the height of his fame and prosperity, helped Akiba to return to European Russia. The veteran cantonist, however, could no longer adjust himself to the habits of a ghetto community and drifted back to Siberia. There he married a Jewish girl and had four children. He remained a pious Jew and tried to carry out faithfully as many of his people's rituals as he could recall from his own childhood. Eliakum corresponded with him until 1884. In that year a fire broke out in the Siberian home and a child was burned to death. When it was buried at the Jewish cemetery, the government discovered officially that Akiba had reverted to Judaism and was raising his sons as Jews. His defense that he was baptized while asleep was rejected. With his removal in chains to the prison at Tobolsk, where a possible sentence up to eighteen years at hard labor awaited him for his apostasy to Greek Orthodoxy, all traces of the much-tried Akiba disappeared.

Eliakum, too, was caught in the net of the kidnapers and faced a fate no less severe than that of his younger brother. But a miracle, which thousands of young Jewish children had waited for vainly throughout almost three decades, saved him from cruel enslavement at the last possible moment.

When Akiba had been kidnaped in 1854, Eliakum's first

thought, as we saw, was to rush home from Bauska to his mother in Vilna. He arrived weary, bedraggled, half-starved. But after a stay of a few months, during which he tried to comfort his despairing mother, he again had to move on. Since he had broken his original contract with the Braiders' Guild, he could not obtain work in his native town in the only trade he knew. Nor could he, at the age of eighteen, endure the sight of his mother depriving herself of barest necessities in order to feed him. He therefore took leave of her in the spring of 1855 and set out on the road to try his luck elsewhere.

Eliakum journeyed on foot eastward and southward, through Lithuania and White Russia. Early in August, he arrived in the city of Bobruisk in the province of Minsk. He expected to get a job as a journeyman with a master-braider in this town. He was disappointed in this hope, however, since he could not produce a document from the Braiders' Guild of Vilna certifying to his satisfactory completion of six years of apprenticeship. For days he walked up and down the streets of the strange city, looking for any kind of work that would provide him with decent food and lodging.

Finally, a stroke of good fortune came his way. A cantor named Yoel Ihumener was invited to Bobruisk every fall to lead the solemn services during the High Holidays. Yoel arrived a few weeks earlier to assemble a choir and rehearse the singing of the prayers. Eliakum, who was growing more desperate each day, mustered sufficient courage to approach him. The visiting cantor immediately gave him an audition, and not only was satisfied with his ability to carry a tune but found his voice to be excellent. Eliakum was engaged as a chorister for the entire holiday season at a salary of two rubles, three meals a day, and the right to sleep on a bench in the synagogue.

Buoyed up by new hope and the brief respite in his search for bread, the young chorister composed two songs, which he entitled *The Candle* (*Dos Likht*) and *Reb Takhnun*. Only the latter has survived. It found instant favor. The president of the synagogue at Bobruisk arranged a festive gathering at his home.

The choir, which had rehearsed *Reb Takhnun*, sang it under the direction of the young composer. The audience joined in enthusiastically. Before the holiday season was over, the entire community was singing the melody, and it spread to Jews in other towns and villages.

The poem is an allegory. *Takhnun* is a prayer which is said only on uneventful weekdays. It is omitted on all occasions when there is the slightest reason for celebrating or commemorating a happy event. Zunser personifies this prayer as Reb Takhnun, the Jew who has to keep away from all happy days but who is called back to participate in all days of distress and drabness. The fifteen stanzas of the poem are full of learned allusions which once delighted the hearts of Orthodox listeners adept in fathoming its many possible meanings.

Reb Takhnun is, however, more than the allegory of the Jewish people, banned from joy, harassed by neighbors, and expelled on every possible occasion. It is also the story of the young wanderer, Eliakum Zunser. When Reb Takhnun laments in the opening stanza: "I go, I know not whither, and wheresoever I arrive, I am not welcome," we can hear the poignant cry of the author, who does not know whether or where he will have a roof over his head on the morrow. When Reb Takhnun exclaims in the second stanza: "Houses, tables, and beds are polished and renovated—but I, alas, may not step over the threshold," we hear the voice of the emaciated composer, whose bed was a wooden bench in the synagogue, granted him for temporary use only. The many compliments paid to Zunser by his Bobruisk admirers when he sang *Reb Takhnun* meant little to him, for these worthy householders never went beyond mere words and never offered him practical assistance in his struggle for physical survival. His thoughts continually revolved about the hardships that he would face during the coming winter, far from his native town and without a friend in the whole world.

When the holiday season was over, the cantor paid his chorister the promised two rubles and told him to go. Neither of them knew exactly which direction it would be best to take. But what difference did it really make? The world was wide and Jews were scattered in all directions. Somewhere or other, Zunser would find shelter among his coreligionists, and a daily morsel to satisfy his appetite. The question of clothing was more urgent. While a young man could get along without a coat in September, he could not brave the cold blasts of the winter months in his summer rags. Zunser had two rubles in his pockets. He decided to buy himself a "fur" coat with this entire capital. A fur coat, Zunser explained, meant an overcoat which had a fur collar or a collar upon which a piece of fur could be attached at some future time. He was so proud of his acquisition that he walked with head high through the streets of Bobruisk, displaying to all eyes his brand-new garment.

One day, he encountered a Jew from a neighboring village who had come into town to find a private tutor for his three children. Zunser saw an opportunity for a winter's shelter and applied for this position. He was employed at a salary of twenty-five rubles to be paid at the end of the semester, and, in addition, the right to sleep on top of the warm stove.

The winter months of 1855–1856 were less pleasant than Zunser had anticipated. The family with which he was quartered lived on a meager diet of bread and cereals all week long. Only on the Sabbath was a symbolic bit of meat added, in order to meet religious requirements. With sardonic humor, the poet later recounted his experiences as a private tutor, when he had to drill three stupid youngsters or, as he put it, when he had to plow and rake with three oxen six hours a day.

After such exhausting labor, even bread made of oats and barley tasted like royal fare. Worse than the poor, inadequate food was the state of Zunser's clothing. Except for his precious overcoat, all his garments were worn to shreds and he was terribly cold in the sub-zero weather. Fear of illness led him to ask the father of his pupils for some payment on his earned salary. Throughout the winter, he was given one excuse after another. Finally Passover came and the first semester was over. His employer gave him the encouraging news that his teaching had been satisfactory and that he would be retained for the following term. As for pay, he need not worry. He could expect to get as much as he required for his essential purchases—soon, but not yet. Since the poor tutor had no choice, he stayed on through the spring of 1856, clad in rags, his shoes full of holes. His mood of this period found expression in the sad verses of his song entitled *The Eye (Dos Oig)*.

When the second semester was in its seventh week and Zunser, growing more and more desperate, continued to ask with ever greater persistence that he be given his promised pay, his employer hit upon a brilliant idea. He would get rid of his tutor without paying him a penny and, indeed, even make a profit. So the respectable villager and father of three sons took a trip to Bobruisk, visited the headquarters of the Jewish community, and told the *Izborshtchik* or presiding officer that, if he were paid well, he would supply a healthy recruit. The Crimean War, which had been raging since 1853, was creating a heavy demand for an ever-increasing number of recruits, and the Jewish authorities were desperately seeking to meet their quota. The villager's offer, therefore, was accepted immediately. He was paid the sum of twenty-five rubles and was given an official "catcher" and two strong-armed Cossacks to help him round up the recruit and bring him to the *Izborshtchik*.

Zunser, unaware of the danger closing in on him, went to sleep in his usual place atop the stove. Suddenly he felt a rough hand shaking him awake.

On opening his eyes, he saw three strangers. One of them was holding a lantern in his face.

"What do you want?" asked the drowsy tutor.

"Nothing, my young fellow! Just get up and dress," answered the official kidnaper.

"Get up? What for?"

"You'll see. Just dress and be quick about it!"

"Why?"

"You'll come with us to town!"

"But I don't want to dress and I don't want to go to town!"

A ferocious blow ended the conversation and left Zunser in a daze. The Cossacks wrapped him in his tattered clothes, threw him into a wagon, and brought him to Bobruisk in the dark of night. There he was locked up in the military detention pen.

The next morning, as he looked about, he saw a heart-rending spectacle. Eighty pale, wretched, haggard, starved children and youths were lying half-naked on the ground. Their bedding was a bit of filthy straw. Most of them, as he soon found out, had gone through experiences similar to his own. Brutal hands had snatched them away, had trussed them up like squirming animals, and had deposited them at the barracks. Here they were waiting for the day of recruitment, which was still weeks away. Some of the younger victims could not yet grasp the full measure of the horrors in store for them. They were becoming accustomed to their prison home and at times they even laughed, joked, and played games. The older recruits forgot their own misery and wept at the sight of these innocent sons of Israel who were to begin their long road of martyrdom at so early an age.

Twice a day, the iron doors were unlocked and vicious-looking guards threw in a few loaves of bread and a few plates of smelly soup, unfit for dogs. If one of the victims ventured to open his mouth to beg for something, he was seized by the hair and hurled against the wall with such savagery that his young bones cracked.

"I want to go back to my mommy," cried a child.

"You'll soon see her in the other world. Just have a little patience," was the guard's brutal answer.

"Let me out! I want to go home!" wailed another little waif.

"Just wait a few days," roared the human tiger. "You'll soon have a big home, extending from Bobruisk to Arch-angel."

When darkness settled on the barracks, all lay down on the ground and said their bedtime prayers. The older boys remembered some Psalms by heart and recited them until they fell asleep. Eliakum looked about and was reminded of a herd of cattle locked up in the stockyards, waiting to be slaughtered. There on the dirty straw lay a heap of humanity, a bundle of wretchedness, with limbs intertwined and sighs commingled with groans. Only the youngest of the lot slept peacefully. An occasional smile crossed a wan face as a child dreamed of home and of the loving arms of his mother.

Zunser himself had no illusions about his future. His recollections of his brother Akiba's experiences were still vivid. Although five weeks were left before the military oath would be administered to him and his group, there was not the slightest chance of salvation from onrushing doom. There was no doubt whatsoever that his detention was illegal—the Czar's decree specifically forbade taking more than one son from each family—but who in Bobruisk would fight for his liberation? There were rabbis in the town, but not one of these spiritual leaders would lift a finger in his behalf. In the first place, some of them held that while the seizure of a stranger could not be condoned, it was a lesser evil than the impressment of a local son. In the second place, rabbis might weep in secret at the flagrant injustice being committed in their midst, but they would not speak out in public against a decree of the Czar or against an action by the *Izborshtchik* and the elders, who had the authority to dismiss all communal employees. Besides, there were informers to be feared. A single word from these moral wretches and Siberia loomed ahead for any Jew, no matter how dignified his position.

Eliakum Zunser knew that he must somehow reconcile himself to the inevitable, to twenty-five years of purgatory in Siberian fortresses. The thought, however, which tortured him most in his sleepless nights was not of his own future but of the effect the news would have upon his mother. He remembered how she had been crushed by the loss of Akiba. When her husband had died, Etta Kayle had found consolation in her three children. Then the little girl had died. And when one son was taken from her, she clung to the other all the more. Now, the second son, too, was being devoured—not by a ravenous wolf in a wild forest but by human beings with the hearts of wolves, in the populous town of Bobruisk.

The more Zunser brooded, the more he despaired. In his helpless wrath against his fellow Jews, who were selling him into slavery for a few bits of silver, he saw himself in the role of Joseph, his patriarchal ancestor who had also been sold into captivity by his own brothers. It was then that the idea of a drama about Joseph in Egypt first came to him, an idea which he developed sucessfully years later.

Zunser's mood of black despair found immediate expression in a song, to which he daily added new verses until it contained one hundred and eight stanzas. It was entitled *Child Recruits or Judged and Found Guilty (Die Poimanes oder Geshtanen zum Mishpot un Herois Shuldig)*. Its theme was the abasement and defilement of the Jewish soul because of its constant contact with a corrupting environment. The poem, which is no longer extant and which was never published, though it may have circulated for a time in manuscript form, dealt with events during the Babylonian Captivity. But its thinly veiled references to the immediate situation were obvious to Zunser's audience. Its biblical inspiration was derived from the prophet Haggai. This prophet of the days of Darius questioned the priests of Israel concerning the law, saying:

> "If one bear holy flesh in the skirt of his garment, and with his skirt do touch bread, or pottage, or wine, or oil, or any meat, shall it be holy?"
>
> And the priests answered and said: "No."
>
> Then said Haggai: "If one that is unclean by a dead body touch any of these, shall it be unclean?"
>
> And the priests answered and said: "It shall be unclean."
>
> Then answered Haggai, and said: "So is this people, and so is this nation before me, saith the Lord; and so is every work of their hands; and that which they offer there is unclean."

In other words, living among foreign peoples, the Jews have acquired not the best qualities and virtues of their neighbors but rather the worst habits and the most horrible vices. Zunser, in this poem, severely condemned the Jewish leaders who were assisting in the outrages committed against their own brothers.

Since 1827 all efforts to evade strict fulfillment of the cruel military edict had been fruitless. The failure to complete prescribed quotas had resulted in the economic ruin of Russian Jewry. Punitive fines had increased Jewish communal debts fifteenfold during the reign of Nicholas I. In the last year of this tyrant's reign, persecution had reached its utmost refinement. No abatement of the evils of conscription was possible. But to offer such an explanation to Zunser, while he was in detention, would have sounded like an explanation to sheep that their flesh was necessary in order to feed others. The poet, recalling the mood in which he wrote his song, exclaimed:

> Not in my blood alone did I dip my pen but in the blood of all my unfortunate brothers. In my verses there resounded not only my individual pain but also the despairing wail of all Israel.

Among Zunser's eighty comrades in misery, there were several with good voices. He selected ten of these and organized them into a chorus. Within a short while, they knew the melody and the many stanzas by heart. They sang the song several times each day. The hearts of all listeners were moved and all eyes were filled with tears. Even the guards, whose nerves were hardened by the constant sight of much suffering, were affected by the tragic text and the sorrow-laden melody, and joined with their involuntary tribute of tears.

The effect of Zunser's song can be likened only to that produced in the early 1940's in the extermination camps of Central and Eastern Europe, when there arose among the candidates for the gas chambers the plaintive chant *I Believe (Ani Mamin)*, which embodied in words and melody the grim tragedy and the undying messianic hope of the eternal people.

Thus five weeks passed. The climax of despair was reached on the ninth day of Ab, the traditional day of wailing, when Jews, the world over, gather to recite the ancient verses of the

book of Lamentations and to mourn the fall of the Temple or
House of God, the loss of national sovereignty, and the dis-
persal of Israel in hostile lands. The helpless Jewish victims of
Russian despotism had reason enough to shed tears on that day,
for on the morrow they were to be finally inducted into military
service. Before the opened ark of the Torah, they would stand
in their prayer shawls. The Shofar or Ram's Horn would
resound in awesome tones which they had heard only at the
beginning of each year when souls were judged in heaven and
dooms were pronounced. Solemnly they would repeat the oath
of allegiance and obedience to the Autocrat of all the Russians,
an oath which was irrevocable and which removed them from
the ranks of civilians for interminably long years. Then they
would be transported to an unforeseeable destiny.

The day of tragedy, however, was fated to be turned into a
holiday of rejoicing. Unknown to the cantonists penned in the
communal barracks, salvation was at hand.

CHAPTER V

Salvation

SALVATION came at the hands of Alexander II. In his Coronation Manifesto the liberal crown prince, who had succeeded to the Russian throne upon the sudden death of his father, Nicholas I, revoked the military regulations that weighed so heavily on the Jewish population. The ending of the Crimean War lessened the need for recruits. Hence, the Jews were no longer to be required to supply double the quota of other subjects. They were not to be liable for service before the age of eighteen. Nor could they be seized for the army on the ground that they lacked registration certificates or passports. For the Jewish community of Bobruisk, this decree, issued on August 26, 1856, meant that no more recruits would be drafted that year. When the happy news reached the town shortly after midnight, Jews ran out of their houses and large numbers converged upon the barracks.

The children were awakened by tumultuous sounds. The noises came nearer and nearer. Soon people were pounding on the iron gate and window-bars. Voices shouted excitedly:

"Children, get up! . . . Salvation has come! . . . You are free, free! . . . The Czar has decreed that you are to be released at once. . . . Thank God! Praise the Lord! Chant psalms!"

The voices grew louder and more persistent.

The sound of the trumpet on Judgment Day announcing the

resurrection of the dead could hardly have produced a more electrifying effect. Shouting and weeping with joy, the children jumped up from the straw-covered ground, washed quickly, and proceeded to recite Hallelujah psalms. Zunser officiated as cantor and his choir accompanied him. They sang hymns of praise to the Almighty Who had delivered them out of the jaws of hell. Then the liberated victims, still laughing and weeping, grasped each other's hands and danced an ecstatic roundelay.

The official hour of release was set for ten o'clock in the morning. But Zunser could not get back to sleep. As he lay awake, he composed words and music to a song which he entitled *Salvation* (*Die Yeshua*).

Men and women, young and old, waited impatiently outside of the barracks for the appointed hour when the gates would be opened. Every one blessed the new Czar who, with a single stroke of the pen, had annulled so many oppressive decrees of his father. Precisely at the stroke of ten, the richest Jew of the town, Isaac Rabinowitz, approached the locked gate. He had made a generous contribution to the synagogue of Bobruisk for the privilege of being the first to enter the place of detention. Reciting the benediction: "Blessed art thou, O Lord, creator of the universe, who releaseth them that are bound," he turned the key and opened the gate. In surged the crowd. Fathers and mothers embraced their children. Tears of happiness replaced tears of misery. The chief cantor of Bobruisk invoked the blessings of God upon the Czar. He followed this prayer with a psalm that glorified the earthly ruler who walked in the ways of righteousness and hated wickedness, and whom God therefore raised above his peers and anointed with the oil of gladness. "Thou art fairer than the children of men; grace is poured into thy lips; therefore God hath blessed thee forever . . . In thy majesty ride prosperously, because of truth and meekness and righteousness."

When the cantor had finished, Zunser was lifted up by the crowd, He beckoned to his ten singers to join him. Standing on the table, the choir sang *Judged and Found Guilty*, Zunser's indictment of the leaders of the Jewish community. The stirring, pathetic verses made a profound impression upon the excited crowd. There was a great surge of anger against the deputies who had been so merciless in their execution of a cruel decree. The people were in a mood for revenge. But the deputies had prudently gone into hiding.

Upon the crowd's insistence, Zunser sang *Salvation*, the song he had composed during the early morning hours. Then he sang *Taking Is Better Than Giving (Besser Nemen eider Geben)*, a ballad of his experiences with the villager who sold him as a recruit for twenty-five rubles. This roused the crowd to frenzy. Some of the listeners were prepared to set out that very moment for the neighboring village in order to seize Zunser's former employer and to take bitter revenge for all the needless suffering he had inflicted upon the honest tutor. Isaac Rabinowitz, the most prominent person present, counseled patience. He pledged his word of honor that justice would be carried out in due time. Then the gates were opened wide and all eighty prisoners marched out of the barracks singing a song of joy.

Zunser was invited by the patrician of Bobruisk to join him in his waiting carriage and to be a guest in his sumptuous house. The youth was glad to have a free roof over his head. He stayed for two weeks, recuperating from his ordeal. During this time he acquired a sum of money which made him feel like a rich person.

The source of his wealth was his former employer, who had also been the source of his troubles. Isaac Rabinowitz had kept his word. He had called in the villager, had greeted him by slapping his face, and had then ordered him to pay the fifty rubles he owed for two semesters of instruction and the twenty-five rubles obtained from the *Izborshtchik* for selling the tutor. All his pleas that he was poor and could not raise such a large sum were laughed at. Several Cossacks were dispatched to his house and removed all his belongings as a pledge for the debt. A few days later, he appeared in Bobruisk with the entire sum and got back his things.

Overnight Zunser became so affluent that, as he later remarked, he felt like a second Rothschild. In addition, he received several smaller sums from guests who came to visit his host and to whom he sang the three songs he had composed while in the barracks. He could now throw away his ill-fitting rags and clothe himself in new garments from head to foot.

In Vilna, meanwhile, his mother had received a letter from an acquaintance, a woman who had happened to be in Bobruisk when Zunser was caught ostensibly without a passport. Etta Kayle was heartbroken but resolute. She immediately presented her case to the Vilna authorities and obtained a passport for her son. She then set out on foot for Bobruisk, a distance of about two hundred and fifty miles. Her brother Abraham Leib, unwilling to let her travel such a great distance alone, walked with her the entire way.

One day, therefore, while Eliakum was sitting in his patron's house, the servant announced that a strange woman and man wanted to see him. They were waiting outside. The joy of reunion was indescribable.

For eight days all three of them stayed at the house of Eliakum's patron. Then they took their leave and began the long trek back to Vilna.

On the way they stopped at the little town of Samokhvolovitz. There Etta Kayle had a sister named Mariashe-Hannah. Eliakum's aunt was most anxious to have her nineteen-year-old nephew as her son-in-law, especially since he was exempt from military service. The bride would not face the danger of having to wait twenty-five years for the return of her mate. Eliakum's mother readily gave her consent to the match. This was all that was necessary. The cousins were engaged. Eliakum could not have been too enthusiastic because the date of the wedding was set, probably upon his request, for two years later and the marriage did not actually take place for six years. The girl was, of course, not asked for her opinion. And she was too cowed by her father's authority to venture any opinion of her own.

Little is known of Rochel, Eliakum's first cousin, but she could not have been much different from most Jewish girls of her generation and upbringing. While boys were sent to school, girls were educated at home, and the emphasis was on homely virtues. Always under her mother's care, the Jewish maiden remained naive, pious, modest, reserved, out of reach of temptation. She was not supposed to be concerned with love. She was to grow up to be a diligent housekeeper and a mother of many children.

Rochel gathered from the conversation of the adults that she was to become engaged—and blushed. She was told that some day in the future she was to wed her aunt's son—and reddened whenever she caught sight of him. She was present at her feast of betrothal and listened to the congratulations being exchanged by the grown-ups in the gaily decorated main room. Then she said good-by to her future husband and his mother, and resumed her accustomed routine while she waited for the years to pass until she should see them again.

When Eliakum arrived in his native town, he was greeted by the same abject poverty with which he had been familiar since his father's death. Again he had to find employment in order to support himself and his mother. He was still barred from the trade that he had mastered so well and that paid better than any unskilled job he might find. The Braiders' Guild still had a record of the contract that he had signed and broken as an apprentice, and no master dared defy the Guild to engage him. Once again Eliakum had to leave his mother alone in Vilna to wander forth in search of work. There was no alternative.

In the spring of 1857 he arrived in Kovno. There he had no difficulty in obtaining employment as a braider. But he was also anxious to continue his studies. At Kovno, he soon discovered that Rabbi Israel Salanter, whom he had admired since his boyhood days in *Ramaila's Yeshiva*, was in charge of an unusual House of Learning, renowned as the *Musar-Stiebel* or Academy of Ethics. There the young man spent his evenings throughout his stay in this Lithuanian town; and the influence of the

Moralist Movement, set in motion by this famed rabbi, affected the poet's creative work for many years.

Rabbi Israel Salanter, who was born in 1810 and died in 1883, had many disciples. From their legends, his saintliness and simplicity shine forth. Before he was out of his twenties, his reputation as a scholar was so great that he was invited to teach Talmud at *Ramaila's Yeshiva.* But the barren elucidation of legal problems and the emphasis on pure logic in the interpretation of Jewish religious rituals did not satisfy his warm personality. On the other hand, he could not approve the neomysticism of the Hassidic brotherhood, who renounced the authority of reason and gave themselves over to religious orgies and to the worship of miracle-working intermediaries between themselves and the Almighty. Hence, he sought to steer a middle course between the Rabbinism which stemmed from Vilna's Gaon Eliahu and the Hassidism of the less sophisticated masses. He emphasized ethical living. Belief must find expression in moral actions. The relation of man to man must be holy. Knowledge was desirable primarily because it led to goodness. "Know thyself" meant: devote some time each day to studying yourself, educating yourself, ferreting out your weaknesses, working at self-improvement, purifying the immortal soul implanted in your mortal body. Pride, wrath, stubbornness, envy, hate, covetousness rise up in every human heart, but daily silent introspection will enable a person to strive successfully with these evil tendencies and overcome them.*

Rabbi Israel Salanter, therefore, founded at Vilna and later at Kovno moral academies, Houses of Learning. Students of all ages assembled at these academies to study books on morality and to listen to sermons on proper behavior towards others. Much of the time was spent in silent meditation on what constituted ideal conduct. Among Salanter's most ardent disciples at Kovno was Zunser, who was encouraged to concentrate his thinking more on eternal verities than on immediate practical problems.

* Josef Meisl, *Haskalah,* Berlin, 1919, p. 175.

Salanter was a great speaker. He insisted that his pupils not merely acquire knowledge, but that they bring this knowledge to the less learned masses in the form of popular sermons on every possible occasion. Natural in speech and in behavior, he moved his listeners because his message always came from the bottom of his heart. It was from Salanter that Zunser learned that a tear in the eye, a frown, and a melancholy smile impressed an audience far more than verbal acrobatics or the most dramatic gestures. This knowledge, acquired so early in life, enabled Zunser throughout his later years to hold his listeners completely under his spell.

Many stories are told of Rabbi Salanter's humility and warm humanity. Since he never permitted himself to be photographed or painted and since he did not publish any of his sermons, it is these stories that have kept his personality alive in Jewish consciousness. In 1848, when cholera raged in Vilna and all the Jews assembled in the synagogue on Atonement Day to pray and to fast and to invoke God's mercy, he ordered the solemn prayers to be cut short so that the men and women of the community could spend more time in the fresh air. Then he announced that, as rabbi, he was granting permission to the worshippers to interrupt their fast and to partake of the sustenance necessary to maintain their physical strength. Cake and wine were ready in the vestry-room. This incident was afterwards embellished by popular imagination. As a tale about Rabbi Salanter, this colorful legend found its finest literary embodiment in David Frishman's narrative *Three Who Ate*.

Salanter's influence upon Eliakum Zunser was enduring. It found immediate expression in the poems composed in the Kovno period. Salanter stemmed the cynicism that had embittered the young man's soul as a result of the injustices he had experienced. Salanter taught him to love his fellow men, even though they often seemed unlovable. Salanter, whose entire life was devoted to making other people happy, impressed upon his young disciple the value of unselfish devotion to humanitarian causes; the gifted wielder of words and the talented singer of songs had a rare opportunity to better conditions and persons. Art became for Eliakum Zunser a medium for inculcating morality and for preaching decency in all human relations.

Beauty was not enough for Zunser. He held that a poem must also conform to truth and reality. It must not conjure up rosy visions and deceptive images. A poet was performing a bad service if he led his readers to revel in sweet dreams; for, when their eyes were opened, the fairy realms disappeared like bubbles. When the rude awakening came, hearts were empty and arid. "Many of the poems of old are but unprofitable flowers, good to smell, nice to touch, but of what import? Yet such poetry has its devotees: the more lies it harbors, the more is it praised as pure poetry."

Both Zunser and his audiences had been most profoundly influenced in their thinking by one text esteemed above all others: the Bible. This collection of books in prose and verse served as their model of what constituted good literature. Hence, they expected from all literary texts an answer to the fundamental question: "How shall we live?" The *Prophets* had constantly wrestled with this question and the answers had not all been uniform. *Job* and *Ecclesiastes* had subjected orthodox explanations to the most searching analysis. Century after century, spiritual leaders of Israel had composed, in the ancient tongue of the Bible, moral tracts which sought to justify the ways of God with man and to explain to the individual how he might best please his Maker by correct conduct. These tracts found especially eager readers in ages when Jews were most oppressed. The victims of injustice wanted to know why wicked neighbors prospered while they, the children of Sinai, bled from a thousand wounds. With all the fervor of despair they wanted to learn how to absolve the God they loved from the charge of guilt, or at best indifference, toward his most faithful believers. Ghetto scholars brooded over the answers supplied in Hebraic texts written by cabalistic seers and rabbinic sages, but the untutored men and women listened with attentive ears and believing hearts to the replies given in the

Yiddish vernacular by the *Magid* or religious lecturer, the *Badchen* or skald, the inspired folksinger or balladist.

Zunser's early suffering, his years of hunger, his wanderings, his imprisonment in the barracks, and his almost miraculous salvation from military enslavement had given him a rich fund of experiences and had brought him ever nearer to the common people. He could sing to them of their melancholy fate in simple words. He could answer their timid questioning of God's ways and their inarticulate pleas for moral enlightenment in parables which they understood. He could offer them solace in their dreary existence and could mirror for them happier days to come. He could rouse their flagging hope of salvation by painting vivid messianic visions. He could castigate the petty exploiters in their own ranks and call down the judgment of heaven upon them. His words and melodies had tremendous popular appeal. Whenever he was invited to a home and began to chant his songs, the Jews of Kovno gathered by the hundreds in the streets about the house. They stood for hours listening to the young braider, until they too knew the songs by heart and were able to sing them to their friends. From Kovno his songs spread by word of mouth to town after town and to province after province, until in a few years all Russian Jewry from the Baltic to the Black Sea was familiar with them. Then the braider of golden lace on woolen coats gave up his unsatisfying handiwork. He returned from Kovno to his native Vilna in order to enter upon his calling as the troubadour of his people, and it was in Vilna that his first volume of verse appeared in 1861 under the title *Shirim Khadoshim* or *New Songs*.

CHAPTER VI

Early Songs

ZUNSER, who was most modest in his claims to creative originality, ascribed the popularity of his early songs and dramatic dialogues to two causes. In the first place, melody and text were so perfectly blended that anyone who recalled the melody also remembered the words. In this magical combination, both could move quickly from house to house and from town to town, until all Lithuania hummed and whistled and chanted these simple Yiddish rhymes. Rich and poor, housewives and their maids, masters and apprentices, the learned and the ignorant, the pious and the freethinkers—all found something in Zunser to delight them.

This perfect blending of tone and word in Zunser's songs resulted from his creating both simultaneously. The phenomenal rapidity with which he was able to transmute a quick image or a sudden insight into a poem and a song astonished all observers. The excitement that seized him when a new concept flashed across his mind and a new melody arose within his heart of hearts, could be recorded by him in its essential verbal and musical outlines before it subsided and ebbed away.

Not all, probably not even most, of his melodies have come down to us. Since he had no formal training in music, he did not at first use the conventional musical notes and symbols. He had to devise his own system of designating musical sounds. In the course of time, he perfected a complete musical alphabet of his own, adequate for his purposes. Only in his later years did he learn to make use of the accepted musical symbols.

His earliest songs, such as *The Candle* and *Reb Takhnun*, were modeled upon synagogue chants, since the only musical experience he had had until then was as chorister on the High Holidays. Zunser stated that he himself was not entirely satisfied with his early melodies and that these consisted mainly of adaptations and variations of motifs used by the cantors of Vilna. The first cantor who served as a model for Zunser had been a drummer before he became a cantor. Zunser's early songs composed under his influence were rhythmically powerful but not too melodious.

In the second place, Zunser said, his songs lacked real competition, since talented poets still insisted on writing in Hebrew. There were three other persons in the mid-nineteenth century who composed their songs in Yiddish, but they were separated from Zunser by the vast distances of Eastern Europe.

In the Ukraine, at Poltava, the Hebrew scholar Michael Gordon composed a few songs in Yiddish before 1861. These songs were not published until 1868, seven years after Zunser's *Shirim Khadoshim*; and certainly were not known to the Lithuanian bard and his audiences in the late 1850's. Zunser remarked that in those years, before the coming of the railroad, the distance between Poltava and Kovno or Vilna was comparable to the distance between Europe and America half a century later. In Lithuania Zunser's reputation was well established before the Yiddish lyrics of Michael Gordon were known.

Zunser's two other predecessors, Berl Broder and Velvel Zbarzher, began their Yiddish improvisations in Austria and Rumania somewhat earlier than did Zunser in Lithuania, but none of their songs was published before his first collection. There is no evidence that Zunser was influenced by them during his Kovno period, although he undoubtedly made use of their repertoire in his later career, just as they made use of his.

Berl Broder derived his name from his native city of Brody in eastern Galicia. He composed songs and rhymed verses, while engaged in his monotonous work of making brushes. Afterwards, when he became a buyer for his firm, he sang these compositions at various inns where he stopped for the night. In 1855, on an extended business trip to Russia, he entertained his fellow travelers and chance acquaintances with his lyrics. Itinerant minstrels imitated and disseminated his texts and tunes. These songs might have reached Zunser after he left Kovno for Vilna and might have strengthened his determination to continue composing in the vernacular Yiddish rather than in the sacred Hebrew. Broder, in the 1860's, organized a group of followers into the first troupe of professional folksingers. This troupe traversed Galicia, Hungary, Rumania, singing in wine cellars and inns. Their initial appearances antedated the theatre of Abraham Goldfaden, who is generally acclaimed the father of the Yiddish stage. The stage of the Broder Singers consisted merely of a table with two lit candles, and their texts were not at first composed entirely in dramatic form. Nevertheless, the success of their acting and singing was phenomenal, and has been ascribed in large measure to their repertoire, in which the songs of Eliakum Zunser soon supplanted those of Berl Broder. As late as 1930, when Khone Strudler, the last of the Broder Singers, died, critics recalled his brilliant renderings of Zunser's ballads and musical monologues.*

Velvel Zbarzher was about a decade younger than Berl Broder and about a decade older than Zunser. His real name was Benjamin Wolf Ehrenkranz, but he acquired the nickname of Zbarzher from his birthplace Zbarzh in eastern Galicia. He was definitely influenced by Berl Broder, whom he is said to have visited at Brody. Like Zunser, he was subjected to a traditional Talmudic schooling and infected at an early age by the spirit of Enlightenment.

According to legend, to please his young wife he translated his Hebrew songs into colloquial Yiddish, which she was able to understand. Driven from his native town by his aroused

* *Forverts*, New York, January 11, 1931.

compatriots, who would not tolerate his scoffing verses, he made his way to Rumania. There he sang his lyrics in Yiddish and in Hebrew, to the accompaniment of his own melodies. His listeners were, at first, merely his drinking companions at various inns. As his reputation grew, however, he was invited to entertain at the homes of the rich. He sang his songs in the sacred tongue for his learned hosts and in Yiddish for the women who were present. He apologized for having to garb his muse now as a maid and now as a mistress. By the close of the 1850's, he decided to make an extended professional tour of the Black Sea provinces of Moldavia and Bessarabia. The story of his success in the South must have reached the ears of Zunser in the North and might well have influenced his decision a year or two later to enter upon a similar career on a larger scale.

Zbarzher was the ablest forerunner of Zunser and he might well have attained the pinnacle of fame reached by the younger bard if he had not squandered his talent in disreputable inns and Turkish coffee-houses. Zbarzher liberated the Yiddish lyric from its dependence upon religious themes. Despite his disparagement of his Yiddish medium, as is evidenced by his publishing his Yiddish songs with a parallel Hebrew translation, Hebrew introductions, and Hebrew titles, his best lyrics did enrich this young literature.

Zbarzher and Zunser had much in common. They were acquainted with each other's songs and borrowed freely from each other's repertoire, even though they never met. At times they treat the same theme in an almost identical manner, and it is not always easy to decide which song was written first. The following example best illustrates the difficulties besetting the scholar who tries to unravel the literary relationship between the two bards.

One of Zunser's most famous songs was included in his earliest collection, published in 1861, under the title *The Watch* (*Der Zeiger*). It was reprinted frequently with slight modifications in words and music.* A song of almost the same content and structure and containing the identical refrain was published under the title *The Golden Watch* (*Der Goldne Zeiger*) by Zbarzher in 1865, four years later. Leo Wiener, the first English historian of Yiddish literature, voiced the opinion that Zbarzher's version was composed earlier and must have reached Zunser in its oral form.† Wiener, however, offered no evidence to this effect in his detailed analysis of Zbarzher. The editors of Zunser's works went to the opposite extreme and, in the two posthumous editions, designated 1854 as the date of Zunser's version, a date which would definitely preclude any Zbarzher influence. However, according to Zunser's own assertion that he composed the poem at Kovno, *The Watch* must have been composed either in 1857 or 1858. Zbarzher wrote in 1865, in his introduction to his first published poems, that he had been making a living from his Yiddish minstrelsy for about seven years. He must, therefore, have begun his career as a folksinger in 1858. If he were the creator of the disputed lyric, he could not have given it wide circulation even in his Rumanian province before the latter date. On the other hand, he could well have taken it from Zunser's printed collection before the former date. The weight of evidence would, therefore, tend to point to Zunser as the probable originator of this popular lyric.

The poet inquires of the watch why it is so despondent and restless, and why its heart beats so incessantly. Surely, it has every reason to be happy. It is garbed in gold and garlanded with diamonds. It is worn by monarchs and fashionable people. It is taken along to dances and splendid assemblies. Its advice is sought on trips and at home. It is the first gift sent to a prospective bridegroom to seal an engagement. The watch replies that its melancholy stems from its inability to determine its own fate. Everyone else has a certain amount of freedom but the watch does not. If it is not wound in time, it cannot go. If it is

* The latest reprint: Janot S. Roskin, *Jüdische Volkslieder*, Berlin, 1922, Heft I, No. 5, pp. 10–12.
† Leo Wiener, *History of Yiddish Literature in the Nineteenth Century*, New York, 1899, p. 92.

overwound, it stops short. Even though its heart beats regularly
and honestly, it is blamed whenever the hands misbehave and
act falsely. On one occasion, it is accused of being ahead of
time and, on another occasion, it is condemned for being
behind time. At the slightest deficiency, it is cast aside. The
moment a single limb fails to function, the grave is imminent
for the entire ticking body. The watch is a symbol of man. His
heart too beats incessantly. He too is full of cares and fears, but
he is also full of overweening ambitions and insatiable desires.
Yet, the slightest breeze may change his course; and his moods,
swinging between hope and despair, may be brought to a sudden halt by the slightest jar.

As the text of the song avoided mentioning specific Jewish
difficulties, no censor could suspect more than harmless generalizations on the state of man. But a Jewish audience read into the
ambiguous phrases its own helplessness, its own dependence
upon others, its own subjection to slanderous accusations, its
own protestation of innocence.

The poems written at Kovno were overladen with moral
sentiments as a result of Zunser's constant soul-searching under
the influence of Rabbi Israel Salanter. Several of these poems
repeated the pattern of *The Watch*. Thus, *The Song of the Eye*
(*Dos Lied fun Oig*) and *The Quill* (*Die Shreibfeder*) also began
with a series of questions and ended with a parallel series of
answers. Each interrogatory stanza recounted the reasons why
the personified object should be supremely happy and concluded with a refrain inquiring as to its apparent discontent. The
answering stanzas listed the misfortunes which rendered contentment impossible. For example, in *The Song of the Eye*,
the poet asked the human eye why it shed tears even when it
laughed. The eye replied that it was cursed with envy, that
it desired to possess all it saw, and that it wept because so much
was beyond its reach. The poet then reminded the insatiable
eye that all life was transitory and that soon dust would cover
its brilliance. Therefore, let it not desire more than was easily
obtainable. Let it rest from overmuch striving here below.

Let it calmly await the peace of the hereafter. There it would sparkle with joy undimmed by tears.

In *The Quill*, the poet asked the quill why it was so worried, why its face was so black, and why its heart was so cramped. After all, kings and ministers made use of it. Millions of human beings were made happy by its slender mouth. It participated in the secrets of philosophers, inventors, architects, and engineers. It announced glad tidings and acted as the intermediary between distant friends. It recorded weddings and final testaments. It inscribed the letters of the holy Torah and the sayings of wise men, thereby enabling people to follow precepts of goodness. Why, therefore, was it so sad and so dark of demeanor? The quill replied that it often fell into the hands of wicked people and had to serve their ill purposes most faithfully. It had to participate in forgeries, in fraudulent correspondence, in hypocritical epistles of praise, in blackmail and slander, in atheistic pamphlets, in signing cruel decrees that condemned God's people to torture, exile, and enforced baptism. Therefore, its heart continually knew sorrow and its face was blackened with shame.

In several allegories or poetic parables, the young bard voiced his own gratitude and that of his entire people to Czar Alexander II, the early years of whose reign were designated by Zunser as the Golden Epoch of Russian Jewry. Alexander II ascended the Russian throne in 1855. While he did not remove all or even most of the discriminatory laws that had weighed so heavily upon Eastern Jewry for many decades, he did display a more liberal spirit toward his subjects of all nationalities than did his predecessor Nicholas I.

Alexander II recognized that the prosperity of Russia could be increased by opening wide the doors of opportunity to all persons of talent, regardless of their ancestral background or their ethnic origin. He, therefore, made it possible for a considerable number of Jews to be admitted to Russian schools, academies, and universities. Within a few years, Jewish physicians, engineers, lawyers, technicians, chemists, and architects began to make their way into the professions and soon acquired national and international reputations. At the same time Jewish men-of-letters, Jewish painters and sculptors, Jewish inventors vied with their Slavic neighbors in furthering Russian cultural projects. Jewish actors and Jewish singers gained fame on the theatrical and operatic stages of the principal Russian cities. Jewish journalists wrote for Russia's influential newspapers and periodicals. A few educated Jews, who were willing to pay the price of baptism, even made headway in the military profession and in government service.

Zunser entertained high hopes for the ultimate abolition of all the legal disabilities under which Jews labored. He had faith in the good will of the monarch who had saved him and others from Siberian martyrdom and military entombment. The best known of the parables expressing this faith were *The Flower* (*Die Blum*) and *The Song of the Bird* (*Dos Lied fun Foigel*).

The former lyric depicted Israel as a flower. Once in the remote past this flower blossomed in a fair garden just like others of its species. The sun warmed it and kind hands watered it. Then came an evil day. The precious flower was uprooted and hurled on the highway. There it rotted away, its petals discolored, its fragrance dissipated. It became prey to wind and weather. It was crushed by all passing feet. But, at long last, an angel heard its plaintive wailing. He lifted it gently from the dungheap onto which it had been blown. He removed the accumulated filth. He revived it with refreshing water. He nursed it back to health. He placed it in his beautiful garden. There it could resume its normal growing and blossoming. There it could regain its splendor and fragrance. This angel was Alexander II.

This early lyric has a strong Zionist undertone, though written in a pre-Zionist period. It was later sung, both in Hebrew and in Yiddish, by the Palestinian pioneers.

The Song of the Bird had an allegorical structure similar to that of *The Flower*. It used the same theme but different symbols. Israel was portrayed as a bird with clipped wings. Once upon a time this bird too had a home of its own and flew gaily

in the sunlight. It sang melodious paeans of praise to its creator,
sweet hymns of thanks to the Lord who gave it pinions with
which to pierce the air and to float high above fields and tree-
tops. Then came an evil hour. Tragedy struck. The bird was
shorn of its wings and driven from its nest. It sought shelter in
various places but everywhere it met with cruelty and vicious-
ness. Deformed by years of maltreatment, it was chased from
place to place as a crippled monstrosity—until a kind-hearted
host took note of its pain and disgrace. He placed it magnanimously in his sunbathed garden, so that it might recover its
former strength, grow wings again, disport happily under the
clouds just like all other birds. This host was Alexander II.

It has been generally assumed by writers on Zunser that his
idealization of Alexander II, as expressed in the above poems,
was an insincere concession to his fear of the censor. This
assumption cannot be maintained. In the first place, an examina-
tion of all the poems written by him during the reigns of
Nicholas I and Alexander III fails to reveal any comparable
praise of these autocrats, even though the censorship they imposed was no less severe. In the second place, Zunser retained
the laudatory verses on Alexander II in all the later editions,
both those that appeared in Russia after the latter's assassination
and those that were published in the New World. In the third
place, in his *Autobiography*, written in America, Zunser criticized severely the policies of other Russian Czars toward the
Jews, but he made an exception of Alexander II, crediting him
with the best intentions toward his Jewish subjects.

There is no denying, however, that censorship did impose
certain hardships upon Zunser as upon every creative writer in
the vast Eastern European realm. Literary men had been suspect
in Russia ever since the first French Revolution, when Cath-
erine the Great, who had at first flirted with liberalism and
enlightenment, took measures to keep dangerous political ideas
far from her borders. No book or pamphlet could go to press
throughout the nineteenth century without the approval of a

censor. The fear of subversive, revolutionary doctrines led to a careful scrutiny of the most harmless texts and even of cookbooks and musical scores.

To write on contemporary themes was fraught with peril. To call attention to weaknesses in the imperial structure or to the failings of governmental institutions might result in immediate banishment to remote Siberia. Nevertheless, the temptation to do so was very strong, especially for a Jewish writer. Just because a Jewish audience suffered more from oppressive measures than did other sectors of the Russian population, it was likely to react with greater intensity to the poet who had sufficient courage to deal with its daily sorrows and afflictions, and who made use of his gift of words to console and to inspire. Great skill was required to circumvent the censor, who himself often lived in terror of supercensors and the ubiquitous, omnipotent secret police.

The device resorted to by Zunser and by others was the lavish use of symbolism. A poem by Zunser might, at first reading, seem to be merely a harmless tale or legend expounded in the traditional manner of the balladists of older generations. But to a listening audience the oral intonation of the poem and the subtle gestures accompanying its musical presentation would carry a contemporary meaning of which a censor at his official desk could never be aware. So essentially were word, melody, and gesture fused in Zunser's art that it is all but impossible to realize from the printed page alone the full magic which he exercised upon an audience.

Zunser's early poems were comparatively mild in their sting and concentrated on generalities rather than on specific issues. His dramatic lyrics, such as *Summer and Winter* (*Der Zumer un der Vinter*) or *Rustic and Townsman* (*Der Yishuvnik mit'n Shtutman*), continued a literary genre which had been popular since the Middle Ages, the disputation or altercation between personified qualities and forces. Opponents, such as virtue and vice, wisdom and folly, soul and body, day and night, met in

debate. In non-Jewish literatures, the former always won and
the latter always had to leave the field of combat routed and
maimed.* Zunser's allegorical struggles were, however, waged
between equally matched opponents and did not result in a
one-sided victory. Zunser did not weight the evidence. He let
each side in alternating stanzas state its case fully and defend its
point of view most vigorously. The audience was left to reach
its own conclusions. Perhaps this approach of Zunser, this dis-
pensing of equal justice to both sides, was the specific Jewish
contribution to this general European theme.

The disputation between the seasons is a theme that can be
traced back through the various European literatures to a fable
of Aesop. Aesop personified winter and spring as opponents in
a verbal duel: Winter mocked spring for its mildness and
friendliness in contrast to its own severity, before which
human beings trembled. Spring accepted these reproaches as
compliments and explained that just because human beings
feared winter they could gladly dispense with it, while they
would always honor and prize mild, friendly spring. As a dispute between summer and winter, the theme was spread
throughout Europe by the *Vagantes* or goliardy, wandering
Christian clerics who wrote in Latin. From their Latin versions,
the various vernacular languages of Europe took over the
theme during the fourteenth and fifteenth centuries. French,
Provençal, and German minstrels always accorded the victory
to summer. The Meistersinger Hans Sachs in the sixteenth century was the first to give the victory to winter. As a German
folksong, this dispute of the seasons penetrated eastward to
Yiddish-speaking territory and was handed down by word of
mouth from generation to generation, constantly undergoing
modifications at the hands of anonymous balladists, until it

* Hermann Jantzen, *Geschichte des deutschen Streitgedichts im Mittel-
alter, Germanistische Abhandlungen,* XIII, Breslau, 1896, p. 96. See also:
H. Walther, *Das Streitgedicht in der lateinischen Literatur des Mittel-
alters,* München, 1920; also: Moritz Steinschneider, *Rangstreit-Literatur,*
Wiener Sitzungsberichte (Philosophisch-literarische Klasse) Wien, 1908,
Vol. 155, Heft 4.

reached young Zunser. Its enduring popularity led him to expand the theme to fourteen stanzas, each stanza consisting of three rhymed couplets.

Alternately, summer and winter sing of the benefits each confers upon mankind and of the ills the opponent brings on. Summer emphasizes its green fields, its warm air, its fruit-laden orchards, its singing birds, its sunfilled days, its refreshing baths. Winter debits its adversary with searing heat, plagues of flies, drenching rains, the weeks of Jewish mourning and lamentation, when even weddings are forbidden; and, by contrast, winter praises its own salubrious air, its blanket of snow which warms the seeded earth, its happy festivals such as Hanukkah and Purim.

Zunser's disputation, *Rustic and Townsman*, went beyond mere generalizations to specific criticism of undesirable moral attitudes. Each adversary, in presenting his case, began by recounting the physical, material advantages and disadvantages of country life or city life, but both soon shifted to a higher level. The townsman praised urban living because it offered better educational facilities for his children and more opportunities to do good deeds. The rustic questioned the desirability of giving every child a Talmudic education, without taking into account the child's mental capacity, and doubted that people in larger settlements really took advantage of their greater opportunities to practice kindness and benevolence.

In presenting the clash of two opposing attitudes through the lips and gestures of two speakers, Zunser was advancing beyond the boundary of lyric poetry into the realm of dramatic dialogue. Unconsciously he had made two discoveries which paved the way for his later pioneering efforts in behalf of Yiddish drama. He had learned that acting was more effective than mere narrating or singing, and he had hit upon the essence of drama: the conflict between antagonists, each of whom was convinced of the justice of his own cause and was ready to maintain his position to the very end.

Zunser's early allegorical poems generally fell into the two patterns discussed above: either the long disputations between personified qualities, which continued an age-old tradition, or the complex question-and-answer type, which he developed in his Kovno period. The finest poem of his early period, however, fell outside of these two patterns. It was the philosophic lyric *The Ferry* (*Der Prom*), composed soon after his return to Vilna in 1858.

The poet, walking beside the Vilia River, which flows through Vilna, sees a ferry conveying people from one bank to another, and he falls to musing about human life and human destiny. The river, in its depth and danger, becomes in his imagination a symbol of the world and the ferry a symbol of time. Within the ferry, human beings are crowded together for the eventful crossing between the banks of birth and death. Near the former bank, during childhood years, they remain confident and unafraid; and, as they come within reach of the latter bank, their aged eyes again know no fear. It is only in midstream that they face real danger, since crosscurrents drive the ferry hither and yon. These crosscurrents are man's fitful desires and erring passions, which seek to take him off his true course. But faith is the compass that saves the boat from floating off to perilous shoals and reefs. Faith guides it unerringly to a safe landing on the farther bank. Faith lends man courage throughout his crossing and points out to him the path of joy eternal awaiting him beyond the river of time.

The poem well deserved its enduring popularity because of its depth of feeling, its comforting message, and its religious tone. The enticing rhythm of its musical accompaniment interpreted the lilting and rocking of the boat on which man journeyed from the cradle to the grave. Zunser avoided critical references to contemporary events and refrained from his usual satiric innuendos. He concentrated on moving the hearts of his listeners by making them aware of the transitoriness of all existence and of the abiding value of their faith. He advised them: "Be a Jew in your relation to God and be a human being in your relation to your townsmen—then you will cross the river safely."

The enthusiastic response of Zunser's audiences to his early songs led to an increasing demand for his appearance at festivals, holiday celebrations, and especially weddings. From beyond Kovno and Vilna came invitations offering compensation far exceeding his earnings as a braider. Since he was still unmarried and unburdened by family responsibilities, he yielded to the persistent clamor for his talents and decided upon the career of a *Badchen* or Wedding Bard, a career which was not then in the best repute because of the unsavory character of its practitioners, but which he was to ennoble by his high idealism and superior artistry.

CHAPTER VII

Wedding Bard

E<small>LIAKUM</small> ZUNSER became famous in the 1860's and 1870's as Eliakum Badchen, Eliakum the Wedding Bard. The term *Badchen* was originally derived from a Talmudic verb, which meant "to cheer up, to make laugh." When Zunser appeared on the literary scene, this term had sunk in popular usage to signify a coarse, uncultured jester. By applying it to himself in his publications and on every possible occasion, he led his admirers to associate it instead with the newer moral type of entertainment, with the singable didactic poetry that he brought to perfection and which added graceful joyousness to solemn wedding rites.

A wedding in an Eastern Jewish community was an event of interest not only to the couple directly concerned and to their immediate families but to the entire Jewish population. It furnished an opportunity to forget temporarily the burdens and cares of drab existence and to enter into a carnival spirit. It was an occasion for gaiety, music, and dancing. The religious leaders, rabbi and cantor, were in charge solely of the serious aspects of the holy sacrament.

A merrymaker, who combined the functions of musician and comedian, came to the fore in the late Middle Ages. He was the Jewish equivalent of the jongleur, troubadour, buffoon, wandering minstrel, court jester, and similar entertainers who delighted non-Jewish audiences in Central and Western Europe.* Rabbis often inveighed against his gay, impudent antics, but they could not stem his popularity. They referred to him in their Hebrew texts as *Letz* or wag. Later on, the merry-maker at weddings was given the more dignified title of *Marshalik*, a word cognate to the English *marshal*, since his function had become that of a marshal or master of ceremonies. By the middle of the nineteenth century, the customs and ceremonies connected with a Jewish wedding had grown so numerous and so complex that only a specialist could guarantee that all the traditional requirements, all the religious prescriptions, and all the local customs would be carried out scrupulously. Certain forms were regarded as propitious, and the slightest deviation from them might invite trouble. The wedding march had to be carefully planned. The order of the various dances had to be meticulously observed. A successful wedding needed authoritative supervision of every detail.

In Eastern Europe the Badchen took over these functions and gradually replaced the *Marshalik*. The Badchen was a pious merrymaker, a chanting moralist, a serious bard who sermonized while he entertained. He emphasized ethical maxims rather than piquant jokes. He had to be a learned person, well grounded in scriptural references, Talmudic sayings, and historic legends. He had to be able to improvise appropriate verses upon the different stages of the wedding ceremony. He had to have a ready stock of riddles, abundant anecdotes, and rhyming compliments for the guests at the long-drawn-out wedding-banquet.

J. H. Bondi, a German physician, described a wedding which he attended at a Russian summer resort, while Zunser was at the height of his career as Badchen. Festivities were spread out over seven days. On each afternoon, a banquet was offered to the revelers. It began at four and lasted until late at night. Zunser

* I. Lifshitz, *Badchonim un Letzim bei Yidden, Arkhiv far der Geshikhte fun Yiddishen Teater un Drama*, Vilna, 1931, pp. 38–74.

had been fetched from a great distance to act as master of ceremonies. He and the musicians kept the guests enthralled
throughout the many hours day after day.*

The most important contribution of the Badchen to the
success of a wedding was his rhymed address to the bride. This
generally took place just before the bride was conducted to the
Khupa or wedding canopy.

A chair was placed in the middle of the festive room. The
bride, whose head and face were covered with a veil, sat down,
and all the assembled guests sat around her in a circle. The
Badchen then addressed her in a chanting voice. He reminded
her that she was now experiencing the most momentous event
in her life, that she was taking leave of her carefree youth and
was about to enter upon the serious responsibilities of married
life. He asked her to look upon this day as no less holy than the
awesome Yom Kippur, the Day of Atonement. He urged her
to turn her thoughts to God and to pray for forgiveness of her
sins. He recalled the names and virtues of her departed relatives,
to whom she had been particularly endeared, and he moved all
listeners with a recital of the fleeting nature of our earthly years,
which pass away like the shadows of a dream. By the time he
had concluded his versified remarks, the spirit of levity had
yielded to the grave solemnity befitting the actual religious
ritual, which the rabbi and cantor were then called upon to
perform.†

The success of a wedding often hinged upon the choice
of the proper Badchen. Eliakum Zunser became, in the course
of time, the yardstick by which all members of his exacting
profession were measured. His services were eagerly sought.
Those couples were most fortunate who could boast that their
married life had been ushered in under the auspices of the famed
bard of Vilna. To attain to this pinnacle of success, however,

* J. H. Bondi, *Aus dem jüdischen Russland vor vierzig Jahren*, Frankfurt,
1927, p. 39.
† S. A. Hirsch, "Some Literary Trifles," *Jewish Quarterly Review*, 1901,
XIII, 602.

Zunser had to surmount many obstacles and to overcome many pitfalls.

When he arrived in Vilna, after his initial triumph at Kovno, he faced two practical problems. In the first place, the patricians of this Lithuanian metropolis did not want to engage a new-comer as Badchen as long as they could afford the services of the experienced Moishe Warshaver, then the brightest luminary of his profession. For a year or two, therefore, Zunser had to content himself with the invitations he received from poor people, and his compensation was far from adequate. In the second place, he could not keep for himself even the small sums he did receive. He needed instrumental accompaniment. The musicians, who cooperated with him during the wedding, would empty his pockets after the wedding. If he refused to give them most of his earnings, they would ambush him while he was on his way home, pin him against a wall, and take all of his coins. The young Badchen must have suffered considerable vio-lence during many a midnight hour, because he had recurrent nightmares about these attacks throughout his later years. Old Zunser often cried out in his sleep and awoke bathed in perspira-tion. In his dreams he was still defending his hard-earned kopecks against a threatening band of musicians.

It was at this time that the poet wrote his *Song of the Ruble* (*Dos Lied fun Rubel*), which he sang at the weddings of the poor. He personified the Ruble as his opponent, with whom he wanted to enter into a dispute. He was eager to inquire into its accursed pedigree and to discover the diabolical magic which enabled it to make the stupid seem wise and the ill-mannered appear as refined. Pride and arrogance accompanied it. Envy and hate were its servitors. All beings from childhood to senility craved its presence, because those who were not graced by this metallic majesty were deemed vile and dishonorable. They were shunned by friends and deprived of courage and joy.

At Vilna, Zunser soon became the idol of the poor and began to make inroads upon the richer territory of his rival, Moishe

Warshaver. Wedding bands that hired any Badchen but Zunser often found the doors of prospective patrons closed to them. The musicians were, therefore, compelled to reach an understanding with him and to substitute true cooperation for persecution. Warshaver, however, could not tolerate a dangerous rival and tried to undermine his achievements. But there were too many witnesses to testify to the younger bard's skill as master of ceremonies, and the songs he originated were on the lips of thousands.

Warshaver then hit upon a clever plan to render his competitor innocuous. He sent emissaries to Zunser with an offer of partnership. This offer sounded attractive to the unwary bard. It immediately opened to him the doors of the richest families of Vilna and enabled him to concentrate on the artistic aspects of his profession, while leaving the business details to the more practical Warshaver. Zunser signed the three-year contract submitted to him by his prospective partner. Only after it was too late, did he learn the full implications of its various clauses. He had agreed, for instance, to accept as his share of the earnings eight guldens a week. This was, in his estimation, a reasonable initial salary. Unhappily, however, Zunser had forgotten to include any provision for a share of the constantly increasing income. He soon discovered that at sumptuous weddings, where he received many times the amount he could claim under the contract, he was required to turn over all the profits to his wily partner.

Such an inequitable arrangement, obviously, could not continue for years. Zunser, before long, felt morally justified in breaking away from Warshaver and in accepting invitations to weddings on his own account. Warshaver immediately sued Zunser for breach of contract. To make sure that the judicial authorities would rule in his favor, he magnanimously offered to contribute any fines collected from Zunser to the general fund being raised among the civilians for the benefit of wounded soldiers. The Poles had just then risen in revolt against their Russian overlords and patriotic gestures were appreciated by the sorely pressed Russians. Warshaver's offer was gratefully accepted. Whenever, therefore, Zunser was invited to officiate as Badchen at a wedding, Warshaver appeared with an escort of gendarmes and forcibly interfered. The repeated disturbances caused by the intrusion of bailiffs, police, and Warshaver, in the midst of the merrymaking, were most embarrassing to the hosts and most distressing to the guests. As a consequence, Zunser found himself with ever fewer invitations and with a rapidly dwindling income. The earnings that he did manage to salvage, for the most part, went to his lawyer Shloime Prudzhanski, since the latter was kept busy defending his client, who after every affair was brought to the police magistrate for questioning.

Months of misery and privation ensued. Zunser despaired of an early deliverance from his bondage to Warshaver. But again, as in the dark days of his military entombment, a miracle took place. The highest administrative authority of the province, the Governor-General himself, freed Zunser from the contract into which he had been tricked, and banished his wily adversary from Vilna. The chain of circumstances leading to this happy conclusion was as follows:

Immediately upon the outbreak of the Polish Insurrection of 1863, Count Muraviev was placed in charge of the four provinces of Vilna, Grodno, Kovno, and Minsk. He set up his headquarters at Vilna and from this town he issued all the commands for suppression of the uprising. The Jews, who had little to gain from either a Polish or a Russian victory, tried in the main to avoid taking sides. Zunser, however, as an ardent partisan of Alexander II, sympathized with the Russian side. He composed a song, entitled *The Polish Insurrection* (*Der Poilisher Miatezh*), and sang it at the Jewish weddings to which he was invited. It found general approval. A Russian colonel happened to attend one of the weddings at which Zunser's song was enthusiastically applauded. The officer asked that the lyric be translated for him, and liked the Russian translation so well that he sent it to the Governor-General. Count Muraviev

was, in turn, so pleased by the patriotic sentiment that he sent
the poet a gift of twenty-five rubles.

A few days later, the Governor-General gave an audience
to one of the prominent and wealthy Jews of Vilna, Judel
Apatov. In the course of the conversation, Count Muraviev
praised Zunser's song and called Apatov's attention to this
talented composer. Soon afterwards Apatov called in Zunser as
Badchen at his daughter's wedding and was delighted with the
bard's brilliant performance. Zunser used this opportunity to
pour out his heart to his powerful and influential patron. Apatov
promised to help. Upon his intercession, the Governor-General
ruled that the contract which Zunser had been enticed to sign
was illegal and unfair, and he ordered Warshaver to leave the
provincial capital. The tables were thus turned, and the harried
Zunser became almost overnight the idol of Vilna.

Released from gloom and from the daily fear of violence,
he now could devote himself more intensely to the creation of
new texts and melodies. These songs quickly spread beyond
Vilna, and the composer's presence was requested in ever more
distant communities. Invitations rained in from Grodno and
Warsaw, from Dvinsk and Vitebsk, from Kovno and Minsk.

Russia was rapidly being covered by a network of railroads,
and Zunser traveled far and wide. His fame and his income rose
steadily. Before he was thirty, he could thank God for having
delivered him from poverty, bondage, and affliction. His happiness and carefree prosperity are reflected in his compositions
of this period. Thus, his *Pre-Holiday Mystery* (*Dos Geheemnis
fun Erev Yom-Tov*) was a gay song of the hustle, bustle, excitement, and confusion in Jewish families on the eve of important holidays. The rushing to butcher and baker, the ordering
of new clothes and wigs, the cooking and roasting of traditional delicacies, all details of a housewife's ordeal were depicted vividly and with broad humor. Another lyric of Zunser's,
The Whiskey Song (*Dos Lied fun die Volvele Branfen*), com-
memorated in a jovial mood the fall in the price of liquor and
the resulting increased consumption. The satiric references were

good-natured, and the crusading spirit completely absent. Drink, he felt, had its value. Why should not the laborer and the poor man also be able to afford once in a while the exhilaration of moderate indulgence?

The growing vogue of Zunser's songs led his colleagues and competitors to use them ever more frequently in their own repertoire. Most of these songs were unpublished. Zunser remarked that heads trained in memorizing the Talmud could very quickly catch on to any text or melody. They needed merely to hear it once or twice. However, his songs easily lent themselves to variations and adaptations by folksingers, talented and untalented. Soon numerous differing versions were heard. The distortions that gained currency because of inaccurate recollection peeved Zunser. He was even more chagrined when he saw his own compositions printed by others without his authorization. He commented: "Our Jews sent abroad and printed my songs anew. They ruined the language. They perverted it. Hardly a verse or a word was recognizable. One could faint, just looking at the product."

To counteract this falsification and plundering of his texts, Zunser decided to publish the best of his songs in penny booklets under his own supervision. His collection *Shirim Khadoshim*, which had gone through several reprintings since its first appearance in 1861, was followed in 1870 by *Kol Rino*. Zunser still followed the learned tradition of using Hebrew titles, but he wrote a versified preface to this new booklet, which ended in a defense of the vernacular. To persons who might ask: "Why do we need this jargon of Yiddish?" the proper reply must be: "You cannot speak to the masses except in their own tongue." Zunser himself was more interested in reaching the masses than in winning the approval of the scholars. Proudly he exclaimed in the opening poem:

> Go, my little book, go out into the world, be everywhere, among pious Jews no less than among the Enlightened. Forget not: a Badchen composed you, a figure disliked nowadays by both groups.

As a protest against this unjustifiable dislike, he called himself
on the title page not Eliakum Zunser but Eliakum, the Badchen
of Vilna.

Kol Rino did not usher in a new development in Zunser's
poetry but rather included further examples of the familiar
genres. The poetic allegory was represented by *The Song of
Satin (Dos Lied Fun die Atlas)*. Satin, in its personified role,
complained that it had fallen from grace. Once the haughty
material enveloping only aristocracy, it had come upon evil
days and was being abused by commoners who did not appreci-
ate its fine texture. Its fate was thus not unlike that of the wise
man who had come into the company of fools, or that of the
learned man who found himself in the midst of the ignorant.

The World in Masquerade (Die farmaskirte Velt), was a
satire on the extravagance of Zunser's contemporaries, who in
their desire to impress their neighbors through finery and outward show, lived beyond their means. He attacked the vicious
habit of buying luxuries on installment, borrowing of money
in order to travel to spas and vacation resorts, strutting like
peacocks in the newest fashions. He praised the simple, sincere
life of the forefathers, who had no need of masquerading and
who thereby avoided much worry and financial embarrassment.

Homely, practical advice was also woven into the verses of
The Old World and the New (Die alte Velt mit die Neie), a
long poetic disputation in the manner of the earlier ones between Summer and Winter or Rustic and Townsman. The
Broder Singers were fond of acting out this song, not only at
weddings but also in wine-cellars, because it lent itself easily
to dramatic presentation. An actor, garbed as the Old World,
and another, arrayed as the New World, chanted alternating
stanzas to the accompaniment of appropriate gestures and movements. Each adversary brought evidence that his way of life
was to be preferred. At the end of an acrimonious debate, both
arrived at the tolerant conclusion that there were desirable traits
in the old order and in the new. Thereupon both Worlds turned

towards each other, smiled, embraced, and danced together, while the delighted audience cheered and applauded.

The lighter tone noticeable in Zunser's poems of the 1860's, when he entered upon his successful career as a Wedding Bard, contrasted sharply with the biting irony of the preceding Kovno period, when he was still smarting under the injustices suffered in his young years, and with the tragic profundity of the succeeding Minsk period, after he was overwhelmed by catastrophe upon catastrophe. The period between the appearance of *Shirim Khadoshim* in 1861 and *Kol Rino* in 1870 coincided almost entirely with the decade of his first marriage, which began in 1862 and which ended so grimly in 1871.

CHAPTER VIII

First Marriage

Zunser's engagement to his first cousin Rochel took place in 1856, shortly after his release from military service. His brief spell of prosperity before he left Bobruisk had made a great impression upon his relatives of Samokhvolovitz, when he and his mother passed through this little town on their way back to Vilna. When Etta Kayle and her sister Mariashe-Hannah, his future mother-in-law, agreed that the wedding was to take place in about two years, it was assumed that during this interval the braider's assistant would become self-supporting.

When Zunser threw his trade aside to become an itinerant bard, the wedding was postponed. Financial uncertainty was probably not the only reason or the main obstacle. Mariashe-Hannah and her husband Reb Hillel, a faithful follower of the Hassidic Rabbi of Kaidanov, would gladly have received their son-in-law as a semi-permanent addition to their household for a year or two, in accordance with the custom in Russian-Jewish communities. But Zunser was not at all eager, after his year among villagers, to bury himself in a town of a few hundred inhabitants, while fame was beckoning to him in the two largest cities of Lithuania: Kovno and Vilna. He, therefore, continued to postpone the inevitable day, in the belief that he would soon be able to earn enough to fetch his bride to a home of his own. Then followed his difficulties with the rapacious musicians and the unfortunate contract with Warshaver. Zunser's dream of a happy family life, free from the dire poverty he had faced so often, seemed to recede ever further.

Reb Hillel, however, was growing more and more impatient. If he had at first agreed to a two years' postponement of the wedding, he was genuinely worried when almost three times the allotted period elapsed. Zunser at twenty-six regarded himself as an old bachelor and was so regarded by others, yet Rochel was even older. When, therefore, in the late summer of 1862, persecution by Warshaver showed no signs of abatement and when Reb Hillel became very persistent in his invitations to his nephew to become his son-in-law, Zunser finally yielded. He accepted the offer to spend the High Holidays at Samokhvolovitz, and on the day after Yom Kippur the wedding took place.

It was customary at the wedding supper for the bridegroom to exhibit his learning to the assembled guests by making a solemn speech spiced with quotations from the Talmud and offering original comments on some disputed detail of religious lore. In this ordeal, Zunser, who was easily the most learned lay person in the entire gathering, acquitted himself with great distinction. Reb Hillel was proud of this new member of his family and eagerly awaited the end of the week of festivities in order to introduce him to the wonder-working Rabbi of Kaidanov.

When Zunser was brought on a Sabbath to the court of the Hassidic *Zaddik*, he was not at all impressed by its ecstatic mysticism. He did not believe in the miraculous powers that his father-in-law ascribed to the holy man. He looked upon the proceedings with the eyes of a rationalist and a sceptic. He did not realize that Hassidism, with its rituals of drinking, singing, and dancing, answered the need for poetry and joyousness in ghetto communities and that, despite its various aberrations, it did bring consolation to the heavy-hearted and new hope to the dejected. He saw merely its abnormal fanaticism and its superstition. He expressed his dislike of the entire movement in a vitriolic satire entitled *The Rabbi's Key* (*Dem Rebbis Shlissele.*) To avoid embarrassing his father-in-law, he transferred the scene of the poem to Galicia and tried to draw a distinction

between the honest, scholarly, religious leaders of Russia and the
dishonest, ignorant rabbis of the remote Austrian province.
Nevertheless, the attack was so withering that Reb Hillel did not
dare to take Zunser along a second time to the holy man of
Kaidanov, and felt genuinely relieved when the young man
announced, two months after the wedding, that he was giving
up all claims to further support and would leave immediately
with his wife for Vilna.

Zunser's decision to return to his native city was wise. It is
true that at first he had to exert all his ingenuity to provide for
himself, his wife, and his aging mother; but a turn in the tide of
fortune came during the following year, the year of the Polish
Insurrection. The Governor-General, as we have seen, freed
him from Warshaver's unfair competition and gave him the
opportunity to enter upon his chosen profession on a grand
scale.

Zunser's hitherto longest song, *The Miser* (*Der Karger mit
Yekele Bass*), was probably started at about this time. Although
it was not published until 1869, when it appeared in a separate
pamphlet, many of its hundred and twelve stanzas must have
been sung or chanted earlier, for they reflect experiences of his
early married years, his difficult economic plight, and his struggle to raise the dignity of the Badchen's calling.

In a rhymed preface of an additional six stanzas, he bewailed
the lot of the Yiddish bards who racked their brains to produce
a song, rich in thought and beautiful in form, only to be nig-
gardly rewarded by miserly patricians. He drew upon his own
bitter memories in telling the versified story of a merrymaker's
revenge upon an ungenerous patron. There were probably
festive occasions when Eliakum, the Badchen, deemed it necessary to intone the stanzas to a jolly host as a gentle reminder
that avarice brought retribution and that whosoever was blessed
with an abundance of earthly goods might act more benefi-
cently towards his less fortunate fellow men.

Zunser portrayed a well-to-do person, whose door was ever
closed to the poor and who even begrudged every coin he had

to spend on himself, his wife, or his only child. When the time came for his son's wedding to a girl in a community some distance away, Yekele Bass, the local merrymaker, begged to be taken along to entertain at the wedding feast.

Yekele Bass had an elastic face and was a most talented impersonator. He could transform himself in a moment into a Russian peasant or an aged Jewish woman. He could appear successively as a policeman, a miracle-working rabbi, a mother in birthpains, a pilgrim from Jerusalem, a coachman, or a ghost. He knew how to evoke laughter and to heighten hilarity. But when he asked to be engaged for the wedding, the rich miser shouted at him that there were plenty of clowns in the world and that it was unnecessary to drag a jester from one town to another. Yekele felt hurt and decided to avenge the insult.

The miser and his family set out on their journey, but no coachman was taken along to drive the carriage. The road led through a village whose gate was closed. An old peasant stood near the gate but failed to budge when asked to open the bars. He remained stiff and mute even when a few pieces of wedding cake were thrown to him. The enraged miser jumped down from his carriage and struck the disrespectful old man. The latter instantly collapsed, covered with blood. The terrified wedding group hid the corpse and fled as fast as they could. Before long, they heard sounds of pursuit. A policeman caught up with them. But he merely wanted them to return to the village to have their passports examined. He was, however, willing to let them continue on their trip, if offered an inducement in cash.

At the wedding feast, a pilgrim from Jerusalem arrived. In accordance with Jewish custom, he was welcomed heartily. He regaled the wedding guests with joyful news of the Holy Land. In the course of the evening, however, he disappeared with the silver candlesticks. The distressed father of the bride rushed for advice to a wonder-working rabbi, who had just come to town. The rabbi promised that the candlesticks would be returned by the pilgrim before dawn, and the grateful father

reciprocated with a handsome reward. The rabbi also mentioned that an accusation was being leveled in heaven against
the bridegroom's father for the murder of a peasant.

When these words were brought back to the miser, he also
went to the miracle man and was told that heaven's judgment
had not yet been pronounced and that perhaps charity might
help to sway the final decision. After he had handed over a considerable sum, the miser was instructed to perform a further
penance, namely, to spend the remainder of the night awake in
a special room in absolute silence. In the early hours before
dawn, he saw the pilgrim enter the room through a window,
deposit the candlesticks, and climb out again. A short while
later, he saw the murdered peasant, his face bloodless, hurl a
bloodstained bit of wedding cake through the window, into the
room. When dawn finally came the horrified miser again rushed
to the house of the godly man for advice. The rabbi asked
him to search his heart: Had he ever hurt or disgraced anyone?
"Nobody of consequence," he replied. "But, how about ordinary
folk?" asked the rabbi. Well, he had thrown out an insignificant
individual named Yekele Bass. "Insignificant?" cried the rabbi
in anger. "Does not a poor man have a heart, blood, veins, a soul
like you, the rich? Why did you hurt him in his profession? Is
it less honorable than your profession of moneylending? How
should God not be wroth, when he sees you mistreat a poor
man who also wants to earn a pittance by entertaining at your
wedding? Return home and placate him with kind words and
substantial cash; otherwise you will forfeit your share of the
world-to-come." The miser did as he was told. After pocketing
the money, Yekele revealed that this was not the only sum he
had received, since he had already appeared as policeman,
peasant, pilgrim, and rabbi.

Not all of Zunser's songs composed during his early professional career as Badchen have survived. Some disappeared from
sight, only to re-emerge in barely recognizable form as anonymous folksongs. Of others, only the titles have come down to us.
For example, Zunser, in his *Autobiography*, mentioned his

composition *At Childbirth* (*Die Kinpetorin*), but text and melody are lost. There are also songs of Zunser's Vilna period that have come down to us in two widely differing versions and even under different titles. The most popular of these is *The Old Father* (*Der alter Foter*), in which an aged parent laments

DER ALTER FOTER

that it is better to be dead than to be dependent upon the whims of children. In six tearful stanzas, the father contrasts his former prosperous years and his complete devotion to the rearing of his children with his present impoverished state and his

ill treatment at the hands of his daughters-in-law and their
maids. He ends his lament with a plea for an early merciful
death. In the repertoire of the Broder Singers, this poem contains eight stanzas. It is entitled *A Father Comes to His Child*
(*Lied vie a Tate kumt zum Kind*).* It lists the ungrateful behavior of children and it ends with the father's plea to God for
restoration of his health and for an opportunity again to earn
his own bread during his few remaining years on earth. The
Broder Singers, entertaining in wine-cellars, needed a hopeful
or happy ending, whereas Zunser, the moralist, could risk
retaining the more effective tragic conclusion.

The moral, didactic tone also characterized the poem *The
Iron Safe* (*Der eiserner Shrank*), composed soon after his first
marriage. Zunser compared human beings who strutted about
pompously without real inner worth to empty safes designed to
store great treasures. Such empty safes were the apparently successful businessman behind whose smiling mask lurked the
worried face of an harassed debtor, the fervent moralist beneath whose learned exterior was lodged the cruel heart of an
exploiter, the dandy whose fashionable clothes distracted attention from his actual shabbiness, the philanthropist whose osten-
tatious charities concealed his neglect of a sick and aged parent.
Zunser enjoyed castigating these hollow pillars of society.

In view of the fact that Zunser's poems were most frequently
composed to be sung at weddings, it might seem surprising that
he touched so rarely upon love, a theme emphasized and overemphasized in all Occidental literature ever since the troubadours and the minnesingers of the later Middle Ages. The
explanation must be sought in the cultural environment of
Zunser's audiences. Among the Russian Jews of his generation,
love before marriage was comparatively rare. Often a boy and
girl did not even see each other before their common fate was
determined for them by their parents. It was assumed that
fathers and mothers who were interested in the welfare of their

* *Shire Zimro, Dreissig herlikhe Broder Lieder,* Warsaw, 1882.

children would arrange the best possible match for them and that young couples, relieved of economic responsibilities during the first years of wedded life, would be able to make successful emotional adjustments and would attain at least moderate happiness. The possible loss of romantic ecstasy and the lack of complete freedom of choice were more than compensated for by the avoidance of perilous pitfalls that beset inexperienced youth set adrift on the sea of love without chart or compass. If Zunser at fifteen, in his first lyric *Jewish Weddings* (*Yiddishe Shidukhim*), had called attention to the misuse by elders of their authority to choose a mate for their children, he did approve, in his later poems, the exercise of such authority. In the rhymed address to the bride, incorporated in *The Sandek*, he asked her to disregard the current journalistic attacks upon practical marriages. In his opinion, a marriage based upon romantic infatuation was more likely to lead to tragic consequences.

> You do not find Jews duelling on account of love, or committing suicide because of longing for a girl, or abandoning wife and children for a mistress. Horrifying is the spectacle of a woman loving another man or a man loving another woman.*

Zunser, the moralist, could not countenance infidelity in marriage, whether in thought or deed. He felt that it was unhealthy to feed the minds of maturing girls with trashy novels that glorified experiments in love. Perhaps a girl should be consulted before she was given in marriage to the man with whom she would have to live a whole life long, and sensible parents should indeed assign some weight to her opinion; but a girl would be courting disaster if she defied parental authority entirely and set out to seek a mate in accordance with her own exaggerated notions of love, which she derived from romantic literature.

> Eyes, dimmed by ecstatic tears of love, cannot see the end

* *Der Sandek*, Stanza 4.

clearly. He sates her with atmosphere until he attains his goal, until he despoils her of honor and gold, and then he derides her according to the latest fashion.*

During the nine years of Zunser's marriage to his cousin Rochel, five living children were born, two sons and three daughters. Each met a tragic end.

The eldest child was a son who died a horrible death in earliest infancy. After his birth, his mother was too weak to nurse him herself and so a wet nurse was engaged. She came from the town of Meretz to fetch the child at Vilna.

Every month Zunser received a letter from Meretz asking him to forward, along with the wages for the nurse, all sorts of necessary articles, such as sheets, pillows, swaddling clothes. The letters listed the many virtues of the infant, who was supposedly growing up to be as handsome as Joseph, as strong as Samson, as wise as Solomon, as modest as Hillel, and as saintly as Moses. The happy father of such a prodigy sent more money than was requested.

One day a young man came to Zunser's house in Vilna to ask for a charitable contribution. Zunser, in his usual cordial manner, welcomed the stranger and inquired where he came from.

"From Meretz," replied the young man.

"Do you happen to know in Meretz a carpenter by the name of Gershon?"

"Indeed, I do. I know him very well. He is my neighbor."

"And how is the little boy his wife is nursing?"

"You mean, how is the little girl?"

"No, my friend, I mean the little boy."

"You must be mistaken," insisted the stranger. "It is true that Gershon's wife did take an infant son of Eliakum Badchen from this very town of Vilna with the intention of nursing it, but a terrible thing happened to this

* *Nokh dem neistem Zhurnal,* Stanza 3.

child. In the course of the long trip from Vilna to Meretz, the woman dozed off. The infant slipped from her arms and fell down from the wagon. When she woke up soon afterwards, she looked about. The child was missing. She immediately ordered the coachman to turn back. Both began to look for the boy. As they again neared the forest through which they had previously passed, she saw the child in the jaws of a wolf, who was devouring it. The woman did not continue her trip to Meretz. She returned to Vilna and there she was able to obtain through an employment agency a little girl to nurse. This is the girl I mean."

Rochel, who overheard the story, collapsed in a swoon. When she regained consciousness, she wept hysterically and tore her hair. But there was nothing that could be done. As a pious Jewess, she had to submit to the inscrutable will of God. In time, she found distraction and comfort in the birth and rearing of her other children.

Zunser too was sustained in this hour of tragedy by his faith in God. He turned in his grief to God's book for consolation. There he found a tale of a father who had gone through a similar experience. To the patriarch Jacob the tragic news was also brought that his beloved child, the son of Rachel, had been torn by a beast in a forest. When Jacob learned that nothing remained of his Joseph save a blood-soaked coat, he rent his clothes and raised his voice in loud lamentation. Recalling this parallel, Zunser was led to give lasting utterance to his own grief through the voice of Jacob:

> God is just in all his works. Solely because of my sins was this innocent blood shed. Rochel brought me the news that beasts tore you apart and that your body is unburied. Where are you, my Joseph, my own? I cry out, I ask, but no answer comes. Naught is left of you, no flesh, no limbs. Teeth are gnawing at your bones. My only joy! My comfort! Gone, gone forever! . . . Rochel, O Rochel, my

darling, beasts sate their hunger on your child! Arise, Rochel, from your grave arise! Look about! Perhaps a trace of his body you'll find. In vain did you weep many a year, desiring a child. In vain did you stake your hope on the birth of your Joseph. Lost all your travail! Only for a brief moment was he our delight, before beasts rent his limbs . . . My sweet dreams are drowned in a sea of pain. My sweet hopes are sunk in a bottomless pit. I dreamed my Joseph would be the staff of my old age, but dreams delude. My Joseph, you feed me with tears this day, and you yourself feed the beasts with your noble flesh.

In this hour of sorrow, the Joseph theme, which had first seized hold of Zunser's imagination when he was sold as a Cantonist, again loomed up before him as a possible dramatic incorporation of his own experiences. From this time on, the subject continued to haunt him year after year, until it found expression in his most ambitious work, the play *The Sale of Joseph* (*Mekhiras Yosef*).

Meanwhile Zunser continued his active career as Badchen and was soon able to provide handsomely for his mother, his wife, and his growing family. He was respected by all classes of Jews from the most orthodox to the most assimilated. He never took an extreme position on the controversial issues that divided his townsmen. He was an adherent of the Haskala, but he did not carry his zeal for Enlightenment to the point of vituperating its opponents. He refrained from indulging in undignified polemics or in personal invectives. He leveled his attacks against principles and attitudes which he deemed harmful, but he never held up an individual to ridicule.

Vilna in the 1860's contained an important group of Hebrew scholars who dreamed of enriching Jewish book-learning with the virile spirit of modernism and of adding health-bringing laughter to the dreary, pious atmosphere which weighed so heavily on young and old. Zunser felt at home in the midst of these *Maskilim* or Men of the Enlightenment, because they were, on the whole, a moderate, tolerant group. They lacked the revolutionary, iconoclastic zeal which led to tragic incidents in so many other Jewish communities. They did not insist fanatically on extreme reforms, as did their contemporaries in Berlin, a century after Moses Mendelssohn's pioneering efforts. They were even less militant than their correspondents and associates in Galicia, who slavishly aped all innovations of Central European Jewry.

Orthodoxy was too firmly rooted in the Lithuanian center. The *Maskilim* did not dare to break openly with it, no matter how radical their personal beliefs might be. They rather sought to loosen a bit the iron grip of tradition by a somewhat more liberal interpretation of sacred texts and ancient rituals. Their striving led not towards assimilation but rather towards Jewish nationalism and messianic Zionism.

The leader of the Vilna group until 1868 was Zvi Hirsh Katzenellenbogen, Inspector of the Rabbinical School and author of numerous works in prose and verse, which were prized in his day but are almost entirely forgotten today. Zunser felt that he was drinking of the pure fountain of truth and wisdom when he was admitted, while still in his twenties, to the Saturday evening gatherings at the home of this revered scholar, then in his sixties. Here Zunser came to know the intellectual elite of the Jerusalem of Lithuania. The Nestor of the group was Abraham Baer Lebensohn, whose Hebrew elegies, published under the pseudonym Adam Hacohen, paved the way for the renascence of lyrical poetry in the ancient tongue. His son, Micah Joseph Lebensohn had flashed as a meteor across the literary horizon and had died in 1852, at the age of twenty-four: but his *Songs of the Daughter of Zion (Shire Bas Zion)* had awakened, in this Vilna circle and beyond, intense longing for the Holy Land and had stimulated a revival of Jewish national feeling.

In the verses of young Lebensohn, who has been called the Keats of Hebrew literature, Zion was a dream and an ideal, to which he took flight whenever sadness and sickess overcame him. It was the Jewish Utopia of a remote past and of a distant future. It was the jewel of creation and its every rock a rune of ancestral history. The lyrics, in which the young poet, at death's door, had expressed his love for this hallowed soil, were often recited by his father. They warmed the hearts of all listeners and especially of Zunser, who was then probably the most receptive and the most impressionable member of the Katzenellenbogen circle.

Zunser paid tribute to the older Lebensohn by translating and adapting for Yiddish readers the latter's Hebrew poem *Dal Mevin (Der kluger Oreman)*. The motto of the poem was taken from Ecclesiastes: "The sleep of a laboring man is sweet, whether he eat little or much; but the abundance of the rich will not suffer him to sleep." The lyric was composed in the form of a long monologue by a poor Jew who was wisely content with little and who did not envy his patrician neighbor the worries that inevitably accompany wealth.

The pillars of the Vilna *Maskilim*, with whom Zunser associated in the 1860's, included Kalman Schulman, Mordecai Plungian, Isaac Shereshevsky, Joshua Steinberg, Matthias Strashun, who possessed the finest private library in the town, and Samuel Joseph Finn, the historian of Vilna's Jews and the founder of the early Hebrew weekly *Ha-Karmel*, which appeared from 1860 to 1881 and which served as the chief organ of the group. Zunser also met Isaac Benjakob before the latter's death in 1863. It was from Benjakob's edition of the Hebrew Bible in seventeen volumes, with the German translation in Hebraic characters by Mendelssohn and the Berlin *Maskilim*, that the young men of Eastern Europe acquired some understanding of the German tongue.

Among the Vilna intellectuals, Isaac Meir Dick displayed the keenest interest in Zunser. Despite the fact that Dick was already in his fifties and Zunser still in his twenties, they were drawn towards each other by a common striving in behalf of Yiddish, the tongue toward which the other *Maskilim* affected a superior attitude. Dick had acquired a moderate reputation as a Hebrew scholar in the 1840's and had at first shared the prejudice of his learned circle towards the so-called jargon of the masses. But, when in the 1850's he stooped to write simple tales in the despised vernacular, he found a response far beyond his expectations. One hundred thousand copies of his booklets were circulated within the first few years and many times this number during the four decades of his literary activity. Such a vast reading audience had never been equalled by the best Hebrew writers. Many of Dick's tales have failed to come down to us, despite their large editions, because they were circulated from hand to hand until they were read to shreds.

S. L. Zitron described, in his memoirs, how as a lad of seven or eight he was sent by his mother every Friday afternoon, when he came home early from Hebrew school, to fetch for a penny a copy of a Dick booklet from a book peddler to whom he had to promise to return it on Sunday morning. Neighbors would gather on Friday evenings at the Zitron home and the mother, often assisted by her young son, would read Dick's tale to them. The listeners, on returning to their own houses or on the morrow in the synagogue, would retell the story to their friends and acquaintances. Sometimes young Zitron would come to the book peddler and would find the stock of tales exhausted temporarily. Then the Friday evening gatherings at the Zitron home would be full of gloom and the neighbors would have to wait impatiently until the following week.

It was to such groups and on such evenings that Zunser's poems, also available in penny booklets, were recited, sung, or chanted. Dick's audience was equally Zunser's audience, not only in Vilna but also in Kovno, in Minsk, in Warsaw, in Kiev, and in hundreds of smaller Jewish communities. Dick's objective, the teaching of ethical conduct and the broadening of the intellectual horizon of the common man, was also Zunser's objective. Dick's use of satire in his narrative as an effective moral weapon paralleled Zunser's similar use in his ballads. Both were primarily interested in ideas. The novelist illustrated his ideas by means of exciting narratives, while the bard clothed his ideas in poetic parables. Both used their literary art to

spread the doctrines of enlightenment among the masses but
neither ventured too far from the beaten path of orthodoxy and
respectability. For example, while Dick joined Mordecai Aaron
Guenzburg and Isaac Benjakob in a secret memorandum to the
Russian government urging it to forbid the wearing by Jews of
their distinctive exotic garments, he himself did not go so far
as to dispense with the *Kaftan* worn by his coreligionists since
the Middle Ages. Similarly, while Zunser ridiculed as Asiatic
the traditional garb worn by the Lithuanian Jews, he had no
less scorn for the ultramodern dress of the assimilated Jewish
dandies.

The struggle waged over the modernization of Jewish dress
was long and bitter throughout the provinces of the Russian
Pale. It had tragic and humorous phases. The more the government persecuted the Jews for their adherence to their strange
medieval garments, the more fiercely did the Jews cling to
them. The clothes, which had in earlier centuries been imposed
upon the pariahs in the ghettos in order to set them apart, to
humiliate them, and to expose them to ridicule, had in the
course of time become invested with religious significance, and
the slightest deviation in style was condemned by orthodox
public opinion as a grievous heresy. Assimilation to non-Jews
in dress was regarded as the first step towards assimilation in
culture, religion, and morals, and was therefore resisted by the
pious masses with all the resources at their command.

Czar Nicholas I, who desired to eradicate all distinguishing
Jewish customs and characteristics, issued a series of decrees in
1835, 1839, 1841, 1844, 1848, 1850, and 1851, imposing ever
harsher penalities upon the wearers of Jewish clothes. Since
these penalties proved to be ineffective, however, governors
of various provinces proceeded to take more forceful measures
in order to carry out the imperial will. They sent out squads of
police to cut off the earlocks and to trim the coats of Jews who
showed themselves on the streets in traditional dress.

Lev Levanda, a friend and admirer of Zunser, described the
procedure adopted by the Governor of Minsk in 1844. This high

official designated a definite final date for the completion of the change to European dress and appearance. When this day passed unheeded, he mobilized the entire police force and sent it forth to the Jewish quarters armed with shears. Upon a signal from the chief inspector, the police took up their positions at every street intersection. The firemen were called out to assist them. Hour after hour passed but not a single Jew appeared on the streets. Even the Jewish stores remained closed and business was at a standstill. All day long police and firemen paced the streets in search of victims but none was visible. Finally, the impatient and angry officers decided to attack. Wielding their shears and scissors, they invaded the citadel of the Jews, the courtyard of the synagogue, and proceeded to cut the *Kaftans* and to annihilate the earlocks of the terrorized worshipers.*

Pauline Wengeroff, in her *Memoirs of a Grandmother,* recalled a scene she witnessed in the marketplace of the same town a year later. A policeman caught an old Jew in a long coat and immediately sent out a call for an assistant to help him in the execution of a most enjoyable duty. The two officers of the law then tore the headgear from the trembling victim. They trimmed his earlocks so close to his ears that the old man cried out in pain. They sheared off the lower half of the coat, so that the underclothes became visible to the gathering crowd. Then they let the disgraced graybeard run off, followed by the jubilant shouts of the street urchins.†

If, as sometimes happened, a policeman was unequipped with scissors when he encountered a Jew of proscribed appearance, he would not let this lack of a suitable offensive weapon interfere with the performance of his patriotic duty. Instead of scissors, he would use two stones. Throwing the Jew to the ground, he would apply one stone to the offending cheek under the earlock and grind the hair with the other stone until the operation was successful. The horrible torture endured by the

* Saul M. Ginsburg, *Jewish Martyrdom in Tsarist Russia,* New York, 1938, p. 303.
† Pauline Wengeroff, *Memoiren einer Grossmutter,* Berlin, 1908, I, 200.

victim merely added to the amusement of the guardian of law and order.

There is a legend that the governor of Vitebsk once saw a Jew on the street wearing a forbidden skullcap or *Yarmulke* and was so enraged that he ordered it to be tacked on to the offender's head with little tacks.

So embittered and outraged were the Jews by these daily, cruel attacks that a revolt might have broken out, if the masses had been powerful and well organized. But the unarmed and helpless Jews had no recourse save to tears and to prayers. They bewailed the loss of their earlocks, their ancient robes, and their traditional headgear as a major national calamity; and they continued to circumvent the ever multiplying decrees with whatever means were at their disposal. In the long run, they won out. The government measures failed to achieve the desired end and gradually lapsed during the liberal reign of Alexander II.

Characteristically enough, as has happened so often in Jewish history, results which tyranny and compulsion could not accomplish in the course of decades were brought about almost overnight when restrictions were lifted. The spirit of Enlightenment, which swept over Jewish youth in the 1860's made them abandon voluntarily their exotic outmoded dress and replace it with the latest garments inspired by Parisian stylists. The revolt of the younger generation against parental authority found its most obvious manifestation in the new clothes tailored after the illustrations in foreign journals. But the change in outward appearance was also accompanied, as the pious had foreseen and feared, by a shedding of old beliefs, morals, folkways, and ideals, and by an uncritical acceptance of every innovation. Zunser sensed the shallowness of the flamboyant representatives of the rising generation and he castigated them in his satiric poem *The Dandy (Der puster Frant)*.

Zunser described a Jewish cavalier in a foppish coat of newest cut, with gloves in his hands and galoshes on his feet, with hair combed to glistening perfection. Honeyed words

dripped from smooth lips when such a dandy visited ladies. He
had a ready stock of piquant anecdotes and sweet compliments
with which to entertain the fairer sex. He could refer learnedly
to Goethe and Schiller, even though he had never read a line of
theirs, and he could fascinate listeners with tales of love and
romance. In reality, however, he had not a penny of his own.
His immaculate cuffs and wide flowing scarf served to conceal
the absence of a shirt and his high galoshes hid his tattered
shoes. If only he had money, he would go to extremes in breaking with the past. He would frolic like a lord and speak French.
He would marry a beautiful lady who could play the piano
and who answered to some poetic name, such as Flora, rather
than to the more commonplace Jewish names. He would dwell
in an apartment in St. Petersburg, decorated according to the
latest interior designs, with draperies and bronze statues all
about. He would drive in a sumptuous carriage to the theatres
and he would sit in a box next to the governor. He would look
through a lorgnette at the faces of the splendid women in the
audience. He would play cards with gentlemen of high degree
and dance with ladies at masquerades. If only he had money, he
could so pleasantly emancipate himself from Jewishness!

The Dandy illustrated a gradual change of emphasis in
Zunser's didactic poetry. The preacher of enlightenment was
becoming wary of too much Enlightenment. The earlier attacks
upon superstition and ignorance in the name of reason were
giving way more and more to attacks upon too hasty and too
extreme sloughing off of tradition. Satires upon mystic excrescences, which had become attached to Judaism, were replaced
by satires upon the young men and women who lightheartedly
threw overboard the wisdom of their millennial ancestral heritage and who uncritically accepted in its stead every innovation
that was trumpeted forth as modern and ultramodern. Zunser,
who in his youth had himself risked persecution and ostracism
in his perilous pursuit of European learning, warned in his
verses against the poison that lurked in an overdose of this
precious elixir of knowledge. The excesses of the radical Jewish

intellectuals and pseudo-intellectuals during the reign of Alexander II led him to stress ever more vigorously the positive values in orthodox Judaism. The bard of the people was gifted with the healthy instincts of the common man. He echoed the rejection of the alien manna by the Jewish masses of Eastern Europe. He fought Russification and Assimilation. He groped his way back to Jewish national ideals.

CHAPTER IX

The Tragic Year

FOR THREE decades Zunser carried on his fruitful activity as poetic intermediary between the learned scholars and the less learned masses. For three decades he brought to the common man in the Russian Pale the treasures of wisdom accumulated by original Jewish thinkers. For three decades he used his literary gifts to instruct, to admonish, and to console his readers and auditors throughout the Yiddish-speaking provinces of Eastern Europe. There was, however, a difference of emphasis in his creative activity in each of these decades.

In the 1860's he was primarily the *Maskil*, interested in enlightening and instructing his people, in aiding them to cast off outmoded habits, medieval dress, queer forms of behavior, superstitious beliefs, and irrational practices. In the 1870's he was primarily the prophet of doom, admonishing his people not to venture too far on the alluring road of Enlightenment and Assimilation, pointing out the dangers of overhasty Russification, warning of probable disaster which might follow too sudden and too passionate infatuation with modernism, radicalism, and worldliness. In the 1880's, when his dire forebodings were realized and disaster did overtake his people, he concentrated on binding up their bleeding wounds, on comforting them in their hour of affliction, and on directing their gaze toward Zion, a fairer goal for their national longing than the inhospitable Czarist realm.

The tragic year 1871, in which Zunser experienced his greatest personal loss, separated the first period from the second; and the calamitous year 1881, when pogroms swept over Russian Jewry, separated the second period from the third.

A distinction is sometimes made between the earlier *Maskilim* of the reign of Nicholas I and the later *Maskilim* of the reigns of Alexander II and Alexander III, when Zunser exercised his strongest influence. The former were lonely individuals completely at odds with their environment. Each one had to defy his parents, teachers, religious mentors, and community leaders. Alone he had to find his way to clarity, alone he had to wade through the morass of ignorance, alone he had to assault the wall of fanaticism that barred his path to free thought, alone he had to defy entrenched power and to put up with social ostracism. Such a *Maskil* was indeed a hero, a martyr to his convictions, a titan of will and intelligence; but he often also bore throughout life the scars of embitterment and frustration. Zunser always spoke with awe and reverence of these intellectual giants of the pioneering generation, and he was proud of his association with some of them, who still survived in the 1860's. He himself belonged to the later *Maskilim*, the gentler souls, the dreamers of messianic dreams, the poetic idealists who lacked the ruthless strength of rebels and iconoclasts, who merely wanted to inject a bit of joy, warmth, and beauty into the sad, cold, and drab ghetto existence.

Zunser was a happy man as he entered upon the fourth decade of his life and he was more than eager to give of his happiness to others. He had succeeded in solving his own personal problems and he was ready to devote himself to alleviating the sorrows of his fellow men. His profession as Badchen or merrymaker gave him an unusual opportunity. At weddings he found receptive audiences that listened with keen attention to his rhymed comments on daily happenings as well as on unchanging religious attitudes. His former pessimistic outlook brightened with his success. He was healthy and prosperous. He traveled far and wide, universally respected and admired. The newly built railroads permitted him to exercise his calling hundreds of miles from his native Vilna. His fame spread beyond the borders of Russia. His chief colleagues and competitors sang his songs and recited his verses. In the Galician town of Lemberg, Yekil Broder published in 1871 six new songs which had been the mainstay of the Broder Singers' repertoire in the late 1860's.* Four of these were Zunser's compositions, even though his name was not mentioned. Book peddlers, who traveled about from village to village with an assortment of devotional pamphlets or *Tkhines* and secular booklets or *Maase-Biekhlekh*, were constantly besieged with requests for Zunser's texts. These emissaries of culture would drive horse and wagon into a synagogue courtyard, display their wares on a hastily rented table or bench, and attract an audience by intoning a Zunser melody. When they left on the following day, mothers and maids, coachmen and tailors were already humming the new tune.

Zunser, however, was not fated to enjoy for many years his fame and good fortune, his tranquility and domestic bliss. In the summer of 1871, in his thirty-fifth year, tragedy struck in the midst of his contentment and deprived him of wife, children, and home. Cholera descended upon Vilna, and among its earliest victims were three of Zunser's children. The first to succumb was his son Akiba, who was four years of age. On the next day Zunser mourned the passing of his older daughter Pessie, and a day later she was followed in death by her younger sister Yente-Leah. Of eight children, to whom Rochel had given birth in the course of eight years, only one remained alive, a girl, Etta Kayle, named for his deceased mother. Husband and wife were in despair. Would their last child also be taken from them?

All about them human beings were dying like flies. Business was at a standstill. Fear gripped everyone. The peasants in the villages ascribed the epidemic to the diabolical concoctions of the irreligious doctors, and in many Russian districts bloody

* Yekil Broder, *Gants neie Broder Lieder*, Lemberg, 1871.

riots broke out. The populace attacked and lynched physicians
and pharmacists. The Jews, recalling how often in former centuries they themselves had been wrongly accused of poisoning
wells and bringing on epidemics, did not participate in these
wild outbreaks of rage and cruelty. They did, however, resort
to strange incantations and superstitious ceremonies in the hope
of warding off this plague, which they interpreted as a severe
chastisement sent by God because of their sins and misdeeds.
Instead of disinfecting their homes they crowded into the synagogues and thus unknowingly helped to spread the dread disease
even more. They organized processions of pious graybeards
bearing Torah scrolls through the streets of the town. They
called upon the Lord to forgo his wrath and to have mercy. As
proof of their repentance and of their return to piety and godli-
ness, they undertook to do good deeds of the strangest variety
and they contributed to charitable causes of the weirdest kind.
For example, in one town a deaf-and-dumb girl and a blind
boy, who had slight prospects of ever being married, were es-
corted to the cemetery and there married to each other, with
the entire community contributing wedding gifts. Every Jew
and Jewess frantically sought the advice and intercession of
rabbis and reputed holy men.

Zunser, in his hour of despair, turned to his former teacher,
Israel Salanter, for succor and comfort, and was advised to
leave Vilna immediately. Moving to another town might ward
off the curse of the plague that hovered over his birthplace.
Zunser came home, packed his belongings in great haste, hired
a wagon, piled his wife and child and furniture on it, and left
for Minsk. He chose Minsk for two reasons. In the first place,
this metropolis of White Russia was still untouched by the
epidemic that was raging in Lithuania. In the second place, his
wife's parents were living there and could provide the homeless
family with temporary lodging.

Just before entering Smargon, a town about halfway
between Vilna and Minsk, Etta Kayle fell ill. The parents at

once recognized the symptoms of the dreaded cholera. They interrupted their journey at Smargon, but were unable to save their last child. They buried her in a lonely grave, far from her brothers and sisters, and then continued on to Minsk. There Hillel and Mariashe-Hannah received the brokenhearted couple.

Eight years earlier Zunser had left the house of his parents-in-law at Samokhvolovitz to establish a home of his own and to raise a family. Now his golden dreams had been converted into a nightmare. The wheel of fortune had turned and had crushed him utterly. In vain he racked his brains to find an explanation. In vain he tried to justify God's actions. In his affliction he cried out through the voice of one of his dramatic characters:

> A father has seen his three children die and now he brings his last one as a sacrifice to death. Who is there to remonstrate with God? God is unbribable. The wheel of the world rolls on as He wills. He directs His universe as He understands.*

Zunser roamed the streets of Minsk dazed with grief. He looked into the faces of children and sought to find resemblances to his own dearly beloved ones. He depicted his mood of those days in *The Sandek*:

> A father had four children and what beautiful children they were! How clever and fine, how modest and pure! In five days the flame consumed them. The father is left alone, a wreck upon the sea of life. Still he floats about in a strange city! Half mad he gazes about. He stops to look at every child: perhaps it is his own. But when he sees only strange faces, he makes his way homeward in anguish. There he beats his head against the wall, and the desolate mother follows suit. When he falls into a stupor, exhausted with grief, his head drooping, his eyes wide open, he sees one child sick, another stretched out on a bench in a shroud, a third with rolling eyes and taut skin, a fourth convulsed in death's fearful grip. The father wants to speak to them but

* *Mekhiras Yosef*, Act I, Scene 3.

his last cry is stifled in the depths of his heart. He knows neither day nor night. His once smiling face is shrouded in woe. He begs for release from life; he pleads to be bedded in his children's tomb; but his wish is unheeded. Death is denied him. He must carry on an existence more painful than extinction.*

The profoundest expression of Zunser's grief, *The Postman's Bell* (*Der potshtover Glekel*), was penned six weeks after his arrival in Minsk. On the day before the Jewish New Year, he looked back upon the dying year 5631. It had begun so auspiciously and had ended with the wreck of all his hopes. He wondered what the new year had in store for him. Would it be another crop of sorrows or could he expect surcease from pain? He thought of the mail-wagon that at regular intervals rolled into town. When its bell rang out merrily, all the inhabitants rushed to get their letters. For some, the tidings were glad. For others, they were sad. Similarly, Time, the postman, delivered every New Year's Day a sealed envelope to each living creature, but no recipient knew the nature of his assignment. When the year was up, the fateful content of the message had been made manifest. Then another year rolled past and still another. All too quickly, all too inexorably time flowed on and on, sweeping us and our deeds and our memories along in its wake.

Where are the people of yore? Where are their pride, their splendor, their wisdom of an hour? Time has flooded all who were: the head that bore a crown, the conqueror who ravaged the cities of men, the discoverer of isles unknown, the artist, the poet, the stargazer, the philosopher. What if they are remembered for a space? And what of the millions of heroes whose monuments the years have choked up with earth? Forgotten their books and their graves. We too shall fare no better.

O earth, how great are your masterworks! You chew us up with your teeth. You change human beings to grass and mountains to metals, but you yourself remain unchangeable.

* *Der Sandek*, Stanzas 32–37.

You seize one of us in your pulverizing grasp and then you reswathe him, and he emerges as a bee. You let the bee go through life's cycle, then you regroup its chemical essence, and it re-emerges as a bit of grain. Then out of the grain human cells are fashioned anew. When I eat, I may, unaware, be eating in the bread the marrow of my dead child. Perhaps my flesh and blood are enchained in the world and who knows how many lives I have already led or how many I may now be leading besides my very own.*

DER POTSHTOVER GLEKEL

* *Der potshtover Glekel*, Stanzas 4–5.

Zunser ended his poem with a plea to the new guest, the year 5632, to be more gracious than his predecessors:

> I beg you: be not as wicked as he. Under the canopy of your wings bring me some kindness and comfort. Say to me: wipe away your tears.*

Zunser's prayer was not granted. The year brought a horrible climax to his affliction. His wife's health had been undermined by her suffering. Tuberculosis developed during the winter of 1871–1872. Her illness was aggravated by her pregnancy. When she gave premature birth to stillborn twins, she could no longer rally. On her tomb, Zunser caused to be inscribed in Hebrew the following epitaph:

> Here rests a loving woman, young in years. Woe the loss! Her ten children she buried in her lifetime, and childless she followed after.

Zunser was for a time completely broken. He compared the misfortunes that had hailed down upon him in rapid succession to those that had befallen the much-tried Job, and he found that his own exceeded those of the biblical sufferer; for the latter was left with the companionship of a wife, while he himself was utterly bereaved. Just as pain had unsealed the lips of Job and caused him to cry out against his Creator, so too Zunser gave voice to his grief and despair. In 1871 and 1872, he composed poems filled with lamentation, questioning the whims of fate, subjecting to deep scrutiny the answers proffered by religion, and ending on a note of resignation. God's will was incomprehensible. What choice had mere man save to submit? Zunser also resumed work on his drama, *The Sale of Joseph*, and completed the greater part of it. He identified himself with Jacob, who also mourned the loss of his beloved wife Rachel and of a son no less dear to him.

Zunser afterwards referred to this doleful period as his most productive. Undoubtedly, his ability to transmute pain into

* Ibid., Stanza 7.

verse and melody aided his recovery and hastened the revival
of his will to live. Furthermore, the adoption of a fatalistic
philosophy, which he was later able to shed, helped to tide him
over his spiritual crisis. He looked out upon the stage of the
world, and he saw himself and his fellow beings as mere pup-
pets in the hand of a supreme puppet-player who pulled the
strings and directed all movements. The ever-changing repertoire might embrace a multitude of scenes, merry and gloomy,
interesting and dull. The text might prescribe for the characters
health and plenty or illness and hunger. Yet, no matter how
humorous or serious the initial acts, the end was uniformly
tragic. In the long run, fortune proved fickle, fame yielded
to calumny, the audience tired of applauding and turned to
booing, the actor awaited the falling of the curtain with increasing impatience, but death was in no hurry to end the drama.
Zunser expressed this pessimistic view in *The World Theatre
(Der Velt-Theater)*. He repeated it in *The World Kaleidoscope (Die Fershiedene Velt)*. Here he reached an extreme of
gloom in his characterization of the world as a prison in which
the unfortunate victims lie fettered in chains. In vain did each
prisoner plead for death. The gate remained heavily guarded
and nobody could break out of his cell. Not even a father, who
had led his children by the hand and who was rendered
wretched and forlorn in the short space of five days, was
paroled from the jail of life.

In *The Sandek*, a poem of 133 stanzas, Zunser painted a
terrifying picture of the sea of pain upon which human beings
were set adrift at birth. Without going to the extreme of
blaspheming God by name, he expressed amazement at the cold
indifference of the Creator toward his creatures. He compared
the master of our destinies to a boy who amused himself on a
summer's day with catching flies. Some flies the boy crushed and
killed instantly. These could account themselves fortunate. But
with most flies the boy loved to disport himself leisurely. He
tortured his victims by throwing them, one by one, into a glass
of water, and he enjoyed watching their contortions. With

every limb they strained to escape from drowning; some managed to reach the slippery wall; a few even got to the upper edge of the glass; but these were blown back into the water, there to struggle on until their strength also ebbed and they too fell to the bottom.

Meaningless was all life and senseless all death. The force that permeated the universe was unmoved by the tears of little children and did not pause in its cruel rampage before the gray heads of the noblest sages.

> Here a father died with his affairs in an unsettled state, leaving his children forever forlorn; there an only son perished, the pride of the home, his mother joining him in a common grave; here a bride descended to a gloomy vault, her marriage had been set for the morrow; there a prince found a resting-place in the earth, though he had been destined for a monarch's crown*

Zunser was in a nihilistic mood. His needless suffering led him to devastating conclusions. Logical reflection upon recent events merely confirmed his pessimistic outlook. In such a frame of mind, he found it impossible to formulate plans for reconstruction of his shattered existence. He had arrived at a dead end in the thirty-sixth year of his life. The well of wisdom from which he had drunk was bitter as gall. He found little nourishment in the fruits of doubt and scepticism. He needed faith and hope to sweeten the bitter cup of life. Slowly, valiantly, painfully, he fought his way back from nihilism and fatalism to a more constructive philosophy. In work he found an effective drug that helped deaden pain, and in a new marriage he found relief from loneliness and retrospective brooding. But the scars of the tragic year remained with him until his last breath.

* *Der Sandek*, Stanza 33.

CHAPTER X

"The Sale of Joseph"

ZUNSER'S drama, *The Sale of Joseph* (*Mekhiras Yosef*), was first published in 1874, but the greater part of it was written in 1872. It mirrored the poet's melancholy outlook during that tragic period and his groping return to spiritual health.

Since Abraham Goldfaden, generally regarded as the father of the Yiddish theatre, did not organize the first troupe of professional actors until a few years later, Zunser could hardly have expected a stage production when he began writing the play. On the other hand, he must have envisaged some sort of performance because he composed melodies for its lyrical passages. Most probably, he planned the play as an evening's entertainment in which he would recite, chant, and sing the various roles, just as he had done in the dramatic disputations with which he had begun his career as Badchen. After Goldfaden's meteoric success as writer, actor, and producer, Zunser did seriously contemplate a stage production. But the acting of plays in Yiddish was prohibited in Russia in 1883, and the prohibition remained in effect until the Revolution of 1905. Zunser's hope could not be realized.

There were, it is true, Jewish dramatic companies which masqueraded as German and which circumvented the law by playing in a Germanized Yiddish. However, the repertoire of these companies consisted almost entirely of musical comedies in the Goldfaden tradition. *The Sale of Joseph* was a serious drama. Nevertheless, although it was not produced on the professional stage, it reached large audiences in such towns as Minsk, Kaidan, Stolptse, and Vilna, when performed by guilds of artisans, in the manner of medieval morality plays. In Kovno, the pupils of the Yeshiva staged a brilliant performance in the early 1880's. The play reached Jewish communities in the Ukraine somewhat later.

Zunser could have found no biblical subject of greater dramatic intensity than that of Joseph and his Brethren. Its appeal is universal. It speaks with no less poignancy to the peasant and the child than to the intellectual and the theologian. It is a tale dealing with passionate love, and it is at the same time a tale which conveys many moral lessons. Writers, from Philo of Alexandria at the beginning of the Christian Era to Thomas Mann in our own generation, have been fascinated by the character of Joseph, now slave and now viceroy, now in a pit or a dungeon and now in the rich house of Potiphar or the palace of Pharaoh. They have delighted to depict not only the extreme changes of fortune in the life of this one human being but also the ripe wisdom he attained as a result of these experiences—his learning to distinguish between the sham and the genuine, his ability to see ever more clearly into the abysses and hidden nooks of frail, mortal hearts, his facing and overcoming temptations of the flesh, his ultimate appreciation of the warm humanity that linked kin to kin.

In addition to these general ideas implicit in the theme and awaiting ever new formulations by literary artists, the tale of Joseph had a special significance for the bard of Vilna and Minsk. Had he not himself been sold, like Joseph, by a brother-Jew into slavery in a military cantonment, and had he not also been saved by the decree of a humane modern Pharaoh in an almost miraculous manner? Did he not experience the same emotional shock as Jacob, when word was brought to him that his own son had been torn by a beast in the forest? In seeking to work his way up from despair to renewed faith in God and in the moral structure of the universe, after the cholera epidemic had wiped out his family, could he not find in the story of Jacob and Joseph the needed affirmation that no suffering was vain and that all sorrows must ultimately be compensated for with joy?

Zunser's chief predecessor in the dramatization of the Joseph theme in Yiddish was Eliezer Favir, Secretary of the Jewish community of Zholkov. Favir had published in 1801, under the title *Gdolath Yosef*, a translation of a Hebrew drama which had been completed four years earlier by a noted *Magid*, or preacher, of Mohilev.* This prose drama began with the selling of Joseph to the Ishmaelites and ended with his elevation to the viceroyship of Egypt and his reconciliation with his brothers. It went through numerous editions throughout the nineteenth century and far into the twentieth, both in the Hebrew original and in the Yiddish rendering. Zunser made it the basis for his own rhymed version, which he interspersed with lyrics set to music.

In a preface, he explained that, whereas non-Jewish authors could give their fancy free rein in dramatizing this theme and could alter the biblical narrative to suit their artistic tastes and philosophic predilections, Jewish writers were severely handicapped by the necessity of making every action and every trait of character conform with legends and traditions recorded by sages in sacred books. These documented events of ancient days could not be questioned or modified at will, even though they contained many inconsistencies and discrepancies.

Zunser owed equal allegiance to reason and to tradition. He would not accept the possibility that there were unbridgeable contradictions between the laws of logic and the beliefs of his people. His task, as he envisaged it, was to resolve all such apparent inconsistencies and to provide explanations that would satisfy both the rationalists and the theologians.

Zunser enumerated at length the inconsistencies which had proved a stumbling block to all previous Jewish dramatists and

* Jacob Shatzky lists all editions in *Arkhiv far der Geshikhte fun Yiddishen Teater un Drama*, Vilna, 1931, pp. 151–158.

claimed that, in his own version, he had solved these satisfactorily. The first of these was the motivation of the brothers for their unbrotherly acts. Zunser held that it was absurd to ascribe their cruel behavior in hurling Joseph into a pit and in later selling him into slavery to their envy of his many-colored coat. Surely, mature individuals, each of whom possessed sheep and oxen and considerable wealth, would not contemplate killing a younger brother for such a childish reason. Such thoughts would have been especially foreign to the holy forebears of the Jewish people. Nor could their hatred of Joseph have been caused by their noticing their father's greater affection for him. Surely, Joseph was as little to blame for Jacob's fondness for him as later on for the love with which Potiphar's wife pursued him. Nor could a Jewish dramatist accept a third possibility, namely, that Joseph's brothers wished to slay him because of his dreams, since dreams came from God, and a person was but the involuntary recipient of these messages from a superior power. Besides, these messages of divine origin were afterwards bound to be fulfilled anyhow. A fourth alternative, that Joseph's tale-bearing set his brothers against him, was also not to be taken seriously, because a sainted ancestor like Joseph could not be presented in the role of a slanderer. If the tales he spread were true, why should he be punished? If, on the other hand, he erred in his stories about his brothers, why could not Jacob examine him in order to find out the exact details?

The attitude of Joseph toward his father during his many years of exile was no less difficult to justify than that of his brothers toward him. For nine years he was Viceroy of Egypt, and not once did he attempt to get word through to his father that he was alive and prosperous. Indeed, he even brought additional suffering upon his aged father when, at the end of this period, he retained Simeon captive and sent the other brothers back to Canaan to fetch young Benjamin.

Zunser claimed that his version in seven acts and seventeen scenes was the only one which satisfied the requirements both of faith and of reason. It did so by discovering, wherever possi-

VILNA: THE STREET OF THE GLAZIERS

ble, a moral motive for each deed; and, wherever this was not feasible, by pointing out that what seemed to be callous or wicked behavior was merely a momentary aberration that was afterwards atoned for profusely. Lessons in ethics abound throughout the play.

The first scene begins with a sermon of 144 lines on the nature of God, addressed by Jacob to Joseph, and ends with a sermon on pride directed at the patriarch's other children. The latter sermon was provoked by Joseph's tale-bearing, but his tale-bearing is condoned as an honest effort by a younger brother to improve the conduct of his older brothers. When Simeon, enraged by the youngster's gossip and arrogant dreams, lays hands on him at Dothan, Reuben, the oldest of Jacob's sons, rushes to the rescue and suggests throwing Joseph into a pit. It is Reuben's intention to save him, after tempers cool off.

Reuben does not have to wait long. Remorse weighs upon the brothers. They would like to undo their impetuous deed. But now they must fear the vengeance of their father if Joseph were to return and if word of his mistreatment were to leak out. Selling him to the Ishmaelites seems, therefore, the best way of preventing his return. Jacob is to be told that a wild beast must have slain Rachel's son.

The final scenes of the first act are devoted to the lamentations of Jacob when he hears the doleful news, and to the wailing of Joseph beside the tomb of Rachel until he swoons away and receives a comforting message from her in a dream:

> Have hope, my son! Not this the end, not thus!
> Affliction, sent by God, endure with patience!
> Your dreams will be fulfilled: a royal scepter,
> A kingly throne, dominion over brothers.
> Your father too will seek you out one day.

These words breathe new courage into Joseph and enable him to face with equanimity all future ordeals.

The second act takes place a year later in the house and

gardens of Potiphar in Egypt. Joseph instructs Asenath, Potiphar's foster-daughter, in the true faith. He plays on a guitar and sings to her of the mournful lot of the captive in a foreign land. Though good fortune has given him a kind master, he still feels the tragedy of the uprooted person. His position is comparable to that of a branch which has been torn from a living tree and bedded among flowers; such a branch, must, nevertheless, wither away. Asenath is stirred by the slave's narrative and feels ever greater affinity toward him.

SULEIKA'S SONG

But Suleika, wife of Potiphar, is even more inflamed by the handsome youth. In an aria, played to the accompaniment of her harp, she sings of her burning passion for Joseph. Again and again she seeks to entice him, but his thoughts are with the God of his fathers and his heart is inclined toward Asenath. Thereupon follows Suleika's revenge because of frustrated love, her false accusation of her slave, and Joseph's imprisonment.

The third act takes place ten years later. Even in prison,

JOSEPH'S SONG

Joseph's wisdom and kindness of heart come to the fore. Suleika, on her deathbed, finally confesses her own guilt and absolves the imprisoned slave of all wrong. Asenath comes to bring to Joseph the news of Potiphar's changed attitude. She has meanwhile also learned from her dying foster-mother her own true origin: she is the child of Dina, daughter of Jacob, and hence Joseph's niece.

In the fourth act, Joseph is released. He interprets correctly Pharaoh's dreams and is then given Asenath to wife and raised to the viceroyship of Egypt.

The fifth act takes place nine years later. During the famine, ten sons of Jacob come to Egypt to buy corn and are accused of espionage. They accept the misfortunes that threaten them as righteous punishment for their sin towards their lost brother.

The sixth act reaches a climax in the recognition scene between Joseph and Benjamin, who has been brought to Egypt. Joseph justifies not having written to his father during all the preceding years on the ground that he assumed his father was angry with him and had instructed his brothers to sell him into slavery. He did not want to hurt his father by informing him that, instead of being punished, he had been elevated to princely rank.

The last act is filled with song, music, and gaiety. The news of the happy turn of events is brought to Jacob, and the aged patriarch intones hymns of praise to God, who is eternally just, even though often mysterious in His ways, and who ever rewards the righteous that put their trust in Him.

Zunser's play has historical, even more than literary, significance. It represents a transitional stage between the primitive Purim plays, acted by amateurs in a carnival spirit, and the professional theatre of Abraham Goldfaden and his followers in Europe and America. It aims to entertain and to instruct. It appeals to the senses by elaborate scenic decorations and gaudy costumes. It appeals to the emotions by the constant alternation of weeping and rejoicing. It appeals also to the mind by stressing ethical conduct and orthodox articles of faith.

Though it is now outdated and outmoded, Zunser's *Mekhiras*

Yosef performed a useful function. For the common man of
Eastern Europe, for the uncritical artisan, the sentimental
maiden, the tired housewife, the pious grandmother, it re-
affirmed in picturesque imagery the lessons of the Old Testa-
ment; it brought to life legendary characters of a hoary past; it
enriched drab reality with colorful visions of heroic experiences.

Zunser continued his efforts in the dramatic field but never
again met with comparable success. He wrote a tragedy in three
acts, entitled *A Victim of Caste* (*A Korbin far Yikhes*), but it
was never produced or published. He read it to a distinguished
audience at Warsaw in 1886, an audience that included Abraham Goldfaden, Jacob Dinezon, and S. L. Zitron. He hoped to
interest Goldfaden, then at the height of success, in a possible
production.

Zitron described the incident in the following passage in his
book *Three Literary Generations* (*Drei Literarishe Doires*):

> Eliakum took the manuscript from his pocket and began
> to read. His manner of reciting was beautiful and effective.
> . . . His heroes and heroines came into real existence. He
> reproduced the intonations of each character with perfect
> fidelity. The greatest impression was produced by a mono-
> logue of the heroine, a girl who had fallen in love with her
> tutor and who was being forced by her fanatical parents to
> marry a Hassidic youngster, a semi-idiot but of wealthy
> family. Eliakum recited the stirring dramatic lines with such
> artistry that all the listeners thought they actually saw
> the unfortunate heroine in the flesh. Goldfaden could
> not restrain himself and interrupted with the comment: "I
> wish I had an actor like you; I would give the best of my
> artists in exchange for a person like yourself." As for the
> play itself, Goldfaden said that he liked it in its broad out-
> lines but that there were specific defects that required im-
> provement. The play's chief fault was excessive length. It
> could stand more concentration. Goldfaden asked Eliakum
> to let him have the manuscript. He promised to write in
> greater detail about the play's defects and how it could be
> staged.

There is no record of what happened to the manuscript after Goldfaden received it. If it was the only copy, it must have found its way back to Zunser, and been the manuscript consigned to the flames in 1889, when Zunser's family was expecting a visit by the police and hastily burned whatever unpublished material was in the house.

Not until Goldfaden came to America for the second time in 1903 did he again meet the bard. By that time, both had experienced many variations of fortune and were drawn together by common memories. A friendship developed, which found its best formulation in Goldfaden's tribute on the occasion of Zunser's Jubilee in 1905 and which grew in intimacy until the death of the noted impresario in 1908.

CHAPTER XI

Second Marriage

ZUNSER'S second marriage on September 24, 1872, ushered in a period of comparative calm after the preceding stormy and tragic year. He was thirty-six and his bride, Hinde Feigel, was scarcely eighteen.

Orphaned early in life, she had been reared at the home of her paternal grandfather Kalman Katzewich, who was also known as Kalman Ritziner, after the village of his origin. Kalman kept an inn and post in the village of Novidvor near Minsk. His son Feitel, Hinde Feigel's father, assisted him in the running of the post. Before the coming of the railroad, the carrying of passengers and of mail by post-chaise was the only means of rapid transportation. There was a family legend that Kalman managed his section of the route so well that Czar Nicholas I, when he stopped at the inn of Novidvor for a change of horses, publicly commended the owner for his outstanding efficiency.

Feitel died of pneumonia at the age of twenty-six, leaving behind two daughters and a third child that was born a few months after his passing. A short time later, Sarah, the young widow, returned with her eldest daughter to the home of her parents in Borisov. Feigel and Faye, the newly born infant, were left in the care of Kalman.

When Sarah remarried, she sought to regain the custody of her daughters, but Kalman, who was particularly fond of

Feigel because of her resemblance to his departed son, refused to surrender the child to the care of a stepfather. Impelled by irresistible longing, Sarah devised a plan for kidnaping her children. One day, while the five-year-old Feigel was playing with her younger sister, a peasant's wagon stopped at the gate, a bearded Jew alighted, and spoke to the children.

"Children," he said to them, "would you like some candy?"

The little girls stretched out their hands to accept the gifts. The stranger lingered on, while the children admired the wagon and the team of horses.

"Would you like to go for a ride with me?" asked the friendly stranger.

Bright-eyed Feigel, ever eager for adventure, jumped onto the wagon and helped her two-and-a-half-year-old sister to climb up. After riding a minute or two, little Faye began to cry and demand that she be taken down. Feigel, older and bolder, continued on. After a while, she too asked the stranger to turn back, but he lured her on with more gifts of sweets and with fabulous promises. After a journey of a day and a night, he brought her to the home of her mother, whom she no longer remembered. The child was inconsolable. She wept whenever she thought of her devoted grandfather. She saw little of her mother, who was busy all day long in the marketplace earning a living for the family.

In the meantime, Grandfather Kalman was filled with grief for the missing child. From little Faye he was unable to get a clear account of what had transpired or a description of the stranger. He sent out searchers on fast horses, upon all the neighboring roads and highways, but no trace of Feigel could be found. Gypsies had camped in the vicinity and rumors of their child-stealing filled the air. Kalman kept up an unabating search.

Two years passed. One day a Jewish merchant of Novidvor, who had frequented Kalman's inn, happened to come to Borisov. In the marketplace he saw Feigel playing near her mother's stall. The child recognized him too. When he offered to take her back to her grandfather's inn, she consented eagerly, and hid in the wagon, joyful at the thought of seeing him. But to Kalman, the sight of Feigel at the door of the inn was so great a shock after two years of lonely brooding, that he suffered a stroke. In the course of time he recovered and continued to live on for two more decades.

At the inn, Feigel often heard guests sing the songs of Eliakum, Badchen of Vilna. When the famous bard came to Minsk in 1871, she was among the many Jews and Jewesses who sought to catch a glimpse of him. She saw a short and slender person with chestnut brown hair, a small beard, and a pale face from which blue eyes peered forth with a kind and melancholy gaze.

When Joshua Feigelson, a friend of Zunser's and of her grandfather's, invited the bereaved poet, a year later, to visit the inn, she instantly recognized him. A short while afterwards, Eliakum asked Kalman for her hand in marriage, and her consent could, of course, be taken for granted. They were married at the inn.

The bridegroom composed for the occasion words and melody for "The Cane-Game" (*Die Shtok Spiel*)—a game, similar to the American game *Going to Jerusalem*. A long row of chairs was placed in the center of the room. Alternate chairs faced in opposite directions, and there was always one less chair than there were participants in the game. All but one of the players were seated on the chairs. The remaining player marched around the chairs carrying a cane. As he marched, he sang *The Cane Song*, in which the others joined. Now and then he rapped the cane in front of one of the seated players, who thereupon rose and followed him. When all the players were marching around the chairs, the leader suddenly shouted "*Shtok!*" (Cane) and all rushed for seats. The one who was left standing was the loser and became the leader of the march for the next round of the game.

The music that Zunser composed for this game was lively and in marching rhythm, but the text was serious. Life, it said, was very much like this game. There were winners and losers.

Someone was always left behind at each round. Who could tell when his turn would come? Hence, let us not fawn upon the winners or mock the losers. All of us, from emperors to plebeians, were in God's hands. God called the signals. We mortals must obey.

Zunser could now again establish a home of his own and could again look forward to happy days. In 1873, a year after his marriage, he wrote that God had compensated him for his loss. A young wife had wiped away his tears and had dispelled the melancholy mood that clouded his days. At night, however, he was still defenseless against the dreams which conjured up the faces and the voices of the ten children that had been given to him and then cruelly taken from him.

Soon these dreams of terror also faded when a son was born to him. This son Feitel (Philip) was followed in rapid succession by four girls, Mollie, Rebecca, Anna, and Rose, and by two boys, Kalman (Charles) and Max. The necessity of providing for his growing family led him to travel far and wide to the weddings of the wealthy, for these alone could afford the services of the most famous Badchen of Russia. When he returned from his trips, which often extended over several weeks, he found release from tension in the pleasant atmosphere created for him by his wife and by a few congenial friends.

Jewish intellectuals of Minsk began to gather about him. As he had looked forward to evenings at the home of Zvi Hirsh Katzenellenbogen in Vilna in the 1860's, so now the young *Maskilim* of Minsk looked forward to admittance into the "Circle of Eliakum." The names of the better known members of this circle have come down to us. They included Joseph Brill, who wrote for Hebrew periodicals under the pseudonym Job of Minsk; Israel Meyer Wohlman, editor of a Hebrew annual; Yehuda Zev Nefach, administrator of the school for Jewish Artisans at Minsk; Jacob Seligman, brother-in-law of the Hebrew poet Yehalel; S. L. Zitron, the literary historian; and four young men—Hurwitz, Heifetz, Zuckerman, and Slepian—who later went to Palestine and helped to found the colony of Gederah, in which Zunser purchased some land with the expectation of settling there ultimately with his family.

On the evening of Zunser's return from a trip, the members of this group would come to his home prepared to discuss the latest articles in the Hebrew and Yiddish periodicals. Heated debates about literary and social problems would continue far into the night. Zunser's role was mainly that of host and listener, but often ideas born out of these discussions found poetic formulation in his songs.

Zunser recalled with pride that, a year after his second marriage, Eliezer Zvi Zweifel, the most beloved teacher of the Zhitomir Rabbinical Seminary, came to visit him at Minsk. The two had much in common, despite the fact that Zweifel was at least twenty years older. Both sought a synthesis of traditional Judaism and the philosophical doctrines of the Haskalah. Both directed their literary efforts towards improving the behavior and widening the horizon of the average man. Both believed in a positive attitude towards Yiddish as a vehicle of education. Both were fascinating conversationalists. The three days they spent together cemented a fruitful friendship. The ethical maxims of Zweifel in his *Musar* booklets became a rich source for Zunser's poetry.*

Zweifel, on the other hand, singled out Zunser as the supreme example of a Jewish poet and paid tribute to him in a much-read didactic poem of fifty stanzas, entitled *The Little World* (*Die Kleine Velt*). The Jews, said Zweifel in this poem, were a distinct nation, a valuable people with brilliant minds and merciful hearts, but, alas, long exile had inflicted upon them numerous vices and follies. Among such vices was the small respect paid by them to their great literary figures. Another people, for instance, would have conferred honor and wealth upon a bard like Eliakum, but Jews failed to prize his lofty striving and dubbed him Badchen, a title devoid of dignity.†

* Eliezer Zvi Zweifel, *Shtruf-Red*, Vilna, 1865.
† *Die yiddishe Folksbibliotek*, edited by Sholem Aleichem, Kiev, 1888, p. 58.

Zitron, the youngest member of the "Circle of Eliakum," was much more critical than Zweifel. He saw in Zunser primarily the virtuoso in rhyme and melody, and denied him genuine poetic talent. Zitron described an evening in Eliakum's house, during which the conversation centered about the nature of poetry. Zunser insisted that poetry could not be divorced from music and that all lyrics must be singable. He even criticized Yehuda Leib Gordon, the best of the Hebrew lyricists, for deviating from this principle. In his own creative imagination, he conceived text and melody simultaneously, and he claimed that he did not need more than two minutes to convert any suggested theme into rhyme and music.

He was immediately challenged to display his prowess. A theme based on a recent magazine article was given him. He improvised a song in Yiddish within the prescribed time-limit and then he repeated the feat in Hebrew. Three more themes were hurled at him in rapid succession. One dealt with a eulogy delivered a short while earlier at the grave of a rich miser. Another dealt with the characteristics of an apple, ruddy without and rotten within. The third dealt with a most dangerous topic: the Czar. Three times Zunser deliberated for a minute or two and then responded with original verses and melodies. This virtuosity so amazed the listeners that Zitron recorded the texts for posterity and later reprinted them in his memoirs.*

In the 1870's, the radical doctrines of the Narodniki or Populist Movement were gaining ground in Russia and were penetrating Jewish circles, including the Minsk "Circle of Eliakum." In contrast to the Nihilists, who were agnostics and materialists, the Populists were believers and idealists. Their motto was: "Everything for the People." They had a Rousseauan concept of the innate goodness of man, especially of the common man who was still attached to the soil and who had not fallen under the corrupting, corroding influence of the artificial civilization which was wreaking havoc among the upper classes. The Narodniki had a naïve faith that Utopia was

* S. L. Zitron, *Drei literarishe Doires,* Warsaw, 1, 32–37.

within reach. They were ready to lay down their lives for their ideal: the bringing of happiness to all human beings. Socialism appealed to them as the best system to hasten human progress, but the socialism they envisaged was based less on the scientific doctrines of Marx and Engels than on the messianic doctrines of Saint-Simon and Fourier.

It was precisely this messianic aspect, the vision of a kingdom of heaven on earth, that had the greatest fascination for Jewish intellectuals. Moritz Winchevsky, who began writing in the 1870's and who was afterwards often with Zunser in America, commented on this earlier period in his memoirs: "We were all Narodniki and the peasants were our brothers." * Unfortunately, however, the peasants who were to be aroused to rebellion, were in the main illiterate. It was therefore necessary, as a first step, to teach them to read and write.

This first step could be dispensed with in the case of Jewish workingmen since every Jewish person, no matter how humble his social position, was at least able to read and write and could, therefore, be reached through the printed word in the Yiddish vernacular. But the only Yiddish periodical in Russia at that time was *Kol Mevasser*, edited by Alexander Zederbaum, and this practical journalist did not want to jeopardize his influential organ by flirting with radicalism. Aaron Lieberman, the most gifted of the Jewish Narodniki, attempted to reach the Jewish masses through a Hebrew monthly, entitled *Truth* (*Ha-Emes*), but the Czarist government forbade its circulation in Russia and thereby forced it into bankruptcy. Besides, Hebrew was hardly the proper medium for agitation among the Yiddish-speaking masses. An opportunity soon presented itself, however, with the founding of a periodical in Yiddish just across the Russian border, in Koenigsberg, the capital of East Prussia. It was entitled *Voice of the People* (*Kol L'Am*) and was edited by M. L. Radkinson. It appeared as a weekly and soon attracted as regular contributors several members of Eliakum's Circle.

At first Yehuda Zev Nefach acted as the principal inter-

* Ibid., II, 109.

mediary between Minsk and Koenigsberg. Then Joseph Brill took over the correspondence from Minsk, signing his articles "Job of Minsk." Before long Eliakum Zunser himself was won over as a frequent contributor in prose and verse. Since the smuggling of socialistic ideas was fraught with peril, Zunser used various pseudonyms. These pseudonyms were generally scrambled combinations of the various letters of his name, as for example, Iakmuel, Kune Roisel Maz, Siman Lukrezia.

A favorite topic for his column, "Correspondence from Minsk," was military conscription. In the Manifesto of August 26, 1856, Alexander II had put an end to conscription. For six years, thereafter, there were enough volunteers to keep the Russian army at an adequate peacetime strength. On September 1, 1862, however, the Czar issued a new Manifesto restoring conscription. To make compulsory military service less onerous than it had been under Nicholas I, the term of service was reduced from twenty-five to fifteen years; the drafting of children was prohibited; and Jews were no longer required to furnish recruits in a greater proportion than the rest of the Russian population. Despite these concessions, military life still proved unattractive to Jewish fathers and sons. The years of terror under Nicholas I were still remembered, and whoever could avoid service did not scruple to do so. Young men of military age fled across the borders, and some of them even made their way to distant America. Jewish communities experienced great difficulty in filling their prescribed quotas of recruits. The *Izborshtchik*, the Jewish official in charge of the local selection of draftees, remained a most unpopular figure since he often had to resort to draconic measures.

In 1873, Zunser was called from Minsk to officiate as Badchen at a wedding in Vilna. In the midst of the wedding-supper, when merriment was at its height and he was entertaining the guests with his rhymed verses, representatives of the *Izborshtchik* appeared, accompanied by a guard of Cossacks, and snatched the bridegroom away. Zunser gave immediate, vigorous voice to the anger that gripped everyone there. When

he returned to his room, he found recruiting officers and
Cossacks waiting for him. He was seized, dragged to the barracks, and placed under military detention, just as in his earlier
days at Bobruisk. This detention did not last very long, however, since he was able to prove that he had a brother, Akiba,
who was still serving in the army, and it was illegal to draft
two children of the same family. He was released with the
warning to refrain from criticizing community leaders.

A year later, a change in the system of recruiting was
decreed by the Czar. Conscription was taken out of the hands of
the Jewish authorities and turned over to Russian officials. The
term of service was reduced once more. The *Izborshtchik* was
stripped of his power. Zunser then composed his most popular
song of the year 1874. It was entitled *Der Izborshtchik*. In nine
stanzas of venomous satire, Zunser gave expression to the fury,
long pent up within the Jewish heart, against this powerful
agent of an oppressive regime. Each stanza consisted of a solo
by the *Izborshtchik*, who lamented the passing of his glory and
the loss of his patronage, and a refrain sung by a chorus of the
town's politicians, who shared in his downfall. Zunser sang
this savage song on every possible occasion, acting out the role
of the *Izborshtchik* with tremendous intensity, while the
aroused audience, recalling former tribulations and inequities,
joined lustily in the refrains.

It must seem strange, therefore, to discover Zunser as the
author of a series of articles which appeared five years later in
Kol L'Am and which defended military conscription. These
articles, published in successive issues between January 17 and
February 14, 1879, argued against the unabating efforts of Jews
to avoid military service by fleeing abroad. Zunser's espousal of
the cause of conscription was, however, more apparent than
real. He first listed the reasons that motivated the flight of young
Jews, ostensibly to refute them. The censor of the earliest article did not interfere with this seemingly patriotic appeal to
Jewish readers, but his suspicions must have been aroused somewhat by the far too detailed presentation of the arguments. In
the second article, a phrase was erased by the censor here and

there. In the third article, entire sentences were blotted out. Finally, an entire article was suppressed. By March, Zunser found it unwise to continue with this subject and to sign his own name to the *feuilletons* he contributed; he substituted the pen name Iakmuel.

Zunser agreed that military service exposed a young man to storms and frosts, to coarse food, to lack of *Kashruth*, and to loss of piety; but, on the other hand, the Jewish religion taught obedience to the laws of the land. He then launched upon a discussion of how the laws of the land might be improved. He pointed out that emancipation of the serfs in 1861 had bettered their character and refined their habits. Emancipation of the Jews would also have beneficial results. It would make them more loyal to the established regime.

> The character of the Jew was wounded by oppression and scorn. It, therefore, decayed. It can be healed only through freedom and the granting of equal civil rights. Then will Jews love their fatherland and become loyal citizens.

Zunser was arriving at the conclusion that political and economic liberation must precede the best-intentioned efforts at enlightenment. As long as all avenues of escape from oppression and intolerance were closed to the Jew, and as long as he was being prevented from making a living by medieval restrictions, there was no use to try to hammer modern philosophy and the new science into his head. Unable to direct attacks openly against the government, Zunser concentrated on the petty local oppressors among his coreligionists. He directed withering satires against the stonyhearted tax-collectors and grafters, the moneylenders who fleeced helpless victims, the dishonest merchants who masqueraded as virtuous God-fearing men, the informers who profited from bearing false witness against their fellows.

In an essay, published in *Kol L'Am* on February 14, 1878, Zunser exclaimed:

> Oh, how unfortunate are you, my people Israel! My

REB YAKOB MESHALEM

FEIGEL AND ELIAKUM ZUNSER, 1904

poor, straying sheep! You roam about in the deep woods in
the darkness of night! You stray ever further into ever
greater dangers! You hear the lions roar and the tigers howl;
snakes open their mouths and pour venom upon you; and
yet you go on, oblivious of everything, and nobody warns
you!

In *The Hypocrite* (*Der Tzvuyak*), he took as the object of
his scorn a supposedly respectable resident of Minsk who, in
1874, had falsely denounced a young teacher to the authorities
and had brought a decent family to the verge of starvation. The
verses that lashed this hypocrite aroused public opinion to such
an extent that the pious old scoundrel was forced to leave town,
while the victimized teacher returned in triumph and resumed
his post.

In *Reb Yakob Meshalem,* Zunser contrasted the many heavy
burdens the Jew had to bear with the few light ones borne by
his neighbors. Every stanza contained the refrain: the Jew pays.
A Jew could not say his prayers or taste a morsel of meat or
even die and receive a decent burial without having to pay a
tax of some kind to a host of idlers and parasites. Feed on the
Jew, you rascals, feed on and on, exclaimed the poet.

> The Jew is a soft bone, full of marrow that melts in the
> mouth. . . . The Jew is a green pasture and tall grass. Oxen
> can grow fat and plump on such fodder. . . . The Jew is
> a mare. Ride on it to your heart's desire. It will carry you.
> . . . The Jew is a sheep. Milk it and fleece it as long as it
> lives, and skin it after death.

In *The Unskilled Moneylender* (*Der Nit-geniter Malve*),
Zunser condemned the financial operations which formed the
basis for business activity in Jewish communities. He described
his own unsuccessful venture into banking. Having saved a few
hundred rubles during the first years after his new marriage, he
was tempted to lend them to businessmen in need of funds.
However, since he was content with low interest rates and since
he refused to take advantage of his debtors who were in diffi-

culties or to drag them to court, he soon lost his entire capital.
As a result of this experience, he felt that moneylending was a
profession to be shunned by sensitive, moral individuals, who
were handicapped by feelings of pity, justice, or fairness.

> One has to be able to rend like a tiger, to suck like a
> leech, to bite like a snake. . . . If you want to live at peace
> with your conscience, what makes you try moneylending?
> . . . You, who still value decency and mercy, truth and
> righteousness!

Zunser's poems on commerce and industry linked practical
problems of every day with universal attitudes toward eternal
questions. He was especially interested in the effect upon the
human spirit of the revolution in transportation. The building
of railroads in Russia extended in the 1860's and 1870's to the
provinces of the Pale and ushered in a difficult period of economic readjustment. Jewish drivers, innkeepers, and middlemen in villages and small towns were deprived of their accustomed livelihood and forced to emigrate to the large cities and
to change their vocations. Crisis followed crisis, and it seemed
to some Jews as though the world were coming to an end.

Zunser at first joined in the lamentations of the stricken
communities. He wrote his *Dirge for the World* (*Sogt Kaddish
nokh der Velt*). In this song, a merchant blamed railroad and
telegraph for hastening the pace of competition and thus preventing him from making a leisurely living. Daily price fluctua-
tions were wreaking havoc on the import-export trade. Foreign
speculators were underbidding native contractors. Goods from
abroad could be delivered in days instead of weeks. The entire
world of industry was in the throes of a cataclysmic transformation. It was time to say the *Kaddish*-prayer for the dead
old order.

A few years later, Zunser struck a more optimistic tone in
his evaluation of the new inventions. In his *Song of the Railroad*
(*Die Eisenbahn*), he hailed the locomotive and the telegraph as
heralds of progress, as great achievements of the human mind,

which would make everyday existence more pleasant ever after. And, if Messiah should one day make his appearance, Jews would not have to drag themselves on foot or by horse-and-wagon to Eretz Israel but would be able to ride speedily and in luxury to this land of their hearts' desire.

Sixteen years after his first *Song of the Railroad*, Zunser composed a second song under the identical title. In a detached, philosophic mood, he compared the movement of life through time to the movement of a train through space. All of us were passengers on the train of life. To some a luxurious compart-

DIE EISENBAHN

ment had been assigned in a spacious car and to others uncomfortable seats had been doled out in overcrowded coaches. Each of us was permitted to travel only a certain distance and not one station farther. The human mind was the engineer and religion was the safety-valve. The poet admonished us not to complain of the accommodations which happened to fall to our lot nor to bewail the brevity of our journey or that of our loved ones, because everything was planned and decreed by the Director of the railroad, the Supreme Authority, whose ways were inscrutable to us mortals but in whom we must have faith.

The last of Zunser's poems dealing with the railroad was entitled *Wherefore?* (*Ma Nishtano?*) and described how Minsk was rejuvenated when it was linked with the net of railroads spreading over the vast Russian Empire. Minsk, which had no port and no commerce of importance, suddenly awoke from its lethargy. Factories arose overnight; industry flourished; rents, wages, the cost of living climbed sky high. The dormant Jewish community was seized by a new spirit. Jews entered the professions of law and medicine in unprecedented numbers. Soon there would arise among them professors, generals, bemedaled artists. Would these intellectuals be bound by the cement of religion that had held them together as long as they remained wholly within the Jewish orbit?

In an epilogue written under Alexander III, Zunser supplied the answer. The bubble of prosperity had burst. Pogroms were breaking out throughout the vast realm. Reaction was in full swing. Minsk was in a funereal mood. Each stanza ended with the refrain: "*Ma Nishtano?*" Wherefore all the hustle and tumult? The lot of the Jew had not improved at all.

Zunser's critical attitude toward a society that exaggerated material values and that lacked faith in the less tangible ideals found embodiment in several lyrics sung by him at weddings. In an apostrophe *To the Ten-Ruble Bill* (*Zu dem Zenrubeldi-gen Billet*), he recounted all the crimes and vices that such a piece of paper must have witnessed in the course of its wanderings from person to person. In another lyric, with the strange

title, *Clever, Polite, and Quiet* (*Klug, Edel, un Shtil*), he compared the poor but honest life of the fathers with the luxurious
and disreputable life of the sons. He felt that the motto of the
new age seemed to be: everything is permissible, provided it is
carried through cleverly, politely, and quietly.

Although Zunser was still in his early forties, a tone of
nostalgia for the days of old was beginning to creep into his
writings. In a *feuilleton* of March 21, 1879, he repudiated the
zealous innovators, who had set out to undermine the faith of
their ancestors but could not offer a happier substitute. He
resented the insolent tone in which frivolous youth mocked
the sacred heritage for which Jewish martyrs had died century
after century. He parodied a high school lad who began a letter
to a parent as follows: "Since the jackasses of former eras believed that the sun moved about the earth, they also made much
fuss over the Books of Moses and they feared Judgment Day
and the world's end. The enlightened generation of our day has
declared, however, that the earth revolves about the sun. Hence,
the laws of Moses are no longer operative today. So, please,
send me a tub of butter."

Zunser saw about him fifteen-year-olds who had acquired a
smattering of Russian or German and who posed as prophets
of a new way of life. He found that some of these immature
youngsters were preaching their shallow wisdom in the very
periodicals that had been established at great sacrifice in order
to bring genuine enlightenment. He was shocked by the
bombastic phrases and absurd metaphors that were parading
in the columns of *Hamagid* or *Hamelitz* or *Hakarmel*. He reproduced a typical verbal effusion: "Just as the sun, the moon,
and the millions of stars course through the blue vault of
heaven; just as the flowers open their chalices and send their
fragrances aloft to the empyrean; just as the shepherd homeward wends his flock and the red cows let their bells resound
across the fields; just as the Atlantic covers half the world with
its waves—even so does the sun of enlightenment shine, glare,
sparkle, glisten, glitter, and its rays wash down the entire heap

of filth and dung which the Talmudists have brought into the Jewish camp."

Zunser agreed that the conduct of people, a generation or two earlier, was not without grave defects; an operation of some kind was indeed necessary; but, when the patient emerged from the operation completely transformed, more serious defects had developed.

Zunser was worried about the increasing rapidity of assimilation and Russification, conversion and intermarriage, among the finest and most educated of his contemporaries. Their participation in non-Jewish activities, especially in ultra-radical political parties, boded ill for all Jewry. Some of his Vilna acquaintances were among forty young men arrested in 1872 as Nihilists. General Potapov, who had replaced Count Muraviev, Zunser's patron, as Governor of the province of Vilna, called in the leaders of the Jewish community for a conference. These included Jacob Barit, Samuel Pieskin, and Matthias Strashun, with whom Zunser had associated in the Katzenellenbogen Circle.

Zunser, in his *Autobiography*, gives a vivid description of the incident. Addressing this deputation in the sternest tone, Potapov shouted:

"To the many, great virtues which you Jews possess, you still had to add affiliation with the Nihilists!"

Silence fell upon the terrified group, when they heard this serious charge.

"We are not Nihilists!" a member of the delegation finally ventured to reply timidly.

"At any rate, your children are Nihilists!" thundered Potapov. "They became Nihilists because of the kind of education you give them."

"Pardon me, General!" countered Jacob Barit. "This is not quite accurate! As long as we were in charge of our children's education, there were no Nihilists among them; but, as soon as you undertook to educate them for us, they became infected with such doctrines."

The effect of this reply was calamitous. General Potapov forwarded this remark, with additional comments of his own, to the central government at St. Petersburg. A short while thereafter, a decree was handed down by the imperial authorities closing the Rabbinical Colleges of Vilna and Zhitomir, which had for a generation trained Jewish religious leaders under the supervision of the Russian Ministry of Education.

Zunser reacted to this unhappy incident with his allegorical song *Shulamith*, written in Yiddish and in Hebrew. The Jews were personified as Shulamith, an aristocratic lady who had fallen from her high estate. Not only was she subjected to poverty, shame, and slander, but her mouth was also stopped up, so that she could not cry out. Nevertheless, she still prayed for her host, because he restrained her neighbors from falling upon her and putting a violent end to her existence.

If I am pious, they dub me fanatical; if I seek education, they teach me self-hatred; if I am dressed in rags, they say I am filthy; if I put on nicer clothes, they resent my display. Why am I considered to be without virtue? I weigh my every deed and watch my every step. A human being of flesh and blood cannot be entirely good, but I surely am not worse than others. I placed my trust in civilization. I saw animals protected; I saw punishment meted out to those people who beat horses; but I found nobody to pity me. When a few Bashibazouks hurt Slovenes, Europe rose up to defend the victims. When Negroes were poorly treated, hundreds of thousands of Americans took up arms in their behalf. Am I not as worthy as a Slovene or as enlightened as a Negro? Why am I free game for everyone?

Similar questions were asked by Zunser in his song *Rachel Weeps for her Children* (*Rokhel Mivako al Boneo*). He depicted Rachel, the wife of Jacob, arising from her tomb near Bethlehem, as night enveloped the earth in darkness. She listened to the weeping of her children, the Jews, who were being ground under the heels of enemies in many lands. She cried out: "How long, O Lord, will you let them suffer thus?"

The song was noted for its beautiful melody, its metrical felicity, and the tender description of sunset and nightfall, which evoked a mood of sweet melancholy.

In another lyric, *A Voice from Heaven* (*Kol Mimromim*), Zunser sought to give God's answer. The Voice from on high called upon the Jews to have patience. God's grace was upon them. The holy faith, which they professed, would one day be acknowledged by all the nations of the earth, and they would receive their well-earned reward for their loyal guardianship down the ages.

These comforting words were most welcome to Zunser's audiences, who saw menacing clouds again darkening the Russian horizon, as the reign of the liberal Czar drew to a close. With the assassination of Alexander II by a group of Narodniki in 1881, the forces of reaction were unleashed and the first victims were the Jews. A wave of pogroms engulfed them, which deeply affected the direction of their thinking. After a brief hour of despair, there followed a sober evaluation of possibilities for amelioration of their plight and then the dawn of a new hope: homecoming to Zion. The bard of the people echoed the spiritual crisis and the glorious awakening of the 1880's as he had reflected the moods of earlier decades.

CHAPTER XII

Pogrom Years

THE ASSASSINATION of Alexander II in 1881 put an end to the so-called Golden Age of Russian Jewry. It was a Golden Age only by comparison with the bleak reign of Nicholas I, which preceded it, and the black reaction under Alexander III, which followed it. The hope, entertained ever since 1861, that the emancipation of the serfs would be followed by the emancipation of the Jews was not realized. The concessions, which were wrested from an indifferent government, had led a considerable sector of the rising Jewish generation to envisage the dawn of an era of political freedom, religious tolerance, and social equality. This vision proved to be a mirage and it left deep scars upon the soul of disappointed Jewish idealists.

Despite Zunser's admiration for Alexander II, he was not blind to the fact that the goal of this monarch differed in no way from that of Nicholas I. This goal was the Russification and eventual conversion of the Jews. The fundamental difference was in the methods used to attain this objective of governmental policy. Nicholas I had used the mailed fist. Alexander II preferred a gentler approach. Nicholas I had heaped one harsh decree upon another but had not dented the determination of the Jews to cling to their God. Alexander had relaxed somewhat the pressure upon them and, as a result, there began a flight from Judaism which soon took on serious proportions. The first group to be assimilated even to the point of intermarriage and conversion to Greek Orthodoxy was the Jewish financial aristocracy of St. Petersburg, Moscow, and Kharkov.

Zunser recalled that in these neo-Christian homes a more hostile attitude toward former coreligionists prevailed than among Russians of the same social status.

A second group to forsake Judaism consisted of university graduates, who sought to make their mark as physicians, lawyers, and journalists. These intellectuals mocked their own fathers and mothers, brothers and sisters, and joined in every slander against Jews in the hope of currying favor with their new associates. Jewish writers, who fell under this spell of Assimilationism, used their literary talent to idealize Russian types and to caricature Hebraic types. Elena was always angelic, while Sarah was diabolic. Ossip was the personification of virtue, while Yossel was a degenerate. A worshiper in a synagogue was a fanatic steeped in superstition, while a dandy with powdered curls and lacquered shoes was a philosopher who espoused progress.

Zunser castigated the Assimilationists who strove to separate their fortunes from those of their people. He laughed and railed at them in poems and articles throughout the 1870's. But when the hour of grief struck in 1881 and the tragedy he had warned against broke upon Russian Jewry, he changed his tone from admonition to consolation.

The first pogrom broke out in Yelisavetgrad on April 15, 1881. Excesses soon spread from town to town and continued until the summer of 1884. During the first year of violence, more than two hundred Jewish settlements were affected, and hundreds of thousands of Russian peasants and workers participated in the robbing and murdering of Jews in the belief that this was a patriotic and religious duty. Whether or not the Russian government actually organized and directed the pogroms, it certainly lent encouragement to them by not punishing the perpetrators of these crimes and by permitting plunderers of Jewish homes and stores to retain their booty.

The psychological impact of the pogroms upon Russian

Jewry was even more profound than the actual physical suffering. Until 1881, the Jews could put their trust in the rule of
law and order. They were not blind to the hatreds and prejudices lodged deep within the hearts of their neighbors. They
also observed ominous signs of a worsening attitude towards
them in the highest government circles. To some extent they
even expected the breaking of a storm over their heads. But
they assumed that such a storm would take the shape of severer
restrictions within the code of the realm. They could not con-
ceive that they would suddenly be placed outside of the law,
exposed defenseless to the brutal ravages of incited mobs. They
could not foresee that, in an empire where police and army
held the people in an iron grip, homes would be set on fire,
business establishments plundered, men murdered, women ravished, and children beaten, while the guardians of law looked
on with indifference, if not open approval. The pogroms of
1881 blasted all hopes of Russian Jews for the amelioration of
their condition through the growth of the spirit of progress.
They could no longer feel secure, even though they obeyed all
legal decrees and police regulations. At any moment, a horde
of neighbors, for some trivial reason or for no reason whatsoever, might fall upon them and destroy them and their posses-
sions without fear of retribution.

Pogroms often had the excitement of a carnival for the
perpetrators. Hunting Jews was not only a good sport for
street urchins but also a profitable venture for respectable
citizens. Wild cheers and joyous shouts of the gay, plundering
mobs drowned out the cries of frightened victims and the moans
of beaten men and ravished women. While youngsters might
content themselves with smashing windows or breaking
crockery, older participants came with carts and wagons and
carried off furniture and valuable goods from Jewish homes and
stores. The formation of self-defense groups among the Jews
was forbidden and, where such attempts were nevertheless
made, the police instantly intervened to deprive the victims of
their weapons.

Zunser, in his *Autobiography*, described the pogrom in which the children of Joseph Sorkin, a prominent contemporary of Vilna, took part, and its tragic aftermath. Sorkin, who was reared in a Jewish orthodox home, had been saved from drowning in his young days by a Christian girl. Some time thereafter, he married her and accepted her religion. For a while he was happy with his wife and children, but when in later years his wealth began to decline, she began to harp upon his "ignoble" origin. He then felt himself a stranger in his own home and, overcome with remorse at his apostasy from Judaism, he sought to atone. He translated into Russian and published at his own expense Isaac Baer Levinsohn's book defending the Jews against the blood-ritual accusations. He interceded on every possible occasion in behalf of his former coreligionists.

Once, when Sorkin came from Kiev on a visit to his half-estranged family at Nizhni Novgorod, he found his sons away from home. Toward evening, they arrived from a suburb, completely intoxicated, and carried into the house big bundles of all sorts of goods. They had spent the day with an hilarious mob, beating up Jews, breaking into Jewish homes, and looting Jewish stores. Their mother greeted them joyfully and praised them for their heroic achievements.

"What achievements? And what are these articles?" asked Sorkin.

"Oh, dear father," answered one of the sons. "We have accomplished a sacred deed."

"We have done what pious Christians should always do!" added another son. "We have wreaked vengeance on the accursed Jews who tortured and crucified our Lord!"

Sorkin was horrified but had to remain silent. He knew that the slightest protest on his part might lead to his arrest and deportation to Siberia, and that his own children would be only too glad to hand him over to the authorities. He, therefore, left his house quietly and went to his old friend Lev Levanda in Vilna. There he poured out his troubled heart to this classmate of his young days. Both wept bitterly as they recalled their early happier years in the Rabbinical Academy and repented their frustrated mature years when they had scorned their forebears. When the newspapers continued to bring daily reports of additional pogroms in town after town, Sorkin sank into ever deeper despair. Finally, he could not stand the horrible news any longer. He locked himself in a hotel room and hanged himself.

Sorkin's suicide made a profound impression upon Levanda. The successful novelist sank into fits of melancholy. From these he emerged in outbreaks of rage. In his madness, he used to smash his furniture, tear his books and manuscripts, and storm at the people about him. In lucid moments he would call for Zunser, in whom he wished to confide. His friends brought Levanda to St. Petersburg in the hope of curing him. But his mind gave way completely. After years of torture, he passed away on March 6, 1888.

Levanda's death stirred Zunser to his inmost depths. He composed an elegy, with piano accompaniment, which was immediately published both in Yiddish and in Russian, and sung far and wide by Jews and non-Jews.

Zunser had known and admired Levanda since boyhood, when the latter, a native of Minsk, had come to Vilna to study at the Rabbinical Academy. They were the same age. Both had spent their youth under Nicholas I, in similar environments. Both had set out on the path leading from Orthodoxy to Enlightenment. But, while Zunser had halted after a short journey along this alluring and dangerous path, Levanda continued on beyond the milepost of Enlightenment, on to Assimilation and complete Russification. In the 1860's and 1870's, he earned an enviable reputation as a Russian writer of great subtlety, rich imagination, and keen wit. His novels and essays of those decades attacked Jewish fanaticism and stagnant ghetto customs. He was then primarily a Slav patriot. He praised the government on every possible occasion. He saw in Alexander II the great emancipator, and he exhorted the Jews to be grateful to him for his efforts to modernize their dress, their speech, their belief.

Levanda held that pehaps the older generation was beyond

salvation but that the younger generation could still be saved. He, therefore, called upon the Jewish youth of Russia to revolt against parental authority, to make its way out of the engulfing swamp of superstitions and taboos, and to step onto the safer, healthier ground of modern science and logic.

Levanda was given an opportunity to put his Assimilationist ideal into practice when he was appointed by the Governor-General of Vilna as chief of the Jewish Department for that entire province. His position brought him into close contact with Jews of wealth, with industrialists who fawned upon bureaucrats, with middlemen who revered ignorant aristocrats, with eternal busybodies who were awed by pompous officials. He hated these unpleasant Jews. He satirized them in his novels. In contrast to them, he liked to call attention to a genuine Jewish personality, whom he truly admired: Eliakum Zunser. In a narrative, he depicted the beneficial effect that Zunser's songs produced upon the Jewish masses.

After the pogroms of 1881, Levanda's Assimilationist ideal collapsed like a house of cards. Reuben Brainin, the Hebrew-Yiddish publicist, expressed the opinion that Levanda's faith in his mission as pathfinder for his people had already been undermined before this catastrophic blow. Describing his only meeting with Levanda, Brainin remarked:

> I was then too young to fathom the tragedy of a serious writer who had devoted his God-given talents and all his spiritual energies to his people in the belief that he was being guided by the bright star of truth which lighted up the only possible or desirable path to salvation and liberation—the tragedy of such a writer, when he suddenly became unsure of himself, when he began to doubt that the path upon which he had trodden for decades and upon which he had directed others, was the correct one, when he could no longer escape the realization that he was not emancipating his people but, on the contrary, was leading them astray and toward a more horrible form of enslavement.*

* Reuben Brainin in *Der Tog*, New York, August 11, 1929.

Levanda was overcome with remorse. The plundering of
the Jews by the unthinking masses shocked him less than the
approving attitude of the Russian intellectuals, his friends, who
looked on gleefully at the destruction. He recognized at last
that for decades he had been dazzled by a mirage, and he at
once found the courage to turn his back upon his Russian past
and to advocate a homecoming of the estranged among his
people. He now referred to Assimilation as a fever which
racked body and soul, and from which he had recovered. As
early as 1883, he preached return to Zion. He urged the revival
of Hebrew as a national tongue for Jews everywhere. He ceased
to be impressed by the volatile emotionalism of his young
admirers, who were prepared to follow him on his new course.
He preferred to place his trust in the unyielding orthodoxy of
the elders. He saw in Zunser a firm branch of the healthy trunk
of Judaism and, when asked for advice concerning a new literary venture planned by S. L. Zitron in 1883, he recommended
that an effort be made to win over the popular bard as a contributor. "Zunser can be very useful with his poems on the
subjects that interest all of us so much nowadays." *

Levanda's remorse and atonement, his psychic disintegration
and tragic end, created an unusual stir in Jewish circles everywhere, but especially in his native town of Minsk. Zunser
mirrored this excitement in his stately dirge. His *Elegy on
Levanda*, (*Elegie Levanda*) opened by solemnly recounting the
blows which an unkind fate had just dealt to the Jewish people.
Gone were the pioneers of the Hebrew press: David Gordon
of *Hamagid* and Peretz Smolenskin of *Hashachar*. And now,
death had removed another of the great spokesmen of the pen:
Lev Levanda.

Zunser read his own soul into that of his friend, whom he
apostrophized in the following words:

    You sought to quench the thirst for diversion—yes—

* *Die yiddishe Folksbibliotek*, edited by Sholem Aleichem, Kiev, 1888,
p. 448.

but you also had another goal that was far loftier. Always, as
you sat alone in your room, you pondered your people's
fortunes. You need no monument of stone, for who can
forget you? All who knew you possess a monument of you,
set deep within their hearts.

Zunser acribed Levanda's end to his overpowering compas-
sion for his helpless people. Their unmerited suffering undermined the novelist's health and spirit. Wherever a Jew was hurt,
Levanda's heart felt the pain. He was the champion chosen by
fate to defend his people when they were infamously attacked
by a blood-ritual accusation. He fought valiantly and saved the
innocent victims of this monstrous vilification. A modern Moses,
he led his people out of the barren wilderness and up to the
banks of the Jordan. He showed them the Promised Land
stretching before them, but God would not let him enter. He
was a leader in Israel who erred and repented. He could not be
denied the tribute of tears, now that he had been struck down
on alien soil.

Zunser pointed out that the recantation of errors on the part
of the assimilated Jewish intellectuals was a common phenomenon after 1881, even though such recantation was fraught with
peril. He called attention to the novelist G. Bogrov, who became a penitent and who devoted his final years to a defense of
the very Jews he had himself vilified in his earlier assimilationist
period. Zunser also saw in the sad end of the Vilna composer
Wolf Ebin an object lesson for gifted Jews who were tempted
to drift away from their coreligionists.

Ebin, the son of a *Klezmer* or musician, had grown up in
Vilna with Zunser and Antokolsky and had displayed artistic
talents at an earlier age than his playmates. At eight, he was
already playing at weddings as a flutist in his father's band. At
ten, he was a favorite violinist at Vilna festivities. The Governor-General of Vilna invited the precocious musical genius to
play before the highest officials of the province. Ebin displayed
such virtuosity that the Governor-General obtained a scholar-

ship for the boy at the St. Petersburg Conservatory of Music and had Anton Rubinstein accept him as a pupil.

Ebin's father was greatly touched by this interest in his son, but he feared that, away from home, the boy might weaken in his devotion to his religion. He, therefore, made him swear solemnly at the grave of his departed mother to continue the sacred Jewish practices throughout life. For many years, young Ebin kept his oath. He did not succumb to the foreign influences all about him. Despite phenomenal success in Russian circles both as composer and as orchestral conductor, he continued to attend synagogues, he never played on the Sabbath, he took an interest in Jewish affairs, he proved that a healthy and harmonious synthesis of faith and enlightenment was possible. When he was once ordered to conduct an orchestra at a reception planned for Alexander II at Minsk on the eve of the Day of Atonement, he did not signify his obedience until he was given a written dispensation by rabbis of Vilna and Minsk.

Success, however, ultimately turned his head as it had done to so many talented Jews of his generation. In the course of time, he associated ever less with his former Jewish friends and ever more with his new Russian aristocratic admirers. Rumors spread that he had become an apostate. Even though he denied these rumors in a conversation with Antokolsky, he was not believed.

After 1881, Ebin found the doors of the Russian aristocrats closed to him. The officers and their wives, who once flattered him, now joined in jeering him as a Jew. He was deposed as orchestral conductor and his compositions were removed from concert programs. Scorned by Jews and Gentiles, the proud musician felt lonely, wretched, and embittered. His health began to give way and he went to Yalta, the Crimean winter resort, for a cure. He failed to rally, however, and the end loomed ever nearer.

Zunser told, in his *Autobiography*, how, when Ebin was on his deathbed, a priest was sent to him. The composer refused to

let the representative of the Greek Orthodox Church administer
the last rites and insisted that he had always been a Jew and
that he wanted to end as a Jew. When he died, the police tele-
graphed to Vilna, inquiring whether Ebin was really of the
Jewish faith, whether there was not some record of his conversion to a Christian sect. Two days later, a reply was received
from the Chief of Police at Vilna that Ebin's name was not
listed among the converts of that city. Jewish officials at Yalta
were, therefore, asked to dispose of the body, but they were in
no hurry to bury the corpse in Jewish soil. They replied that
they wanted to make a thorough inquiry of their own. Since
the corpse could not be kept indefinitely, it was put on a garbage
truck and dumped in the Christian cemetery.

Zunser concluded his story with these comments:

> Thus ended the great Ebin, the world-famous artist
> whose musical fantasies, waltzes, and other compositions
> are still a source of delight everywhere. In the bundle of
> things sent on to his heirs at Vilna were found his manu-
> scripts, in which he poured out his bitter heart, full of
> remorse for the sins he had committed against his people.

Was the exchange of the old forms of Jewish behavior for
the modern, so-called progressive, culture really an improve-
ment? The repentance of Sorkin, Levanda, Ebin, and others
furnished evidence to the contrary. Zunser contrasted the old
way of life and the new in a poem, entitled *The Interchange*
(*Der Khiluf*), and concluded each of the sixteen stanzas with
the refrain: "Surely, the change was not worth while." Zunser
observed that in former generations a young man generally
followed in the footsteps of his father, he was embedded in his
people's culture, he acquired at home and in *Kheder* training
in morals, love for his forebears, pride in his traditions. The new
education, however, sought to do without religious training,
without ethical precepts, without reverence for the past. Formerly, women were devoted to their husbands; they performed
their household duties; they reared their children; and they

found happiness in these limited activities. Now, they insisted on widening their horizon. This meant flirting, skating, dancing, and seeking various amusements outside of the home. Formerly, synagogues were crowded day and night with learned Jews who were engaged in heated disputations based on Talmudic folios. The new reforms introduced into the synagogues prescribed silence for the worshipers, while services were conducted by a choir and by paid officials in black costumes. With these innovations, religious fervor somehow flagged, and houses of worship were never filled save on Atonement Day. Formerly, every Jewish family had its collection of books, because learning was held in highest repute. Now, card-playing was taking up the leisure time once devoted to the study of holy texts. Formerly, a Jew avoided participating in politics or mingling with non-Jews outside of the sphere of business activities. The closer association in common cultural activities, evident in recent years, was to have led to a bettering of relations. Actually, it gave rise to undesirable consequences, to more violent brutality. Surely, the exchange was not worth while.

The pogroms of 1881 evoked strong protests from abroad. The European press attacked the Czarist regime for its inhuman policies toward its own subjects. Mass meetings in the principal English cities called upon the British government to intercede in behalf of the innocent victims. In London, outstanding representatives in the various fields of politics, science, literature, and religion, under the leadership of the Lord Mayor, voiced their profound indignation. Relief funds to help Jews emigrate from Russia were started in several countries. Victor Hugo was head of the French committee. He appealed to his countrymen to speak out boldly against the savage actions of the Russian government. In Washington, the Congress of the United States passed a resolution on March 6, 1882, calling upon the President to request the Czar to protect his Jewish subjects against the violence of their enemies.

The Russian Minister of Interior, Count Ignatiev, felt that something had to be done to quiet the mounting storm of

protests. He, therefore, convoked a series of conferences for
the purpose of discovering the underlying causes of the pogroms. In Zunser's opinion, the primary aim of these conferences was to whitewash the regime. Hence, Jewish delegates
were also invited to attend, in order to convince foreign opinion
that absolute objectivity would prevail. Since the Christian
delegates were recruited from the ranks of notorious anti-
semites, these used the conferences as pulpits from which to
level slanderous accusations against the victims. The Jews were
declared to be, in the main, swindlers, thieves, parasites, enemies
of the state. Pogroms were not exactly condoned, but merely
explained as the inevitable reaction of the Russian masses to
Jewish exploitation. When Jewish delegates sought to refute
these monstrous charges, they were not permitted to speak.

The Jews became convinced that the pogroms were not
spontaneous and accidental. Apparently, the government itself
was in large measure responsible for these outrages. Indeed,
Czar Alexander III openly boasted that he hated Jews and that
he would like to cleanse Russia of them. When a Jewish deputation appealed to his Minister of Interior for mercy, it was told
that the border to the West was open to the Jews and that they
were free to get out if they did not like the treatment accorded
them. Steps were actually taken to compel emigration. A series
of decrees deprived the Jews of certain civil rights and of the
economic freedom which they had enjoyed to some extent
under Alexander II. They were prohibited from living in
villages. They were restricted from entering institutions of
learning by the adoption of a stringent quota for Jewish
students.

The reaction of Jewish intellectuals to these coercive measures was a rebirth of national pride, a return to piety, a reaffirmation of their kinship to their coreligionists, a reversal of
their scornful attitude toward their mother-tongue Yiddish, a
renewed longing for Zion. Zunser described this changed mood
in his poem *The Aristocrat* (*Der Aristokrat*).

The hero of the poem was a Jew who had emancipated

himself from his ghetto environment. He regarded himself as an aristocrat and behaved accordingly. A Christian atmosphere prevailed in his home. His children were educated in Russian schools. His son excelled at a Russian university. When the mobs assailed Jews, however, this aristocrat was the first to suffer. His own servants despoiled him of his belongings and wrecked his house. His refined son, beaten up in a pogrom, asked in amazement: "Are we also Jews?" Impoverished and disgraced, mocked by his erstwhile friends, and expelled from his native land, the would-be aristocrat finally found refuge in

DER ARISTOKRAT

Palestine as a tiller of the soil. His misfortunes cured him of his
delusions of grandeur and brought him back to the Jewish fold
as a hard-working colonist in the land of his ancestors.

The return to health and sanity after the disillusionment of
1881 was also treated by Zunser in a long allegorical poem,
entitled *Yudeshke*. As so often before, Zunser used the allegorical form to circumvent the censor. Under the mask of
Yudeshke, the Jewess who had become enamored of a Russian
who scorned her, the poet could allude to contemporary events
and reach the hearts of all listeners without risking an involuntary trip to Siberia.

Yudeshke had the insane notion that her neighbor's son was
destined for her, and so she pursued him with her love. He never
gave her any reason to feel encouraged. He even went out of
his way to hurt her. But still she did not desist. In every other
respect, Yudeshke was a decent girl, kind, intelligent, thrifty.
In her infatuation, however, she imitated slavishly the behavior
of her idealized young man. If he brought a Christmas tree into
his home, she must do likewise. If he attended balls and masquerades, she followed suit. If he went to church, she too
yearned to do so. She grew ashamed of her own parents, her
own language, her own faith. Her adored hero finally tired of
her intrusiveness. He fell upon her, tore her clothes to shreds,
beat her black and blue, and threw her out of her own room.
She then recalled a similar experience of earlier days: her
infatuation with a Spanish cavalier, an experience from which
she had barely escaped, after being knocked down by the Inquisition and driven from her apartment. To a suggestion that she
now try to obtain a new dwelling in America, her reply was:
"Who can assure me that, in exchanging Europe for America, I
shall not some day go through the same ordeal?" No. Yudeshke
had enough of rented dwellings. She wanted a home of her
own, where she could determine her own fate. She wanted to
return to her ancestral soil. There she hoped to regain her looks,
her happiness, her courage. There she expected to find her true
mate: Messiah.

Zunser reverted to the same theme in *The Bridegroom Reconsiders (Kharuta fun Khosens Tsad)*. He merely varied the allegorical symbols but not the lesson he wanted to emphasize.

After 1881, it was obvious that Russian Jews were unwanted in the land of their birth and that they would have to plan a reconstruction of their communal existence elsewhere. The pogroms were causing a panicky flight across Russia's western borders, but neither in Central Europe nor in Western Europe was there room for mass immigration, since these regions were themselves seeking an outflow of their excessive populations. Palestine and America were the most promising possibilities. Palestine was preferred by many because of its historic connection with the Jewish people and because it filled a mystic longing within the hearts of religious Jews. America was preferred by others because it could more immediately offer a haven of refuge and economic rehabilitation to large masses who were already in flight or who were preparing to flee as soon as possible, and because of its ideals of freedom and equal rights.

In the debate between exponents of Palestine and America as the goal of Jewish emigration, Zunser took a most active part. His songs of Zion and his songs of the New World mirrored the mood of Russian Jewry on the march to a new destiny.

CHAPTER XIII

Pioneer of Zionism

THE POGROMS of 1881 changed the thinking of Russian Jewry. Until this catastrophic year, three main tendencies could be distinguished. Each was the expression of a distinct social group among the Jewish population, and each had a definite philosophy of life, well buttressed by seemingly logical arguments.

The advocates of the first viewpoint, and the most vocal, were recruited largely from the ranks of the middle class. They believed in the inevitability of progress. They expected developments in Russia to follow along lines similar to those of Central and Western Europe. They foresaw a gradual lifting of the restrictions which reduced Jews to pariahs, a steady amelioration of economic and political disabilities until the final complete emancipation of the Jews. Then, all social and racial distinctions would disappear. Humanity would consist of equal, free cells, whose reactions to all situations would be motivated by reason, tolerance, and mutual good will. During the reign of Alexander II, Zunser had for a brief time believed in this roseate dream of the approaching era of the brotherhood of man. However, he soon recognized this dream as a dangerous delusion. Evil was a potent force in human affairs and could not be conjured away. Untamed, savage impulses still persisted within the human breast; the millennium was not in sight. Moreover, Zunser questioned the desirability of a "Utopia" designed to put an end to religious or national differentiation. He did not want to give up his Jewishness in order to enter as a naked cell into the stream of humanity-at-large. Nor was he interested in converting his Russian neighbor to his own views of God. In his lyric *The World Kaleidoscope (Die Fershiedene Velt)*, he pointed out that, though one earth bore all of us on its wings and though one sun shone upon every human being, nevertheless, in the eye and in the mind of each one of us, every phenomenon was mirrored in a unique way and no two beings experienced exactly the same fate. Differentiation of groups and of individuals within groups was the law of life, and hence God's way with man. We should pray for a lifting of tensions between groups, not for a melting pot in which historic and religious groups would lose their identities. The pogroms of 1881 reduced the Utopian dream of a symbiosis of Russians and Jews to a grim nightmare.

The advocates of a second movement struggling for supremacy on the Jewish scene were recruited mainly from the ranks of academic youth, the so-called intelligentsia. They preached revolutionary action, the violent overthrow of the oppressive autocracy. They held that the liberated Russian of the post-revolutionary generation, the noble proletarian and peasant, would embrace the Jew as his brother and would usher in a golden age of justice, equality, and creative labor. In the 1870's, some members of the Circle of Eliakum at Minsk debated this solution of Jewry's ills, and for a few months Zunser wrote in the periodical *Kol L'Am* articles not far removed in their revolutionary intent from those of his friend Moritz Winchevsky, then an active disciple of the Narodniki or Populist Movement. It was, therefore, a great shock to the Jewish intellectuals when the Narodniki hailed the pogroms as a popular movement worthy of support by revolutionists and their press praised the peasant-heroes for their participation in plundering Jewish shops. These radicals looked upon the uprising against the Jews as the first step in the awakening of the long-dormant masses, a step that would be followed by riots against landlords, feudal aristocrats, and despotic officials. This cruel attitude of the Russian preachers of socialism and cosmopolitanism towards their Jewish comrades led to a decline of Jewish revolutionary zeal and a defection of many Jewish followers of the Narodniki.*

The third tendency among Jews was an expression of the will of the common man to seek salvation in hours of adversity in closer ties with his fellow Jews. Disappointment with Russia led to an intensification of longing for a Jewish homeland, where the individual Jew could help to determine his own destiny. After 1881, the cry of self-emancipation became ever more audible in Jewish communities. It was given its clearest formulation in Leo Pinsker's pamphlet of 1882, entitled *Auto-Emancipation*. It found its warmest expression in Zunser's songs of Zion. It led to the rise of the Khoveve Zion movement and the beginning of agricultural settlements on a large scale in the ancient land of Israel.

Pinsker's pamphlet, originally published anonymously in German, became available immediately in Yiddish and Russian translations. Zunser was among its first readers and found himself in agreement with its conclusions. Both Pinsker and Zunser had started from the same assumption—that the Jews comprised a distinctive group among the nations on whose territory they dwelt, a separate group which could neither assimilate nor be readily digested by any nation. Both thinkers, therefore, sought the solution of the Jewish question not in the adjustment of the individual Jew to his non-Jewish neighbor, but rather in the adjustment of the Jewish people as a whole to the family of nations. In other words, both called upon the Jews to cease wandering under compulsion from one exile to another, and rather to concentrate all efforts upon the acquisition of an extensive, productive land as a permanent refuge, as a national center where they and their descendants could lead an autonomous life on their own soil. Pinsker, the physician and scientist, used logical and practical arguments to emphasize his thesis.

* E. Tcherikover, *History of the Jewish Labor Movement in the United States*, New York, 1945, II, 174.

Zunser, the poet, appealed also to religious sentiments and to messianic longings in order to bolster Jewish self-respect and to revive the Jewish will for self-regeneration. Pinsker was equally willing to accept a large tract of land in the New World or in Palestine as the goal of Jewish colonization. He was prepared to leave the decision as to the exact territory to agricultural and financial experts. He even voiced the opinion that the purchase of land in the United States would, because of the swift rise of that country, be not a risky but a lucrative enterprise. Zunser, on the other hand, placed greater weight upon tradition and upon romantic, mystic factors. He was, therefore, more insistent upon Palestine as the inalienable home of the Jewish people.

Zunser's arguments in behalf of a union of the people of Israel with the soil of Israel were embodied in a lengthy essay, written soon after Pinsker's pamphlet and entitled *Endowing the Bride (Hakhnoses Kalle)*. Since Zunser recited his essay at public gatherings, he could not have the protection of anonymity, which Pinsker resorted to. He, therefore, fell back upon the device he had perfected, the allegory.

The bard's essay purported to be an appeal by a poor sister to her wealthy, assimilated brother to contribute to her daughter's dowry, so that she could marry her chosen bridegroom in *Eretz Israel*. Zunser listed seven reasons for this match. These reasons still carry weight and are still regarded as standard arguments in behalf of Zionism, even though the essay itself, because of its obsolete symbolism, can no longer appeal to contemporary taste.

The following paragraph best illustrates the style of the epistle by Judith, descendant of Abraham, the Hebrew patriarch, to her brother Yaphim. Invoking his assistance in her hour of distress, she cries out to him:

> Help me, because you are of my flesh and blood, born of the same parents, reared in the same surroundings, and subject to the same illnesses. Strangers are welded together by common hardships, but we are brother and sister, and the suffering of our family cannot be compared to that of

others. Our history is older and more tragic: every page is inscribed with tears and blood. We have borne all pain for the sake of our heritage, bequeathed to us by our ancestors. Recently, however, you have become estranged from me; you have garbed yourself in a masquerade in public and in private, so that nobody will suspect you of being your father's child. When you see me in the street, you puff yourself up like a peacock and turn away from me. You have changed your name from Yankel to Yaphim, and you are angry when reminded of your Jewish origin. You ignore your sister and her family. You hate us like the pest. May I ask, dear brother, what have our forefathers done to earn your displeasure? Is our ancient, honorable lineage too ignoble for you? It seems to me, our parents were wiser, more gifted, more cultured, more moral than you are; yet they were not ashamed of their family. On the contrary, they sacrificed their lives for their kin. Indeed, the very people you are flattering claim some relationship to one of our forebears, even if it be a mythical relationship. You, on the other hand, are ashamed to acknowledge your genuine relationship. But, regardless of your attitude and your masquerading, you are still recognized as a son of our people. Though you placed ikons in your windows during the recent riots, you were not spared. You may trim your beard and change your name, but your face will still reveal your origin and background, and you will be punished doubly for decking yourself out with false feathers. Come back, my brother, to your family. Befriend your kin. Recover your pride in your ancestors. Remember that, while others lived in primeval forests as primitive cannibals, your forefathers were outlining the course of the stars and philosophizing about the one and only God. The memory of our glorious past should rouse you from your assimilationist delusions and should warm your heart for your family.

The appeal of the afflicted sister to her prosperous brother ended with a warning that he should not feel too secure in his aristocratic quarters. There was no security for Jews anywhere on the globe save in a territory of their own. If the nineteenth century could give rise to pogroms, the twentieth might revive the Inquisition and resume expulsions of Jewish populations. There was no guarantee that efforts at extermination might not be attempted even in liberal countries and in enlightened generations. A haven of refuge, a permanent, inalienable home for the Jewish people, was a necessity. The outcast daughter, who was now begging for a pittance from her wealthy kin in order to reach the Land of Israel, might one day be the last source of salvation for the relatives who, in their haughty hour, scorn her.

In 1882, the first organized efforts were made to further large-scale emigration of Jews from Russia to Palestine and to America. Zunser lent his support to the pioneers who were heading eastward. These early pioneers came from the ranks of young, disappointed idealists, university students who had for a time fallen under the spell of the Narodniki and who had wanted to labor in behalf of the Russian masses. However, when these would-be saviors were assailed by the masses and beaten up in pogroms, they became convinced of their unalterable alien status in the land of their birth—that their people were not the Russians but the Jews. In a mood of remorse, they left the academic halls and set out for Palestine, to devote themselves to the regeneration of their ancestral soil and to the rebuilding of the Jewish nationality. They called their movement BILU, after the initials of the biblical motto: *Beth Iacob Lekhu Unelkha*—"House of Jacob, come and let us go."

Twenty-five students at the University of Kharkov formed the first group. They set out for the Holy Land via Constantinople. En route through Russia, they sought to win converts to their idea, and they helped to organize other groups. They stopped for three days at Minsk and paid tribute to Zunser as the singer of Zion. They recalled his lyric *The Flower (Die Blum)*, which had been on the lips of Jews for two decades and had voiced nostalgia for the ancient garden in which the Jewish flower had once blossomed in full vigor, before it was uprooted and trampled in the dust. They sang his pathetic elegy

Rachel Weeps for her Children (Rokhel Mivako al Boneo), in which he had expressed the lament of the desolate land for its exiled children and the hope for the return of the eternally afflicted wanderers.

Zunser responded to the tribute of the heroic pioneers of BILU by composing for them, in Hebrew and in Yiddish, his song *Return to Zion (Shivas Zion)*. He selected a motto from Isaiah: "Lift up thine eyes round about, and behold: all these gather themselves together and come to thee."

The poem was in the form of a monologue by Mother Zion. Widowed for many years and deprived of the sight of her beloved children, she now beheld the first of her offspring returning to her. God had performed a miracle: the long night had ended, darkness was yielding to dawn. Oppression that

SHIVAS ZION

seemed unbearable was in reality a means of Providence to compel homecoming to Zion. If the Jews had not been violently uprooted from foreign soil, they might not have begun the re-building of their own national center and might not have re-affirmed so vigorously their ancient covenant. Though foes might laugh at the modest beginning—a few youngsters attempt-ing to restore the splendor of yore—it might be well to keep in mind that the mightiest rivers began as tiny rivulets, which grew ever wider and deeper, until they could carry splendid ships onward to the sea. The coming of enthusiastic colonists, eager to engage in physical labor, would rejuvenate the ancient land. Blessed were the youthful pioneers who were leaving behind the glamor and the tinsel of their individual careers in order to sacrifice their lives for the common welfare of their people. These young men would, in time, remove the stones that barred their path. They would suffer and endure and create until there emerged a Jewish commonwealth no less re-splendent than the one which arose in the days of the prophet Ezra.

Zunser's vision, in *Shivas Zion*, was prophetic. Twenty years later, he remarked that his comparison of the stream of Zionist immigration to a tiny rivulet which would grow until it became a mighty flood was indeed appropriate. The first colony, sym-bolically named Rishon le-Zion (The First in Zion), was founded on July 30, 1882, near Jaffa, by ten pioneers, who over-came all political and economic obstacles set in their path. Others followed. When, in 1884, settlers of Rishon le-Zion founded Gederah as a model colony, Zunser participated in the purchase of the land and prepared to settle there with his family. Among the first nine colonists of Gederah were four young men of Zunser's circle, members of the Khoveve Zion organization of Minsk, which had been formed in 1882 in the home of the poet. For this group Zunser had written *The Plow* (*Die Sokhe*), his most famous lyric. It was soon sung by Jewish mothers in Russia as a cradlesong and by the first pioneers in the blazing heat of the subtropical sun. It is still heard in Jewish homes

from Biro-Bidjan on the banks of the Amur to the prairies of
Argentina and the farms of Saskatchewan.

The theme of the song is the joy of labor. In the plow lies
bliss and blessedness, life's true essence. When morning comes,
the tiller of the soil goes forth into God's world, full of health
and cheer, breathing the clear air of freedom. Unknown to him
are the worries of the city dweller, who has to engage in
speculative ventures and rack his brain to eke out an unproductive livelihood. In stanza after stanza, the wholesome and in-
vigorating life of the colonists in Palestine is contrasted with
the unhealthy, parasitical existence of petty traders in ghetto
communities. The poem ends by invoking God's blessing upon
all who support Zion and who rebuild the land of Israel, and
by praying that the colonists increase and multiply until millions
are again settled on the soil of the Holy Land.

Zunser saw the main achievement of modern Zionism in its

DIE SOKHE

reawakening of Jewish national feeling. After centuries of
lethargy, the Jewish soul was stirring again and Jewish pride
was reasserting itself. A single idea was again uniting Jews of
all the corners of the earth. Individuals who formerly wallowed
in self-hatred were losing their feeling of inferiority and re-
acting with greater dignity to the scornful attitude of their
neighbors. Even if the Zionist ideal should ultimately prove to
be a Utopian dream incapable of ever being realized in actual
practice, Zunser felt that the moral gains would be enduring.
Zionism was weaning Jewish youth away from the false road of
assimilation. Zionism was the cement that welded millions of
grains of sand into a pillar of strength capable of withstanding
the hammering of hostile storms.

"Back to Zion!" was the slogan underlying Zunser's poems
of the 1880's. How much longer should Jews submit to the
tortures of Europe and the horrors of Occidental civilization?
Was it not time for them to return to Asia to the cradle of their
own precious culture? Zunser asked these questions in the lyric
On the Old Road (Uf Dein Alten Veg), and he replied:

> It is time, O my people, to inscribe on your heart what
> Europe has meant to you: persecutions, accusations, plunder-
> ings, expulsions, all in the name of civilization. . . . Your
> natural inclination is toward Asia; there you swim in your
> native waters. . . . Leave all commerce and trade, and
> betake yourselves to the soil that awaits you. . . . Return,
> O my people, return to your ancient ways.

In the hymn *Our Fatherland (Unser Foterland)*, Zunser
reminded the Jews that no country save Zion could ever be
their fatherland. Israel was scorned and despised because it was
scattered and dispersed. Let it re-establish itself in Zion and
let it have a government to defend its interests. Then all vilification would cease. In Zion none would dare to call the Jews
strangers or to scold them as intruders. There they would be
masters on their own estates. There they would enjoy the

products of their labor: corn and fruit and wine. There they
would not be molested by Cossacks. There they would not have
to pay dearly for rented, squalid quarters and still fear expulsion.
There a vacant home lovingly awaited its rightful owners.
There every blade of grass beckoned intimately and every stone
was a monument to a glorious past. There every step stirred the
soul to happiness. The Land of Israel was the warm heart of
Israel reviving all the limbs throughout the world. The paralyz-
ing blow of 1881 had at least one good effect: it initiated the
Jewish trek homeward, to the Jewish fatherland, to Zion.

Zunser's passionate avowal of love and longing for Zion
reached its climax in the lyric *My Longings* (*Meine Gefeelen*).
With every nerve he reacted to his people's happiness and

MEINE GEFEELEN

sorrows. When his fellow Jews were hurt he too was hurt. He did not claim that his people were entirely blameless. He knew there must be divine punishment for their transgressions. But, why did God have to inflict such severe drubbings for the slightest infractions by his chosen people? Why was God more wroth with his favorite children than with their merciless oppressors? Surely, the waywardness of the Jews was nearing an end; they were anxious to sow the seeds of a new life in their Promised Land, to plant trees on its mountain-slopes, and to fill its valleys with verdure.

Oh, take Israel's hand again and lead him back to your land. I shall fly like a dove and feel the sweetness of each blade of grass. My family will sow and plant, and I shall sing psalms to you. . . . Wings, oh, give me wings, that I may float beneath Zion's blue sky, in the shadows of Lebanon, and near gently flowing Shiloh, where the atmosphere is resonant with divinity. There, there is the goal of my longing.

Zunser's language took on an intenser glow when he sang of Zion. His usual melancholy was transformed into a joyous mood. His imagination swept onward to dizzy heights. Gone was every trace of timidity and humility. The Badchen became a proud poet and prophet, calling upon his people to arise from filth and poverty and despair, to turn their backs upon their European hosts, both the humanitarian and the cruel, and to fashion a new life with their own hands in Israel.

In a philosophical poem, entitled *The Pyramids or The Eternal People (Die Pyramiden)*, he reminded the Jews that they were an immortal people and had no cause to deem themselves less than others. If the ancient Egyptians built mighty pyramids as mute monuments to outlast the centuries, the ancient Hebrews were riveted together by Moses into a living pyramid, a holy people to endure through all historic cycles. Before their ageless eyes, other nations arose, paraded a moment on the stage of history, and were then wafted away as dust and smoke. Unlike other peoples, who passed through the stages of youth, maturity, senescence, and death, the Jewish people never got beyond the third stage. When this people grew old, it was seized with fever and emerged, phoenixlike, rejuvenated. It entered on a new historic cycle. But what if the Jewish people should intermingle with others? Would it not succumb like the others and cease to be immortal? No, replied the poet, complete assimilation was impossible, because God instilled in the Gentile nations a sense of difference. Hence, the stronger the urge of Jews to assimilate to their neighbors, the greater the resistance of the latter. But, if all the nations among whom Jews dwelt harbored resentment against these strange, uncanny persons, was it not possible to destroy the Jews by enacting discriminatory laws to deprive them of a livelihood? No, replied the poet, because God had endowed the Jews with resourcefulness which enabled them to find means of subsistence where another people would starve to death. But, if the Jews were so intensely hated by their neighbors, was there not danger that these might rise up and annihilate them utterly? God foresaw this danger, too, and scattered the Jews over the face of the globe, so that, if they were attacked and exterminated in one country, those in other lands would still survive.

Let not, therefore, the Jews despair in facing the onslaught of their enemies. Let them not be panic-stricken by the momentary wave of pogroms. Let them seek solace in their religion and in their history. Beneath the surface of European culture, savagery still prevailed and the nations of the earth were not yet wholly divorced from primitive brutality. But a gain had been achieved: these nations were already paying lip service to Christianity and Mohammedanism, religions sprung from Israel's loins. Some day, the nations would realize how grievously they wronged their benefactor, the people that gave to the world monotheism and the moral laws.

What if a gifted Jew, under the stress of circumstances, strayed from the fold and forsook his heritage! Let but danger threaten his people and his old love for it would revive. Despite his apostasy, he would rush to its defense. Historic experience had proved that, whenever a Haman plotted the destruction of the Jewish people, a Mordecai was at hand to frustrate his evil designs. The storm passed away and the Jews resumed their historic role as witnesses of the unitary God among the nations of the globe.

Zunser affirmed the necessity of Jewish survival both in Palestine and in the Diaspora. The poetic pioneer of Zionism saw the Jews as a world people, whose heart was in Palestine but whose limbs encircled the earth. Without Palestine, the Jews were a sick people. But Palestine alone as the expression of the Jewish historic fate did not entirely satisfy his religious conscience.

Zunser was profoundly religious. He divined a moral meaning in all happenings. Naught was accidental. Naught could occur against the will of God. There was no absolute evil. In two poems, entitled *Dayenu*, he maintained that what seemed evil to us often bore results which were good. As proof, he pointed to the evil of pogroms and to the Zionist revival as a good consequence. Hatred was evil, but the hatred surrounding the Jews was also forging a greater unity among them. The new discriminatory laws directed against Jewish students were evil, but they also favored Jewish survival. Students, formerly alienated from their faith and scornful of their fathers' ways, were increasingly retracing their steps in the direction of orthodoxy and were assuming leadership of the constructive Khoveve Zion movement.

Probing ever deeper into the meaning of all historic changes, Zunser was able to appraise the striving of his mid-century generation more objectively. With the realization that no evil was wholly devoid of good, there came also the insight that good was not unmarred by evil and that truth lost much of its pure whiteness when it descended into the realm of practical human affairs. After his early enthusiasm for Enlightenment and after his subsequent disappointment with this panacea of his generation, Zunser arrived at the mature conclusion that it was

one of several necessary stages in the evolution of the modern
Jew.

In a panoramic poem *The Nineteenth Century* (*Der Nein-
zenter Yorhundert*), written by him in his fiftieth year and regarded by some as the classical description of Jewish disillusionment with Christian civilization, he reviewed the errors and the
achievements of the Haskalah. Israel was represented as a
wanderer from Asia who came to Europe and stopped at an inn.
There he fell into a deep slumber. For seventeen long centuries, he slept on and on, unaware of the passage of events.
Suddenly he was awakened by the cry: "Arise! Day has
dawned, the day of humanism and enlightenment! All nations
want to win your friendship and to bestow equal rights upon
you. Wash away your grime and acquire a modern look and a
worldly education."

Israel rubbed his eyes and gazed about him. He heard the
singing of telegraph wires and the rushing of locomotives.
Humanism beckoned and modernism lured. Quickly he gave
up the old rags of fanaticism, discarded the Talmud, donned
modern clothes, entered academic halls, and emerged as a free-
thinker. Believing himself no longer in need of the lamp of his
religion, he extinguished it and waited for the radiance of the
rising sun. For half a century he waited, but darkness continued
to reign all about him. He sought to fraternize with his neighbors on the assumption that they too had awakened and had
cast aside their medieval prejudices and were ready to receive
him in their midst as a member of the same human brotherhood.
But his hope was short-lived. When he ventured out of the inn,
he saw black clouds moving across the sky and horrible ghosts
clawing at him. When he returned to the inn, he discovered that
the other guests were still asleep, as though deep midnight were
still upon them. When he tried to awaken them, he was beaten
and ejected from the inn as a disturber of the peace. Alas, the
day of human brotherhood and genuine enlightenment had not
yet dawned! And now he regretted bitterly that he had extinguished the lamp of faith which had illumined his rooms so long,

and which might still have relieved somewhat the prevailing gloom.

To the pessimism voiced by the disillusioned Jew, the Nineteenth Century made the following reply: It was true that all did not go too well with the Jew in the modern world; unforeseen ills had cropped up; but, nevertheless, there was no cause for despair. Enlightenment was not at fault. Progress was not to be condemned. Would we had more of both! The wheel of history did move forward and could not be reversed. The old days of blissful ignorance were gone beyond recall. The need of the hour was for a synthesis of reason and religion, modernism and ethical conduct, secular education and respect for ancestral traditions. Then the Jew could face his foes with calmness, self-reliance, and dignity.

Zunser thus did not repudiate the achievements of Haskalah, but he did repudiate its excrescences and heresies: Assimilation and Russification. Beyond the ideal of Haskalah, the purification of the Jewish soul of ignorance and superstition, there shone before his eyes the ideal of Zionism, the rebirth of Jewish creativeness in a Jewish commonwealth. Zunser had begun as the champion of Haskalah. He reached his highest peak as the singer of Zion.

CHAPTER XIV

Composer

ZUNSER'S songs of Zion raised his popularity to its highest peak. His hymns of Palestine appealed more poignantly to the Jewish soul than did his earlier lyrics. The succession of pogroms from 1881 to 1884 had bared Jewish homelessness in its most tragic aspects. The poet and musician could reckon on an enthusiastic response when he sang of the coming idyllic life in a Jewish homeland where Jews could till their own fields and enjoy the wine from their own vineyards, unafraid of a rapacious, envious population all about them.

Besides, Zunser had at his disposal for his imagery of Zion an almost inexhaustible treasure of material. From the prophets of the Bible and the sages of the Talmud to the contemporary writers in the Hebrew press, Jewish imagination had endowed the landscape and the atmosphere of the Holy Land with glowing warmth and with fabulously rich coloring. The vocabulary and the tunes associated with the Land of Promise were charged with the emotional electricity of many generations. The bard who achieved an original combination of the traditional words and sounds was assured of an instantaneous vogue.

Whenever Zunser traveled to a city or town, in pursuit of his profession as Badchen, the Lovers of Zion there called together the Jews in the synagogues, so that all might hear him sing his hymns of Zion. Public assemblies outside of a synagogue would have aroused the suspicion of Czarist officials and might have been banned, but there was normally no interference with religious gatherings. On several such occasions, Zunser's presence furnished the incentive for the founding of new Khoveve Zion groups and for the collecting of funds for the movement. In his own city of Minsk, the mere announcement that Zunser would chant Zionist lyrics brought thousands upon thousands to the synagogue, far more persons than could be admitted. Such announcements were not posted or printed because of fear of police interference but were spread by word of mouth.

The text of Zunser's poems alone, as it has come down to us, does not, however, explain adequately his hold upon audiences. The music was no less important than the words. He himself recognized this fact. In a quatrain, addressed to the reader, as distinct from the listener, he reminded the former: "If you read my songs in my booklet and the melody is not reproduced for you, it is as if you were looking at a photograph: all features are accurately delineated but, alas, there is still lacking—the breath of life."

Artchik der Khazan, the ex-drummer who so strongly influenced Zunser's early melodies, probably owed his position as cantor in Vilna less to his own rather limited talent than to the well-founded reputation of his brother, who was known as Fiedele Khazan and who delighted the congregation of Slutsk with his liturgical compositions.

A new musical tradition came to Vilna, however, with the arrival of the cantor Khaim Wasserzug, better known as Khaim Lomzher. Zunser spoke of him with great reverence and acknowledged his own indebtedness to this talented composer, who introduced greater lyrical feeling and sentiment into the religious services. This cantor adapted for religious texts the simple melodies of folk songs current among the common people. In his transformation, these melodies returned to the marketplace, the inn, and the workshop. They brightened dull moments and penetrated through the outer bark of hearts embittered by hunger and privations. Zunser's songs of the 1870's were composed in the spirit of the new musical tradition. They were simple, soft, pleasant, caressing, sentimental.

The chief cantor of Minsk, Israel Shavelson, a friend of Zunser, was also an adherent of this school of liturgical music. Shavelson's successor, Moshe Levinson, called attention to the similarity of Shavelson's style to that of Zunser and saw in this fact an additional explanation for the enduring popularity of both in the White Russian metropolis.* Their melodies were like balm that soothed the wounded Jewish heart; they were appealing, and where they were heard, they were sung. The cobbler sang them at his last, the porter trudging along the street, the tailor at his ironing, and the carpenter to the accompaniment of hammer, saw, and plane.

The close relationship between the early music of Zunser and that of the cantors of his generation was not at all surprising. It was, of course, a relationship of give and take, of mutual influence. As Badchen or master of ceremonies at weddings, he came into constant intimate contact with cantors of many communities, who also officiated at these affairs. A new tune, picked up in the course of his travels, would remain in his subconscious until, evoked by a favorable mood, it emerged in some modified form. Similarly, his own musical creations would stimulate cantors, folk singers, and *Klezmorim*. There were many professional popularizers of his songs, and they did not always give credit to their master. If the Broder Singers only occasionally made use of his repertoire, the wedding bards of the late nineteenth century were more dependent upon him. Hillel Klebanoff of Borisov, Pesakh Eliahu of Bobruisk, Jacob Zizmor of Vilna, Israel Sadrunski or Sonia of Bialystok, and many a Badchen in other towns earned wide applause with interpretations of Zunser.

Perhaps the most erratic interpreter and popularizer of Zunser was the first violinist of the Pinsk Band, who also officiated at weddings as Badchen under the name of Dark Yehuda (*Yudel der Shwartser*). He could play with his gloves on, holding his fiddle behind his back. He would learn of a new song by

* Moshe Levinson, *Khazonim un Khazonos in Minsk*, Zukunft, April 1947, p. 206.

Zunser even before it was printed and would present it with great fervor to audiences keyed up to a high pitch of expectancy. He sang to the rhythmic accompaniment of his violin and improvised constant melodic variations as he continued on and on, stanza after stanza.

No interpreter could, however, equal the musical creator himself, according to the testimony of his listeners. Abraham Cahan, the noted publicist, recalled an evening in Vilna in the 1870's, when as a youth he first heard Zunser perform some of his famous songs to the accompaniment of a *cappella*.

It was an evening of thrills for me and I beheld the entranced faces of the other members of the audience. A dense crowd was listening spellbound in the street outside. And for weeks and weeks afterwards I would often catch myself humming one of the tunes I had heard on that divine evening and evoking the never-to-be-forgotten image of the wizard of rhythm as he stood singing and beating time for his own voice as well as for the instruments.*

Abraham Cahan also attended a wedding at which Zunser participated, and he described the remarkable scene in his autobiography. When Cahan arrived, a short while before the religious ceremony, he was astonished to find Zunser lying on a bench in an adjoining room, apparently fast asleep. Closer observation revealed, however, that Zunser was merely keeping his eyes closed so that he might concentrate better and so that other guests, who also thought he was asleep, would not disturb him. He was at that moment preparing the versified lines he would have to recite and chant in the course of the elaborate ceremony.

A little later in the evening, Zunser opened the official ceremony with his address to the bride. He moralized on the solemnity of the occasion. His verses included references to her name. As he proceeded, each letter of her name became a most

* Eliakum Zunser, *Selected Songs*, New York, 1928, p. 1.

significant word, about which an appropriate proverb or moral sentiment could be woven. Then followed rhyming couplets about the bridegroom, the parents of the couple, and other relatives of prominence. All this Zunser had improvised during the few minutes when he seemed to be lost in a trance.

During the wedding meal, he sang some of his songs. These were already familiar to his audience from previous occasions. He appeared to be transformed suddenly into a human dynamo. While singing, he beat time with his foot and directed the orchestra with both hands. He sang in such an enthralling way as to compel the participation of the assembled guests. The incomparable rhythm of his verses was irresistible. All who were within hearing range had to join in, keeping time with him and singing or humming the refrains.

At times, the bard would sing the accompaniment between the stanzas as well as the verses, and the audience would hum along with him. As a result, strange interpolations developed. For example, in singing the lines of *The Nineteenth Century* (*Der neinzehnter Yorhundert*), Zunser would turn to the orchestra at the end of each line and direct it to play three chords. Since he used the words *eins, zwei, drei*, to emphasize his gestures, the audience picked up these words as a refrain and interpolated them between the verses. Although these numbers were entirely unrelated to the text, they continued to be handed down from year to year.

The wedding songs of the 1870's, when Zunser was so successful in his career as Badchen, still retained a close association with religious ritual. His songs of the 1880's were, however, more national than religious. They reflected the sadness of the pogrom-years, but also a nascent hope in a brighter Jewish future. They ranged from the elegiac tone of the dirge for Levanda to the triumphant marching tempo of *The Plow* (*Die Sokhe*). While these songs still lacked classical form, they always maintained a certain melodic interest. Zunser's strength lay not in his mastery of form but rather in his unerring instinct for music. This led him to write captivating tunes of a haunting

DER NEINZEHNTER YORHUNDERT

quality. Furthermore, like many a famous cantor of his day, he invented new musical themes for every section of his poems, thus avoiding repetitious monotony as stanza followed stanza.

A. Z. Idelsohn, the author of *Jewish Music in Its Historical Development*, believed that he could trace in Zunser's tunes a certain kinship with Slavic and with Spanish-Oriental forms. Idelsohn held, for example, that the tune of the *Elegy on Levanda* could be traced back to an old Iberian folk song of the fifteenth century, which was published in 1575 by Francesco di Salinas of Burgos and which was set to a satiric text dealing with the Jews expelled from Spain in 1492. This tune must have persisted for centuries among the Jewish refugees from Spain and must have been transmitted by them to their non-Sephardic coreligionists, ultimately reaching the bard of Minsk. Idelsohn maintained also that the melody of *The Plow* (*Die Sokhe*) showed Slavic influences and that German musical characteristics were traceable in such songs as *Contrasts* (*Die Kontrasten*), *After the Latest Fashion* (*Nokh dem neisten Jhurnal*), *The Answer* (*Die Antwort*), *Certain I Am* (*Ikh bin shon sikher*), and *Clever, Polite, and Quiet* (*Klug, Edel, un Shtil*).

Salomo Rosovsky, the musicologist of Palestine, on the other hand, was inclined to minimize the influence of foreign melodies upon the Yiddish bard. But, whatever the ultimate source of Zunser's melodies from the viewpoint of musical history, there was no doubt that in his hands these underwent a modification or transformation which was distinctively Jewish. He varied and combined musical phrases in such a manner that his listeners felt a kindred Jewishness in them. Only thus can one explain their unerring, instantaneous appeal to the Jewish heart.

A. W. Binder, who made a study of Zunser's music, emphasized that the bard possessed to a high degree the gift of musical improvisation. He was perhaps the last and greatest improviser of Eastern European Jewry. In the cantoral style of former centuries, improvisation was extremely important. Just as in the Commedia dell' arte, actors were briefed only on what they were to talk about in a given situation on the stage but were expected to find the exact words on the spur of the moment, so too cantors were expected to go beyond the traditional melodies and to improvise continuations and variations, to the delight of their audiences. This art of musical improvisation or *Zugekhts*, has practically died out in Europe and America. It survives to an important extent only among the Oriental Jews in Yemen and Palestine.

Abraham Goldfaden, who experimented with many musical forms in his operettas, complained that all his efforts to graft classical melodies of European composers upon the Yiddish words of his musical dramas ended in failure. Somehow his audiences remained indifferent to these alien compositions. No matter how beautiful these melodies might seem to musical connoisseurs and no matter how singable, they did lack certain familiar Jewish qualities. These qualities were not easy to define, but his audiences sensed the strangeness, the incongruity, and reacted coolly. Thereupon Goldfaden decided to try the kind of folk tunes with which Zunser, Zbarzher, and their followers had aroused audiences to a high pitch of enthusiasm. Immediately he met with a warmer response. This taught him a lesson that Zunser had learned before him—that, whether a melody be simple or sublime, it had, above all, to be perfectly in harmony with its words and the ideas they expressed, if it were to exercise a magnetic influence upon the emotions of a people. Yiddish words and characteristic Jewish moods could not normally be happily wedded to German or French operatic airs. They rather craved embodiment in chants and tunes stemming from the synagogue and from Jewish historic experiences. A Jewish *Nigun* (melody) had a charm and a sadness of its own. It might be associated with the fragrance of the Torah and the holiness of the Sabbath, or it might echo with the wailing of countless generations of enforced exile. Zunser instinctively felt this mystic relationship between the Jewish soul, the melody of the synagogue, and the Yiddish word. He, therefore, became the most popular singer of Jewish faith and Jewish sorrow.

A generation ago, George Selikovitch expressed the wish that some day a composer might arise who would weave Zunsers' melodies into a grandiose Jewish symphony. This wish still awaits fulfillment.

CHAPTER XV

Philosophic Poems

INSECURITY is inherent in human fate, but there was an additional insecurity to which the Jews as a homeless people were subjected throughout their long exile. Misfortunes assail all human beings, but a pogrom was an additional hazard with which only Jews had to reckon. A fire may break out accidentally in any home and destroy in a single hour the material prosperity and the accumulated resources of an entire family. But Jews alone suffered from incendiary conflagrations set in motion by the majority group of the population, which had the government apparatus in its hands and which sought to bring about the economic ruin of enterprising competitors. Zunser managed to escape pogroms but, during his Minsk period, he was a victim of both types of fires, the accidental and the planned.

In January 1879, a fire broke out in his home. Immediately friends and neighbors rushed to his assistance. They saved everything that could be saved. His wife Feigel, who was in the house with her four children, ranging in age from five and a half years to a few months, succeeded in rescuing them all and in getting them to safe quarters. Her maid, however, who had been with her for four years, paid no heed to the frantic appeal of her Jewish employers and was interested only in getting her own belongings out of the house. Not until an hour after the fire, when her things were safely stored in a friend's house, did

she return to the Zunser family. Eliakum was angry at this heart-
less behavior. A few weeks later, in an article in *Kol L'Am*,
he used this incident as the starting point for a sermon on
mutual aid. He was probably also hurt financially by this accident, but his professional skill enabled him to recover any such
losses quickly and to refurnish his home in comfortable style.

Two and a half years later, his house again burned down, but
not as a result of an accident. The Jewish quarters of many
Russian towns were swept by large-scale conflagrations in 1881,
as an aftermath of the pogroms or in lieu of pogroms. It is difficult to establish the extent of government connivance at this
wanton destruction, which did not spare the city of Minsk. It
is certain, however, that the government took no steps to
punish the perpetrators or to relieve the suffering of the Jews.
Relief had to come from their coreligionists abroad or from
Jewish communities in Russia that managed to escape similar
horrors.

Minsk in 1881 numbered about fifty thousand inhabitants, of
whom at least two-thirds were Jewish. The great conflagration
of July destroyed more than a fifth of the town. In the course
of a few hours, sixteen hundred houses burned down, and ten
thousand men, women, and children were made homeless.
Twenty-one large synagogues were destroyed. Of some streets
in the Jewish quarter, not a trace was discernible. The
wooden houses disappeared from the surface of the earth, leaving merely rubble and half-burned beams. Among the ruins, the
walls of the more massive houses jutted forth like ghosts.

When the great fire occurred, Zunser was out of town,
officiating at a rich wedding in Homel. The festivities lasted
several days. When Zunser returned, he found his house and
family gone. He finally located his wife and children at
Novidvor, the village outside of Minsk where she was born and
where his brother-in-law now resided. There he heard the
dramatic news of his family's rescue. His wife, who had given
birth to her second son Kalman (Charles) two weeks earlier,
was in bed with the infant on the upper floor and was cut off

by the fire. While the other children, who were on the ground floor, got out easily, Feigel and the infant experienced a few harrowing moments before they were rescued by the Chief of Police, who carried them down a ladder. Since she was in her night clothes, Feigel laid the baby down for a minute on a market-stall in order to put on a wrap. As she did so someone in the crowd of gapers cried: "Look! An unmarried mother is trying to abandon her baby!"

The realization of the hazards to which his beloved wife and children were subject while he was away from home, made Zunser most reluctant to leave Minsk and its environs. At the same time, the gutted and impoverished town alone could hardly furnish him with sufficient occasions to use his talents as Badchen to support himself and his growing family in the manner of the preceding, prosperous years.

In the fall of 1881, therefore, Zunser temporarily abandoned his profession. When the reconstruction of the Jewish quarter was begun in Minsk, he returned with his family and opened a textile store. He believed that, with the knowledge of textiles he had acquired in his young days as a braider, he was more likely to succeed in this business than in any other. Besides, he reckoned with an increasing demand for linens, as conditions in the Jewish community returned to normal. Unfortunately, however, the time did not prove to be as opportune for new enterprises as he had anticipated. The panic-stricken Jewish population was preparing for flight from Russia and was merely waiting for some haven of refuge to be opened up. For eighteen months Zunser struggled on as a businessman, until he lost his entire capital and had to close the store.

This financial setback forced him to return to the profession he had sought to give up. Again he accepted invitations to weddings and other festivities hundreds of miles from home. Wherever he made his appearance, immense crowds gathered to listen to him. His songs of Zion had made of him a living legend. The weddings at which he officiated were converted into national celebrations and demonstrations. Since no special

permits were necessary for wedding songs and since a Badchen
was regarded as a religious functionary essential for the ritual,
Zunser was able to carry on as fiery national agitator for a year
or two without falling under any government ban. The police
began to be suspicious, however, when they realized the immense influence he was exerting upon the masses. Secret agents
began to shadow him when he arrived in a town for a wedding
or for a concert. Gendarmes at railroad stations exchanged
knowing glances when he boarded or left a train.

As early as July 1883, Zunser felt himself to be in danger of
arrest. In that month, on the occasion of the coronation of
Alexander III, he had been more outspoken than others regarding this despot, and he could not be sure that informers had
not overheard and reported his remarks. Although Alexander III
had ascended the throne in 1881, the actual coronation ceremony did not take place until two years later. The Russian
Government had expressed the wish that the main public bodies
in all the communities of the vast land should forward congratulatory resolutions to the Czar on this occasion, expressing
their love for the fatherland and their loyalty to the throne.
Obviously, no communal group could risk opposing such a
wish, or command, of the imperial authorities. Had any group
done so, it would thereby publicly have proclaimed itself in
rebellion, and its members would have been punished most
severely.

Zunser happened to be in Vilna, as he informs us in his
Autobiography, when its Civic Council, or duma, was preparing a congratulatory address to the Crown. On this Council
were representatives of the Russian, the Polish, and the Jewish
communities, since these three ethnic groups formed the bulk of
the city's population. The Russians and Poles, in an upsurge of
superpatriotism, refused to permit the Jewish deputies to sign
the official document. It was, therefore, sent off to Moscow
without bearing a single Jewish name.

The Jews of Vilna were horrified. They realized how tragic
the consequences might be, if the central Government should

notice that the Jewish community had failed to send an expression of devotion to the new Czar. The Jewish inhabitants of the town would be denounced as revolutionists and treated accordingly. An emergency meeting of Jewish leaders was called to take some kind of action to avert the threatened catastrophe.

A cousin of Zunser, named Cahan, invited the poet to be present. As a teacher in a Russian school, Cahan had previously been among the delegates chosen to confer with the Governor-General of Vilna regarding Jewish matters when pogroms threatened. At the meeting, he suggested that the Jews prepare a congratulatory address of their own and send it off to Moscow immediately, so that it would arrive in time for the coronation. This suggestion was approved unanimously. Cahan sat down and wrote out a beautiful laudatory document. He read it aloud to the assembled deputies. It began:

> Who can recount the many favors conferred upon us Jews since your gracious Majesty ascended the throne?

As Cahan read on and on, Zunser found it increasingly difficult to control himself. He thought of the soil that was still moist with the blood of pogrom victims. He recalled the new restrictions and the severer persecutions that were daily being promulgated in the name of the Czar. Gracious, indeed! Kind, indeed! As one flattering phrase was heaped upon another in the bombastic eulogy, the pure-hearted poet was seized with disgust and helpless rage. A sudden awareness of the depths of Jewish degradation overcame him, and he burst into tears. In his eyes, Alexander III ranked with Pharaoh, Haman, and Torquemada. Nevertheless, his victims were cruelly compelled to sing the praises of the imperial scourge whose hands were soaked in Jewish blood. The deputies interrupted the reading of the document and asked Zunser why he was weeping. He evaded a direct reply. He offered an explanation in the form of a parable, to which all listened, deeply moved:

Once upon a time there lived in Vilna an old Jewish widow, who used to go about the streets with a basket of baked beans, which she sold to little children. This "business" yielded her a profit of one or two gulden a day, a sum which was more than enough for her ordinary needs. She even managed to put away a trifle for a rainy day.

Now, this widow had a son, a cobbler by trade, an invalid, blessed with half-a-dozen children. Almost every day she would come grumbling and complaining to him. She insisted that he must give her a part of his earnings, since the law required a son to support a mother in her old age. He explained that he was in no position to help her, because his own household was in abject poverty, and his children were often without bread.

The old woman became very angry one day when rebuffed, and rushed off to the police station. There she told the captain that she had a son who neglected her and permitted her to starve. The police official, who welcomed an opportunity to flog a Jew, sent two constables with her, with orders to bring her son to police headquarters and there to flog him mercilessly until he promised to provide for his old mother.

As the woman was on her way with the tough-looking constables, a sense of pity awoke within her maternal breast. Her poor child would soon be whipped! Her own, dear son!

What was she to do? How could she save her child? A sudden idea flashed across her mind. She saw a young man crossing the street and she pointed him out to the constables as her son.

The constables seized the innocent stranger by the collar and hustled him off to the police station. They brought him before the all-powerful captain.

"Is this your mother?" asked the official, pointing to the old woman.

"No, sir!" replied the young man.

"Twenty-five lashes!" thundered the captain.

The young man was thrown to the floor and the constables began to belabor him with the knout.

When they reached the count of fifteen, the captain again asked:

"Is this your mother?"

"No, sir!" the young man replied again.

"Work away!" bellowed the captain.

A few Jews, who happened to be present, looked on at this savagery and finally one of them said to the victim:

"What a fool you are! Why don't you say she is your mother, and they'll stop beating you? Otherwise, they'll flog the life out of you."

The young man saw that he really had no alternative, and so he cried out:

"Yes, captain, the old lady is my mother."

"In that case," replied the captain, "you must sign a statement that you will give your mother four gulden a week for her maintenance."

The victim signed the statement and was released from custody.

Zunser concluded his narrative with the words: "We Jews in Russia are in about the same situation as the young man. Pogroms are inflicted on us; we are flogged; we are forced to pay taxes; and we are made to shout: 'This is our mother!'"

The parable made a profound impression upon the deputies. Several of them were near to tears.

The emotional tension it created was all the greater because there was no alternative for the Jewish community of Vilna. The text of the eulogistic address could not be altered. It had to be forwarded exactly as written by Cahan.

Zunser was conscious of the risk he was running in expressing subversive thoughts and sentiments. But, on the other hand, how could he maintain silence when on every trip out of Minsk he saw fresh examples of the Government's injustice and cruelty? Looking back upon his years under Alexander III, he remarked:

> Daily my heart bled when I saw my unfortunate Jewish brethren lying on the ground like innocent lambs under the the knives of the slaughterers, and I protested publicly with all my vigor against the savagery of the regime toward an

entire people. I was in a constant ferment of agitation, in a ceaseless state of anxiety. I expected to be arrested at any moment.

Zunser did not yearn to be a martyr. He did not relish an involuntary trip to some Arctic province. Hence, he avoided encounters with the police, whenever possible.

A. Litvin recalled Zunser's circumspection at Vilna, where the young Zionists arranged a meeting at which the famed bard was to appear and to sing newly composed national songs. The meeting had been camouflaged as a religious ceremony, and the members of the Khoveve Zion circle spread word secretly to one another that Zunser would come. Only a small group was expected. But when the doors were opened, crowds began to drift in. Soon every seat was occupied and hundreds milled about the entrance. Men and women peered through the doors and the windows to catch a glimpse of the poet. But Zunser did not show up, and word had to be passed around that a singer would substitute for him. The audience, which had waited patiently until ten o'clock, began to disperse at this disappointing news. Actually, Zunser had arrived on time but, when told that the police had become inquisitive because of the size of the crowd, he had quietly slipped away in order to avoid possible, unpleasant repercussions.*

In the mid-1880's, when Zunser felt the eyes of the police upon him, he composed lyrics which dealt with generalities and so-called eternal problems rather than with specific abuses that might call down retribution upon his head. The very titles of these philosophic poems were to serve as an index of their political innocuousness: *The Keys to the Heart* (*Die Hartz-Shlisslen*), *The Moon* (*Die Levono*), *To the Stars* (*Zu die Shteren*), *The Contract* (*Der Kontrakt*), *Contrasts* (*Die Kontrasten*).

The Keys to the Heart was a poetic parable which linked events at the birth of the universe with happenings of con-

---

* A. Litvin, *Eliakum Zunser*, Zukunft, 1940, XLV, 114-119.

temporary life. On the morning of the sixth day of creation, after having fashioned all the beasts of the earth, all the birds of the air, and all the things that creep and crawl and swim, the Lord decided to attempt the shaping of a new species, a middle species between ape and God, a composite species that would contain characteristics of every living creature.

> All traits in him will now be found:
> Of wolf and lion, bee and cat,
> Of snake and spider, cock and hound,
> Of horse and jackal, fly and rat;
> With mind to pierce the universe,
> To scan the heavens and the earth,
> To know the better from the worse,
> And brood on life and death and birth.

Unfortunately, God did not mix in equal proportions the materials which were placed at his disposal by all the living things. He used whatever was nearest at hand. As a result, human beings did not emerge with identical characters and tastes. They were not uniform like drops of rain or blades of grass. They did not harmonize with each other. One was more snakelike and another more foxy, one was more sheepish and another more piggish, depending upon the way the elements were mixed in him. From the actions of a person, it should be possible, however, to discover which animal predominated in him. Zunser, therefore, proceeded to outline, in the thirty stanzas of the poem, the various types of human behavior. These were the keys that unlocked for us the recesses of the heart and enabled us to penetrate to the beastly or saintly core within each being.

> To you, my friends, I give a key,
> Into their heart of hearts to reach.
> May God preserve you ne'er to be
> With vermin, cattle, wolf, or leech;
> But, if you must consort with them,
> This key will tell you whence they stem.

The Contract was also composed in the mold of a poetic fable. It spanned the vast reaches of time from the creation of the universe to its ultimate extinction. Its basic idea was as follows:

When God fashioned the world, he established a balance between matter and man. He permitted the human species to receive from earth exactly as much as it returned. As long as man's tastes were primitive and simple and as long as he contented himself with little, the duration of his life was nine hundred years and more. But when his wants increased and he demanded of earth greater luxuries, finer dwellings, gaudier dress, he used up his account in a shorter space of time. His maximum life-span was reduced to a mere three hundred years. As the centuries rolled on and man exploited the earth at an ever faster tempo, the years of his life continued to shrink more and more. To live in six rooms rather than in one meant to use up six times as much of earth's bounty. It meant to fell much more wood for firelogs and for furniture. It meant to clear the forests at a faster rate than they could be replenished, and thereby to hasten the process of erosion. The earth, denuded of its soil, ores, and stored-up treasures, was becoming withered and anemic, devoid of fat, and lacking its pristine strength. A time could be foreseen when our entire planet would be over-populated, when every village would be a city, every mountain drained of coal, and every forest reduced to a desert. Perhaps the span of life would then be limited to a single decade. The human species, continuing its parasitical way of life and consuming more than it produced, would grow ever more feeble. It would ultimately disappear and be replaced by a new grouping of the eternal elements. For, God's law was immutable. This law, or contract, insisted on a balance of forces. It did not tolerate abuse of God's resources.

In the poem *The Moon*, Zunser let the terrestrial satellite look down upon earth and survey the strange phenomena of conscious life here below. As earth's nearest neighbor and as its traveling companion for countless aeons, the Moon bewailed the outrages that daily came into view. The crawling little microbes that called themselves human beings were spending their lives quarreling, intriguing, and trying to wrest from one another bits of the earth, which was, after all, their common heritage, God's gift to them. The climax of cruelty was reached when a tyrant set upon a weak people, desecrated its name, deprived it of its natural rights, denied it elementary justice, and drove it out into unknown regions. The poem ended with a prayer by the Moon for a cloud to appear and to veil from its sight the deeds of horror and shame perpetrated on the earth.

To the Stars, composed in the same year as *The Moon*, resembled the latter poem. The earth reported on the state of civilization attained on its surface and inquired of the stars whether conditions were better there. Assuming that the stars also harbored a human species, the poet wondered whether it too was divided into quarreling nations and races, each armed to the teeth and each eager to drench the soil with the blood of its neighbors. Did the stellar beings succeed in solving the mystery of existence or were they still groping in darkness and ignorance? Were they feeding on each other, the stronger consuming the weaker? Did justice prevail among them, or was bribery as rampant as on our globe, clouding the face of justice? Were honesty, simplicity, uprightness their ideals, or had they too learned to betray and to deceive? Did they enjoy social equality, or did they also suffer from a caste system, with the noblemen despising the serfs and the rich the poor? Were they blissfully unaware of religious hatred, or did they too destroy peoples in the name of God? The poet ended with a prayer for the early fulfillment of the messianic Jewish dream, for the coming of the reign of universal peace, justice, and good will on earth, the era foretold by the prophets of old, when swords would be turned into plowshares and sorrow would be banished from our midst.

Although Zunser's philosophic poems deal with universal problems, they still manage to include allusions to the specific situation faced by the Russian Jews. But these allusions are, of necessity, veiled in nebulous symbolism and deliberate ambiguity in order to lull the suspicion of censors. They are forceful and clear only when Zunser speaks to the conscience of his own people, calling attention to their acquired faults, and urging them to cleanse themselves of moral impurities.

In the poem *Contrasts*, for example, Zunser begins with the generalization that in nature opposites are mutually exclusive. Thus, fire and water cannot exist together. Each must war upon the other, and only one of them can be victorious. From this generalization, the poet proceeds to a discussion of the Jewish heart, in which contrasting qualities do exist side by side, in contradiction to the universal law. The amazing contrasts in the character of the Jew include his groveling humility before Gentiles and his arrogance at the synagogue when communal honors are at stake; his thrift and temperance, on the one hand, and his extravagance in dress and finery, on the other; his charity towards the sick and needy, and his ruthlessness towards a business rival; his gregariousness and his disunity; his capacity for martyrdom in defense of his faith, and the ease with which he abandons this faith when it is no longer under attack. Enumerating these contrasts, the poet ends each stanza with the refrain: "Believe me, my people, I do not understand you."

In the poetic sermon *After the Latest Fashion (Nokh dem neisten Jhurnal)*, Zunser again assails Jewish follies and aberrations, Jewish aping of foreign fashions and mannerisms. He approves educational innovations, the teaching of secular subjects such as English, physics, geography, and mathematics; but he regrets that the newest fashion in education is accompanied by a negative attitude towards the sacred tongue, towards Biblical studies, and towards Jewish history and religion. He points out that good manners require us to be chivalrous to women, but that the latest fashion modifies this to mean chivalry to young and pretty women only. He agrees that a father should consult his daughter before giving her hand in marriage, but he holds that the latest fashion goes too far in permitting a girl to choose a husband in total disregard of a father's wishes. It is just that women should enjoy equal rights with men, but the latest fashion is to be deplored, which encourages women to look upon themselves as the superior sex and to treat their mates as slaves and underlings. It is an enrichment of a Jew's personality, if he sloughs off old prohibitions against attending dramatic and operatic performances. The latest fashion, however, goes too far, if it encourages men, and especially unaccompanied married women, to frequent cabarets and masquerade-balls. Tolerance towards one's neighbors is desirable, but the latest fashion interprets tolerance of others to imply intolerance towards one's own kind. As a result, Jewish self-hatred is on the increase.

The sermonizing tone characteristic of Zunser's philosophic verses also dominates the poem *Moses and His Generation* (*Moishe mit sein Dor*). Zunser starts with the assumption that the greatness and the weakness of the Jews have not changed throughout their long history, and then he proceeds to prove this generalization. He points out that when Moses, the leader and lawgiver of Israel, emerged from Pharaoh's palace, the first sight that greeted his eyes was that of an Egyptian beating an Israelite; the second, that of two Israelites fighting each other. This pattern has prevailed ever since. The Jewish people may be compared to a ship on fire in midsea. This ship is threatened both by waves of hatred—anti-semitism—raging ouside, and by fires of discord and dissension raging on board. Nevertheless, miracle of miracles, the people survives. After thousands of years, it shows no trace of age or feebleness. It is as youthful and energetic as when it was first established as a nation under Moses at Sinai and in the desert. Israel is eternal. "I see in thee again the generation that emerged from the desert. Ageless art thou and young shalt thou remain unto the end of time."

Zunser's faith in the eternal destiny of his people was unshakable. It is true that much of his poetic effort seemed to be devoted to castigating the Jews for their moral faults and their erring ways. But this was only because he expected of them a Utopian or divine standard of ethical conduct and cooperative living. His audiences sensed this and did not falter in their affection for him. He resembled in this respect the prophets of old, who were forever thundering against Israel's waywardness and religious backsliding, despite the fact that spirituality and morality were considerably further advanced in the ancient Jewish commonwealth than among its neighbors.

Zunser dreamed that in Palestine a state based on the Biblical principles of justice, tolerance, and labor would arise as a haven for Jews from lands where they were unwanted and unhappy. In his fiftieth year, he still hoped that he himself could begin with his family a pioneer's rugged existence on the holy soil. Fate, however, willed otherwise. Though his eyes were turned to the East, necessity drove him to the West. His life's pilgrimage was to end not in Israel but in the New World.

CHAPTER XVI

America Bound

I N 1886 Zunser celebrated his fiftieth birthday and the twenty-fifth anniversary of the publication of his first collection of songs, *Shirim Khadoshim*, which had launched him upon his successful career as the People's Bard.

The Circle of Eliakum at Minsk decided to honor this occasion. S. L. Zitron and Yehuda Zev Nefach sent a communication to the principal centers of the Khoveve Zion movement. They called attention to the impetus that Zunser's songs had given to the movement from its inception, and they suggested that organizations throughout Russia participate in the celebration by sending congratulatory messages to the Minsk Committee. The response was overwhelming. The telegram from Vilna bore the signatures of Samuel Joseph Finn, the historian of the Jewish community, Lev Levanda, the repentant Russian novelist, and I. L. Goldberg, the philanthropist. It ended with a Hebrew sentence paraphrasing a verse of Yehuda Halevi: "While we dream the dream of our salvation, you are the violin for our songs." The Warsaw admirers of Zunser included the novelist Jacob Dinezon, and such pioneers of Polish Zionism as Shefer (S. P. Rabinowicz), Yasinovsky, A. S. Friedberg, and Eliezar Kaplan. Moscow sent eulogies by J. M. Pines, who was soon to leave for Palestine as the representative of the Lovers of Zion; the industrialist Wissotsky, who was later to help establish the Haifa Technicum with his magnificent gift;

and the physician E. M. Tchlenov, who was to play an important role in political Zionism from the first Basel Congress in 1897 until his death in 1918, a few months after the Balfour Declaration. From Odessa, the Hebrew writer M. L. Lilienblum, who had been transformed in 1881 from an assimilationist to a fiery champion of Jewish rebirth in the Holy Land, hailed Zunser as the poet of Zion. From Kovno, from Riga, from Libau, and other cities came additional messages of praise. A moving letter from David Gordon, the editor of *Hamagid*, was read to the Minsk gathering by the presiding officer, Rabbi Abraham Khanalish. Zunser was deeply touched as he listened to the words of affection by his admirers. When he arose to reply, he spoke for an entire hour in rhymed verses and concluded most effectively with the oath of the Psalmist: "If I forget thee, O Jerusalem, may my right hand wither!"

In the same year, Zunser was feted at Warsaw. Jacob Dinezon, who was among the sponsors of this evening, brought Abraham Goldfaden along as his guest. When Zunser sang some of his songs of Zion, Goldfaden was very much impressed and voiced his admiration. A friendship, free of pettiness and envy, began between the two popular minstrels, which was to endure until death.

Reports have also come down of Zunser evenings in other towns during the years immediately following. L. S. Gamze, the Dvinsk correspondent of the Hebrew press, discussed in an article the phenomenal success of Zunser's Zionist songs when recited by the poet to a large audience in that town's big theatre. When an article directed against Zunser appeared in the influential Hebrew organ *Hazfira*, Gamze replied with a spirited defense of the bard.

In Kovno, the poor people complained in 1888 that they could not honor their adored poet, because the tickets of admission were too high. A second evening, therefore, had to be arranged. The proceeds of both evenings were contributed to the Khoveve Zion movement. A letter of appreciation by the Kovno Zionists contained the following sentences in Hebrew:

PHILIP AND ELIAKUM ZUNSER, 1890

"Your precious words, which glow with love for our unhappy people and its land, the cradle of our historic life, were not uttered in vain. They have brought forth fruit. You have breathed the breath of life into our dry bones. You have transformed us."

Zunser was much in demand throughout 1888. He gave successful concerts at Homel, Suvalki, Lomzhe, Tomashev, and Lublin. At a concert in the theatre of Riga, he made the acquaintance of the famous cantor Boruch Leib Rosovsky, father of the Palestinian musicologist Salomo Rosovsky. Sixty years after the concert, the latter still remembered the great enthusiasm with which the audience greeted such songs as *The Plow, The Aristocrat,* and especially *Shivas Zion.* Zunser was able, through the medium of his art, to buoy up the flagging hopes of the Lovers of Zion, who were becoming depressed because of the inadequate results of years of strenuous efforts to colonize the Holy Land.

The following year, however, Zunser sensed a growing apathy towards the ideas he espoused. The Zion movement was experiencing a crisis. Leo Pinsker, its dynamic leader, was forced to retire for reasons of health. Achad Haam launched an attack upon its entire ideology and method of approach in a sensational article in *Hamelitz* on March 4, under the provocative title: *This Is Not the Way (Lo Zeh Haderekh).* Theodor Herzl, the theoretician of political Zionism, had not yet appeared upon the scene and the feeling was growing that Palestine could not, within a reasonable time, offer a solution to the physical distress of Russian Jewry. The average man, who had affiliated himself with Zionist groups because he wished to emigrate to Palestine, was not enthusiastic about Achad Haam's efforts to solve the spiritual distress of the Jews. He turned his eyes to America as the more promising land, which was ready to receive him immediately.

A mixture of motives—fear of the police, temporary decline of Zionist agitation, changing public taste—led Zunser in the fall of 1889 to contemplate a concert tour of America. Palestine still remained the goal of his longing. But, until his Palestinian plans matured and colonization in Gederah or in some other new settlement along the Mediterranean proved practical, America appeared the most promising home for the immediate future.

Zunser's plans for his trip across the Atlantic were kept secret from all except his closest friends as long as possible. One evening in October, just before he was to leave, he invited the members of his literary circle to his home. The doors were locked in fear of eavesdropping secret police, and then the poet broke the news to his friends. When someone inquired why he was leaving so abruptly, since the main incentive did not seem to be financial, he replied by reciting the verses of a ballad he had just composed, entitled *The Three Doves (Die drei Toiben)*.

The action of the ballad took place a decade before the expulsion of the Jews from Spain. Only the first clouds of the coming storm were as yet visible. Most Jews believed that the efforts of the Inquisition to destroy Jewish freedom would fail, especially since Jews had recently risen to high military and political positions and were bringing blessings to the land.

In that year of 1482, a Jewish patrician of great wealth invited his friends to a farewell banquet. When the feasting and the toasting were over, the question was put to him, why he was leaving the city of Madrid where he had evidently prospered. In lieu of an answer, the host invited his guests to an upper room which contained three cages. In the first cage, a lively dove was hopping about. In the second lay an enfeebled dove, plucked of its feathers from head to foot. In the third was a dead dove, also bereft of all feathers. The patrician explained that these doves symbolized the three stages through which Jewish life in Spain was likely to pass. It was true that the Inquisition had not yet unfolded its entire dangerous program, but he preferred to get out in time, while he was still free and in full possession of his wealth and feathers. The Jews who did not leave voluntarily would before long be stripped of their capital and houses and would be forced into exile against their will. There would still remain, however, a third group of Jews. These would change their religion because of their love for everything Spanish, but theirs would be the worst fate of all. They would end at the stake as unwilling martyrs at autos-da-fé.

Zunser himself did not want to wait for the second or third stage. He called upon his coreligionists to heed the parable of the three doves and to emigrate from Russia at the earliest possible moment.

When Zunser in 1889 began a correspondence with the Khoveve Zion group in New York, he at first had in mind only a concert tour of America, but he was soon led to consider a longer stay in the New World. His friends who had exchanged Russia for America painted in glowing colors the free and secure life of Jews in the land of unlimited opportunities. There pogroms were impossible. There a person was not subjected to discrimination because of his origin, nor did anyone need to fear imprisonment because of a mere expression of opinion. There children of immigrants could obtain a free education to the fullest extent of their mental capacities.

To Zunser, whose oldest son Philip was sixteen and whose other children were of school age, this last consideration carried much weight. In the fall of 1889, Philip was at Vilna, where he had been apprenticed to an engraver and where he was also studying the violin. He received word from his parents at Minsk to come home immediately. When he arrived, he was told that he was to leave with his father for America. His joy was boundless. He would no longer have to dread several years of service in the army of the hated Czar. He would be with his father in a land of marvels, a country where adventurous youth could make quick headway. He would help to prepare a new home for his younger brothers and sisters.

The thoughts that coursed through the minds of father and son as they set out across the Atlantic found expression in the song *Columbus and Washington*, begun by the bard during his last days in Minsk and completed on board ship.

The two historic figures were hailed as among mankind's greatest benefactors, because Columbus discovered and Washington fought victoriously for a continent where unfortunate men and women of all nations could find refuge and freedom. Each of the six long stanzas into which the song was divided recounted the fate of a typical European person or group that had reason to bless the two heroes. Thus, the artisan, who labored diligently but who was not allowed to enjoy the products of his toil, turned to America and there his diligence was rewarded most handsomely. The honest burgher, who was wrongly accused by professional informers and who faced years of imprisonment as a result, escaped with wife and child to the secure haven beyond the Atlantic. The maiden, who deserved a fine husband but who could not obtain one for lack of a sufficient dowry, left Europe for the land of opportunity, where dowries were less important than genuine gifts of personality. The bankrupt, who feared a debtors' prison, preferred the risk of making a fresh start on the new soil and was soon prospering as a respectable American citizen. The Jewish actor, plagued by the Russian police for performing in the forbidden Yiddish tongue, followed the stream of emigration westward and was soon performing on a stage where his tongue was not scorned and where there was neither censorship nor any other restriction of free speech. All these persons and a host of other human beings, liberated from European gloom, invoked blessings upon Columbus and Washington.

Upon Zunser's arrival at Castle Garden, the receiving station for immigrants in New York, he was met by a large delegation of the Khoveve Zion group as well as by other admirers. A concert had been arranged for him at the Turnhalle on the East Side of New York. Two weeks after his landing, he faced his first audience. The evening must have been successful, because a manager undertook to arrange an entire series of concerts for him in several of the large cities in the East and the Middle West.

At Rochester the greater part of the Jewish population

turned out to hear him. At Pittsburgh he was less successful, because of an unfortunate misunderstanding. A rabbi, who resented Zunser's failure to pay a courtesy call upon him, announced to his congregation that anyone attending the scheduled concert would be excluded from the synagogue. He gave as a reason the fact that a few tickets had allegedly been sold on the Sabbath, a serious infraction of a religious regulation.

At Cleveland a more dangerous incident occurred. The theatre had been sold out. Zunser appeared on the stage and recited some of his best-known songs. Soon he noticed a growing restlessness in the audience. He was somewhat disconcerted, but continued to the end. When he came out of the theatre, he found a large crowd gathered at the exit. He heard a voice: "It isn't the real Eliakum! . . . He is an impostor." He heard other voices shouting: "Let's lynch him!" The crowd kept on increasing and was becoming more menacing with each moment. A woman, who had known him in Minsk, recognized him and was ready to vouch for his identity, but nobody listened to her. She did manage to draw him back into the theatre and enabled him to escape through a stage exit. Before daybreak, she brought him to the railroad terminal and saw him leave town safely. Later on, Zunser learned that the ugly rumor that he was an impostor had been spread by his own manager. The tour was nearing its end and the shrewd, unscrupulous entrepreneur sought to avoid payment. When Zunser asked for an accounting in Cleveland, the manager planned the near-riot and got away with the entire proceeds.

When Zunser returned to New York, he was invited by representatives of the Yiddish press to contribute a few of his songs. Unversed in the politics of the New World, he gladly assented and soon found himself in trouble.

The Russian-Jewish intellectuals were then espousing various radical causes. In the closing days of 1889, they had convoked a national conference on the lower East Side of New York in order to compose their divergent views. This conference ended in an uproar on January 2, 1890, when the assembled delegates divided almost evenly between a Socialist and an Anarchist wing. These two groups then proceeded to battle each other vigorously throughout the coming decade. When the Socialists, early in 1890, founded the *Arbeiterzeitung,* the Anarchists followed a few weeks later with an organ of their own, *Die Freie Arbeiter Stimme.* Zunser contributed to the former newspaper, which was the first on the scene; but he saw no reason for rejecting an offer of publication by the latter organ, when it made its appearance. Since the conflict of ideologies was then at white heat and each of the contending parties was anxious to win new recruits, *Die Freie Arbeiter Stimme* published a poem of the immigrant bard under the sensational heading: ELIAKUM ZUNSER IS OURS—AN ANARCHIST.

Among the New York readers of this new gazette was a former resident of Minsk who sent a copy of this issue to his native town. There an unscrupulous informer forwarded the featured poem to the office of the Governor-General of the White Russian province. One day Feigel Zunser received a summons from a high-ranking official to appear for questioning by the government authorities. Not knowing what to expect and fearing a possible raid by the police on her home during her absence, she gathered together whatever manuscripts of her husband she could find and burned them before leaving for the dreaded interrogation. Among the irreplaceable manuscripts, which were thus destroyed, was the only copy of the completed play *A Victim of Caste (A Korbin far Yikhes).*

As a result of her encounter with the authorities, who wanted to know all about her husband's political activities in America, Feigel Zunser realized that it would no longer be safe for him to return to Russia. Although she managed on this occasion by the exercise of her keen wits to extricate herself from the toils of the dreaded police, she determined not to subject herself to similar or worse dangers in the future. She cabled her husband that she intended to join him as soon as possible. She then journeyed to Vilna, her husband's birthplace, in order to obtain the necessary passports for herself and her children. By selling her household belongings, she obtained enough money for passage to America. The bard had left her his accumulated savings of more than ten thousand rubles, a magnificent sum in those days, but this money she wished to retain as a reserve. It gave her a sense of economic security as she set out for the distant continent.

With her five children, Feigel traveled to Berlin and then on to Hamburg. There they boarded the *S.S. Augusta Victoria* of the Hamburg-American Line. After a rather rough voyage of ten days, the vessel docked at Hoboken on August 10, 1890. Nine-year-old Charles was the first to catch sight of his father, who was waiting at the pier, handsomely dressed in a tan topcoat, despite the hot weather.

A tenement flat at 63 Canal Street, in the heart of New York's Jewish district, had been rented and furnished in modest fashion. The reunited family, liberated from fear of Russian officialdom, prepared to enter upon a new existence in the New World.

CHAPTER XVII

Poems of the New World

THE POEMS written by Zunser during his first
years on American soil mirrored the moods and the problems
of adjustment faced by Russian Jewish immigrants in the closing
decade of the last century. Three stages in this adjustment
could be distinguished: idealization, disillusionment, integration.

Jewish immigrants arrived in the New World with a legend
of America constructed out of romantic tales and wishful
dreams, a legend so glowing, so colorful, so entrancing, that
reality could never approach it. Many factors had in the course
of generations entered into the shaping of this legend. Fantastic
narratives of the discoveries and conquests of Columbus, Cortez,
and Pizarro had seeped into the ghetto communities of Eastern
Europe centuries after the actual historic happenings and had
been transformed by popular imagination during this long
interval of time into glamorous visions of towns whose streets
were paved with gold and whose inhabitants were noble savages
devoid of guile. Upon this earliest layer had been superimposed
Utopian concepts garnered by *Maskilim* from Defoe's *Robin-
son Crusoe,* from Rousseau's challenging tracts, and from
Jewish messianic lore. The dreamland beyond the fabled Samba-
tion, where descendants of Moses lived unmolested and unafraid, enjoying the fruits of their labor, was transplanted to the
hemisphere beyond the Atlantic, which was still partly un-
explored and from which ever new marvels were fed to Jewish

readers by popular periodicals and penny booklets. The exploits of George Washington in overthrowing the yoke of a European power and of Abraham Lincoln in emancipating the victims of slavery confirmed Jews in their idealization of America. Zunser's poem *Columbus and Washington* was an embodiment in word and song of the legend of America as seen through the eyes of Russian Jews throughout the nineteenth century.

The second stage through which the immigrant passed was one of disillusionment. The struggle for mere physical survival on the foreign soil was generally much more severe than anticipated. The necessity of working from dawn to sunset and even far into the night in a sweatshop or as a peddler left the newly arrived person little leisure to enjoy the vaunted freedom of America. In the narratives of Abraham Cahan, in the auto-biography of Morris Hillquit, and in the sociological studies of Lillian Wald and Jacob Riis, are found harrowing details of the life of the Jewish masses on the East Side of New York in the 1890's. But the mood of these masses, their disillusionment, their tears of sorrow, and their helpless submissiveness, was best recorded in such songs of Zunser's as *The Golden Land (Dos goldene Land)* and *The Greenhorn (Der Greener)*. These lyrics were sung in factories and courtyards. They were in-toned in tea houses frequented by men and women during cold winter evenings, and on tenement rooftops where families sought refuge from stuffy rooms on sultry summer nights.

The Golden Land contrasts the golden vision of America, entertained since childhood days, and the sad reality of the immigrant's lot. Zunser sees parched lips and tears of despair on faces that crowd the narrow lanes of the New York slums. He notes that in the Golden Land there are individuals who collapse of hunger and families who are thrown out into the gutter when their rent is unpaid. In the Golden Land, a worker's life is of no more account than that of a horse that draws a streetcar. Like a horse, a worker plods on and on until he collapses or is maimed by an accident. In the busy season he labors beyond his strength, and in the slow season he knows

want. Every new machine throws hundreds of honest people
out of work. In the Golden Land, urchins pursue the foreigner
with jeers and blows. The policeman is indifferent to these
pranks and pretends not to notice; but he acts when a poor
peddler seen with a pushcart on a Sunday can be jailed for
breaking a city ordinance. In the Golden Land, industrial
accidents, mine explosions, and tenement fires are a common
occurrence. Children, subjected to factory enslavement, age
quickly. Girls, seeking in marriage an escape from the sweatshop, find the burden of caring for a home and babies and
boarders even worse slavery. Their strength ebbs all too soon
and their blossoming figures wither away.

> Look down upon New York's downtown, where the air
> is pestilential, where human beings are pressed together like
> herring in a barrel. . . . Who can calmly watch children
> jump from streetcars with batches of newspapers in their
> hands, risking their lives for a penny? The bitter need in
> their homes takes them from school prematurely and con-
> demns them to coarseness and ignorance. Yet this is called
> the Golden Land.

Disillusionment with America is also the dominant tone of
The Greenhorn, but Zunser remains an admirer of American
ideas and fundamental political institutions, even when he de-
picts with sadness the difficulties that beset the newcomer. He
compares such a person to a newborn babe that must go through
the diseases of infancy. On board ship the immigrant is vac-
cinated against smallpox; on arrival he contracts the measles.
The vaccination causes only a slight fever, but the measles is
rather unpleasant and may be long-drawn-out. Ignorant of the
language and the customs of his new home, without a trade in
hand, surrounded by strangers, confused and distraught, he is
quickly depressed. Nevertheless, he carries on the hard struggle
for survival.

Zunser surveys the various trades open to a poor immigrant.
He finds it almost axiomatic that every Greenhorn must start

out as a peddler. But a legitimate peddler needs some capital. He has to make an initial investment of at least ten dollars: five dollars for an official license, one dollar for a basket, and four dollars for his stock. Lacking this sum, the immigrant must set out to acquire it as an unlicensed peddler of matches on Hester Street, in constant fear of the police; or as a newspaper vendor, crying out his penny-ware throughout the night; or as a rag-picker with a pack on his back, climbing up and down tenement stairways. He might try to sell lemonade; or he might get a job in a tin factory or as a glazier or as a clothing worker, and survive an apprenticeship without pay, only to find seasonal work at an end just when he was to earn his first wages. Applying for relief to Jewish philanthropy, he will find himself scorned by officials of German-Jewish origin, who regard the influx of Russian Jews as a major catastrophe. Zunser ends with an appeal to his fellow-immigrants to organize for mutual help in a "Jewish Alliance."

The third stage in the adjustment of the newcomer, the successful integration into American life, also found expression in Zunser's songs. These songs do not deal with mere generalities but espouse a definite cause. They seek to promote an exodus of the Jews from the large cities and their rehabilitation on the soil as farmers. This was the main purpose of the "Jewish Alliance," an organization formed in the early 1890's by a group of social workers and publicists. Zunser was one of most active supporters, participated in its conferences, and wrote its hymn.

In August 1890, the very month when Zunser's family landed in America, he joined with several Russian-Jewish intellectuals under the leadership of Dr. Hyman Spevack of Philadelphia in planning constructive aid for the stream of immigrants that were expected to seek refuge from renewed persecutions in Russia. After six months of preliminary discussion and diligent effort to gain the cooperation of the more successfully integrated Jews of German origin, the organizing group called a conference for February 15, 1891, at Philadelphia.

Over a hundred delegates from twenty cities attended. The chairman, Dr. Spevack, formulated the objectives of the Jewish Alliance of America as follows: 1. to end the dole and charity approach towards the immigrants; 2. to discourage Jews from peddling and from concentrating in large cities, where they were exposed to sweatshop conditions; 3. to attract Jews to agriculture by awakening in them a love for the soil. Although these objectives were approved with great enthusiasm and thirty-seven branches of the Jewish Alliance were formed in smaller communities, the movement was short-lived, because it was overshadowed by the establishment of the Baron De Hirsch Fund a few months later. This fund had similar objectives and, with millions of dollars at its disposal, it promised to accomplish much more.

Several of Zunser's poems were written to further the ideals of the Jewish Alliance. The first of these bore the title of the movement and was its campaign song. It pointed out that while Irish and German immigrants were united in federations and were thus able to influence American political life, Jewish immigrants might be compared to scattered and dispersed sheep. They were unable to present a united front to their detractors. Yet, Jews above all other groups needed a strong Alliance to bind them together. Furthermore, while newcomers of all other nationalities settled on the land and founded colonies as centers for their common cultural activities, Jews let themselves be led astray and be exploited in factories and slums by avaricious bosses and landlords. The Alliance would prepare them for a free existence on free soil. In addition, the Alliance would counteract ultra-assimilationist tendencies: the efforts of the younger generation to escape from the faith and the traditions of their fathers. For two thousand dreadful years Jews were deprived of the right which America was at last granting them, the right to band together in autonomous cultural alliances. "Use the time well! Remember: if you make your bed aright, you will sleep as peacefully as all others, but, if you are apathetic now, remorse may come too late, when your sleep is disturbed."

Zunser continued in stanza after stanza to hammer away at the concept that there is strength in unity, that five weak fingers clenched together make a mighty fist, that the pennies of the masses, added together, can accomplish as much as the formidable funds of a philanthropist. The firm will for creative constructive social living was all-important. Achievement would inevitably follow.

The most popular of Zunser's American songs was undoubtedly *The Peddler*. It stressed one of the main objectives of the Jewish Alliance: the liberation of the Jewish immigrants from an occupation generally held in ill repute. This song was far more influential among the masses than all the formal resolutions passed at the Philadelphia Conference. The Yiddish

DER PEDLER

writer Joel Entin reported that, when he arrived in New York
in the spring of 1891, he heard the melody of *The Peddler*
wherever he went. Even the Chinese laundryman played it on
the harmonica. From the lips of old and young came Zunser's
verses portraying the bent figure of the Jew, trudging on with
his heavy pack from lane to lane, up and down dreary tenement
stairs, bathed in sweat, hounded by street-urchins, and jeered by
his somewhat more fortunate neighbors.

> O poets, cease singing of flowers and birds. Such songs
> time has passed over. Such songs may lull children in cradles.
> Our sick crave other, healing pills. Our people are in danger.
> Tensions are rising. Where will this end? Oh, add a note of
> pity to your lyre and lead us to a better path. Could I but
> gaze afar and see the happier days ahead, when the peddler
> will become a farmer and Jews will live united in peace and
> joy! Then my heart would be content and I, the singer of
> *The Peddler*, would sing a Song of the Reaper.

The last of the lyrics inspired by Zunser's interest in
The Jewish Alliance was entitled *Hindsight Comes Too Late*
(*Fersehn-Fershpielt*). In this poem, he called attention, on the
one hand, to the multiplicity of *Landsmannschaften* and lodges
that stimulated nostalgia for communities of the Old World,
the birthplaces of the immigrants, and, on the other hand, to
the utter lack of Jewish political clubs similar to those formed
by the Irish and the Germans of New York. How could one
ask American officials to give due heed to specific problems
faced by the Jewish inhabitants of the metropolis, if the Jews
did not become citizens at the earliest possible moment and did
not exercise intelligently their right to vote and to influence
their government? While it was true that the American constitution guaranteed freedom and equality to all, it was equally
true that reactionary forces were constantly attempting to
annul these fundamental rights. The poem ended with a call for
vigilance.

> Post pickets! Be alert! Know what goes on all about you!

Your foes neither slumber nor rest. Their mutterings reach
the White House. Nor is the Constitution unalterable. Truth
grays when falsehood flares. The world has often erred and
strayed. And we have always felt the blows. Be alert! Hindsight comes too late!

The ever-recurring theme of the need for greater unity
among Jews was also the concluding thought of *Our Heritage
of Dissension (Hakhaluka Uamakhlokes)*. Zunser pointed out
that since the division of the ancient Kingdom of David and
Solomon between Rehoboam and Jeroboam, Jews have suffered
greatly from constant division into dissenting groups. They
have the finest heritage in the Book of Books, their source of
strength and inspiration; but they also have the less noble
heritage of rugged individualism, which has resulted in unending
feuds down the centuries. If only they could cease their internal
dissensions, they could enjoy fully the blessings of America, the
sanctuary of freedom.

The failure of the Jewish immigrants to rid themselves of
the unpleasant traits acquired in Eastern Europe and to experience a moral regeneration in the land of unlimited opportunity
filled the poet with anger and sorrow. He lamented the fact
that there were newcomers who forgot all too quickly their
own flesh and blood, their less fortunate brothers abroad, and
who pursued petty personal ambitions and advantages. In the
poem *Summer's Drouth (Bekharbuni Kaitz)*, composed when
America was negotiating a commercial treaty with Russia
despite the Czarist crimes against the Jews, he lashed out against
the callous indifference to moral values when profits were involved, and bewailed his own helplessness as a wielder merely
of verbal weapons.

Zunser felt that a Jewish poet could not afford the luxury
of writing purely for aesthetic enjoyment. A Jewish poet must
ask himself the question: in what way will my song benefit my
people? It was the height of absurdity for a literary spokesman
of a persecuted people to sing of the loves of Jupiter, Mercury,
or Venus, or to transport the modern reader to an Elysian vista

beyond imaginary seas. Zunser was a forerunner of Naturalism, and he defended his position. He maintained that a poet should concentrate on the reality about him, on the landscape of cavernous streets, gloomy tenements, noisy market-squares, and belching smokestacks. He should aspire to photographic veracity and vivid clarity. He should reproduce honestly the poverty and wretchedness about him, the brutality of dominant power, the inspiring humanity that coursed through the hearts of the weak and oppressed. He should personify contrasting qualities, such as justice and injustice, truth and falsehood. He should place these personified abstractions on the stage and have them engage in controversies modeled upon actual situations of daily life. Above all, a poet should always ask himself before beginning to write: whom will my song profit? For, to seek merely for beauty in a song was as foolish as to seek merely for good looks in a bride. More solid and more lasting qualities were also needed. No matter how sublime a verse might appear at first glance, unless it also taught a moral lesson, it must be likened to hollow noise, to glittering tinsel, to a momentary dream that left the heart empty and unsatisfied. If this conclusion applied to poetry in general, how much more so to Yiddish poetry written for Jews who were everywhere victimized!

Shame and scorn is our share; hunger, need, and pain our daily lot. Here we are driven forth with cudgels and there the doors are closed to us. We fare far worse than in medieval days, for if a Jew was then expelled from one land, he was received with open arms in another. Today, however, all gates are tightly barred and locked, from the frozen Arctic to the torrid Equator. A beast has arisen that feeds on Jews, a monster that kills with its foul breath, its sharp fangs, its vicious claws. Its throat spews poison in all directions and it spawns eggs wherever it moves. Not a corner of the globe is unaffected by its ravages. It swims across the Atlantic and often appears in our midst. Yet, in this hour of distress, there are Yiddish poets who still fail to ask themselves: how does my song help my people?

Standing: JACOB ADLER (B. KOVNER), JOEL SLONIM, JACOB MARINOFF, JOEL ENTIN
Seated: YEHOASH (SOL BLOOMGARDEN), ELIAKUM ZUNSER, MORITZ WINCHEVSKY

Zunser refused to yield to self-deception. If hypocrisy, false-hood, and cruelty flourished supreme among the human species, this fact had to be faced honestly. If the two-legged creatures, even in the free atmosphere of America, were still motivated by selfishness, avarice, and lust for power, more was to be gained by exposing these unpleasant tendencies than by denying their existence. Zunser did so by means of specific illustrations, as in his song *The Three Stages* (*Die drei Stantzies*), one of his few American compositions which did not end on a note of hope, probably because it was written at the height of the depression of 1893.

He himself suffered severely from the economic dislocation of that year. Ever since the arrival of his family, he had found it increasingly difficult to eke out a living for its members purely by creative work as a writer and on concert tours. The birth of his youngest daughter Sadie had added to his responsibilities at a time when he was least able to assume new ones. Fortunately, Feigel had managed to retain unspent the ten thousand rubles that she had brought from Minsk, and this money—five thousand dollars—could now be invested in some enterprise.

The poet had never been averse to earning his bread by manual labor. In this respect, he followed in the footsteps of great Jewish sages, who preferred to engage in a trade or handi-craft so that they might devote their leisure hours to the rab-binate without compensation and thus be better able to resist any undue influence by the rich and powerful members of their communities. Though already in his mid-fifties, Zunser took the bold step of starting out in a new business. He set up a printing shop at 138 East Broadway on New York's lower East Side. There he worked day after day, year after year, assisted for a time by his oldest son Philip, and by George Offin, his oldest daughter's husband, a typesetter, while his other children were completing their schooling. The family had moved from its original home on Canal Street to new quarters at 162 Henry Street, two blocks away.

By 1894 the economic depression had run its course, and

the healthier mood of cautious optimism communicated itself
to Zunser. In his poem for the Jewish calendar year 5654, he
speculated on the inscrutable mystery of God's universe and
expressed the wish that he, though a mere human being, could
some day fathom this mystery and return to his work on earth
among the people here below.

As the singer of the masses, Zunser continued to voice their
grievances in the New World as he had done in the Old. When
efforts were begun to unionize the sweatshops and to improve
the harsh working conditions then prevailing, Zunser wrote
poems in behalf of the proletarians and against their exploiters.
These poems, however, lacked the revolutionary ardor found
in the contemporary Yiddish lyrics of Moritz Winchevsky,
David Edelstadt, or young Morris Rosenfeld. One poem, of
which nine stanzas have survived in manuscript form, was
entitled *The Lament of a Rich Manufacturer (Die Kinos fun a
reikhen Manufacturer)*. It had many structural resemblances to
Zunser's earlier song *Der Izborshtchik*. It voiced an employer's
grief at the loss of his former unlimited power over his employees since the latter had become organized and were cowing
him with their threats of a strike. These helpless creatures of
yesterday, whom he was wont to call "hands," had suddenly
sprouted "heads" and were no longer helpless.

Since Zunser's social poetry was not wedded to a single
political or ideological movement, he was no less popular among
the Socialists and Anarchists than among the pioneers of
American Zionism. All were his friends. None spoke or wrote
unkindly of him. Many sought his advice. Some imitated his
literary style and utilized his melodies for their own texts.
Abraham Cahan, who in the 1890's was already a leader among
the Jewish Socialists, composed his only Yiddish lyric, *The
Operator*, to the melody of Zunser's *The Plow*.* The text was
sold in the New York shops by peddlers at two cents a copy.
The music did not have to be reproduced, since Jewish workers
were familiar with the Zunser melody. Morris Rosenfeld also

* *Forwerts*, June 6, 1948.

found, in the 1890's, that the vogue of his poems could be increased by adapting them to Zunser's music.

The shop of the aging bard, at 138 East Broadway and,
somewhat later, at 156 East Broadway, became a center for the
Yiddish-speaking intellectuals of all shades of opinion. The
Circle of Eliakum thus rearose on new soil and with a new
membership. Charles Zunser, in his recollections of the stimulat-
ing years at the turn of the century, listed some of the visitors.

Here came Morris Rosenfeld, then a rising young labor
poet, with a shock of black, curley hair and burning eyes,
to read his early effusions to one he greatly admired. Here
came Leo Wiener of Harvard to gather material for his
forthcoming book *History of Yiddish Literature in the
Nineteenth Century*. Here came Moritz Winchevsky, poet
and rebel. Here came Abraham Goldfaden, who had visited
father in Minsk and now, an aging but still handsome dandy,
with a roving eye for beauty. Here came Shomer, the
pioneer novelist and for a time business competitor—for he
too attempted to make a living out of a printing shop,
though with marked unsuccess. Little did father and mother
think that their son, the writer of these recollections, would
later fall deeply in love with the novelist's daughter Miriam.
Abraham Cahan, now the venerable editor and novelist, then
a fiery rebel and crusader for the Socialist cause, came often.
Some of the non-Jewish literati came in search of local color,
having heard in some way of the last of the troubadours,
who was living out his last days on the East Side. Of these,
Hutchins Hapgood best caught the essence of the man and
his message in his fine book *The Spirit of the Ghetto*. Here
too came Will Carlton, the poet and friend of Walt Whit-
man, and one day he brought along Edwin Markham.
Edward King, editor of the *Sunday Journal* of pre-Hearst
days, was brought in tow by Joseph Barondess, orator and
fiery tribune. King later wrote a novel *Joseph Zalmonoh*,
in which father was a leading character. Later also came the
newer Yiddish writers: Yehoash, Abraham Reisen—long an
ardent devotee—and Sholem Asch, who said that to him
Eliakum Zunser was always a legend, not a living being, and

that now he was coming face to face with the legend. Here too came young Abba Hillel Silver, Abraham Feldman, Barnett Brickner, Morris Rothenberg, and other youths who subsequently attained fame in American Jewry. They were then members of a Zionist youth club, and placed printing orders for their society "The Flowers of Zion," and talked to father.

To this formidable list can be added Peter Wiernik, literary editor of the *Jewish Morning Journal* and historian of American Jewry, the columnist David Hermalin, the poets Naphtali Herz Imber, author of Israel's national hymn, *Hatikva*, M. M. Dolitsky, Jacob Marinoff and Joel Slonim, the critic Joel Entin, the humorists Tashrak and Kovner, the Hebraic wit Gershon Rosenzweig, the journalists Mordecai Danzis, A. Litvin, Kalman Marmor, Professor George Selikovitch, and Johann Paley. The last-named was editor of the newspaper *Volksadvokat*, and his association with Zunser dated from 1890 when both were involved in a public debate concerning the establishment of Jewish colonies in Zion. Paley had expressed doubt as to the wisdom of continuing Zionist agitation in America. Zunser's reply, written seven years before Herzl launched the political movement on a world-wide basis at the First Basel Congress, defended the basic concepts of Zionism and foresaw the revolution in Jewish life everywhere that could ultimately result from the success of the first modest ventures at Palestinian colonization.

Paley had characterized the proponents of Zion as impractical visionaries who suffered from the delusion that Jews could establish a state of their own in the land of Israel. Zunser countered that, while it was still premature to speak of a Jewish state, there was nothing absurd about the idea itself. In the first place, several new states had already come into existence in the territory of the Ottoman Empire in recent generations: Rumania, Bulgaria, Serbia, and Montenegro. It was not impossible that a comparatively small section of the vast land mass of Asia Minor should some day be set aside for Israel. In the

second place, history had shown that the Jews were never safe
for long periods of time among Christian nations, while they
were always treated tolerably in Moslem countries.

Every Christian child is conditioned from infancy to
dislike Jews. This dislike remains, even though the grown-up
may afterwards cease to believe in Jesus. The best proof
may be seen in Germany and Austria, where many of the
anti-semites are professors and students, who had high
academic training. The Jew can find a secure home only
among those nations who do not worship a God supposedly
tortured and crucified by his forefathers. Turkey is such a
nation. In the Koran there is no trace of Jew-hatred. In
Eretz Israel, therefore, a secure Jewish home can be erected.

In analyzing Paley's pronouncement that America had
solved the problem of Jewish homelessness by granting freedom
to all nationalities, Zunser warned against jumping to conclusions. America had indeed gone further than other countries in
incorporating humane laws in its statute books, but anti-Jewish
prejudice still persisted to a considerable extent.

We know enough editors who daily incite the populace
against the Jew, and we are certain that more editors would
join in if it would not hurt their business. We have as yet no
guarantee that the calm days we are now experiencing in
America will always remain. If hostility towards us should
ever flare up in America, the aftermath would be worse than
in Russia. In the Czarist realm there is a ruler who can put a
stop to outrages by a single word, but in America the government is in the hands of the people who are being fed
anti-semitism by the Germans, the Irish, and other European
immigrants infected by this virus. Today we are blamed for
having too many Socialists in our midst. Later on, a thousand
other reasons will be found. Dark clouds are hovering over
the Jewish future in America. It is not too early for Jews
to get together to consider counter-measures, before hatred
has become too manifest. It is no consolation to be told: it
can't happen here. We heard this in the Hellenistic Period,

in Spain under the Arabs, and elsewhere. And how did these tolerant eras end? Who would believe that in Germany, which produced Goethe, Schiller, Lessing, Börne, Heine, Zschokke, Kant, and Humboldt, and where the Jew Lasker is a leader in the Reichstag, the monster of anti-semitism should arise and spread its pestilential breath over all Europe? Let us, therefore, prepare for ourselves a place of refuge in Palestine, whither we can escape in time of peril. Never will we find lasting peace in the Christian world.

Since Paley agreed with Zunser that there was no hope for the Jews under Czarist oppression and that they would all have to emigrate from Russia in the course of time, the Zionist bard asked what objection there could be if a million less refugees came to America. He himself believed that Palestine might in the distant future offer a healthier economic basis even than America, that the freedom of enterprise of which the United States boasted constituted a great danger for coming generations. Since the government refused to socialize the railroads, the banks, and the basic industries, the growth of trusts, monopolies, and huge capitalistic aggregations was inevitable. In time, big business would swallow and digest the small enterprises, and ultimately America would fall into the hands of a few multimillionaires, perhaps no more than three or four persons. These would dictate policies in accordance with their own interests. Such a development could not take place in Palestine, according to Zunser, since its colonies were founded on the principle of universal labor and cooperative living.

In short, the idea of Palestine is being propagated by practical thinkers. The colonists can rightfully look foward to a brighter future than we can in this country. It is a disgrace that American Jews still show so little sympathy for Zionism and are so overconfident of their future in this free republic, with which they are head over heels in love and for which they are sacrificing their own national past and forgetting their own prophets, heroes, martyrs, poets, philosophers, and lawmakers. Yet, Palestine will be colonized, if need be, without their help. It is only eight years since we have launched the movement and already Palestine has twenty flourishing settlements, whose inhabitants are the happiest and healthiest Jews in the world. Read the letters from Acre, Zikhron Yakob, Rosh Pina, and other colonies, and you will shed tears of joy. The progress made by the settlers there, we in America will never be privileged to see. The children grow up to be heroes. They are of the stuff of the Maccabees. The Arabs fear them. If we here stand aloof and fail to lend our help, they can quote to us the words of Mordecai: "Help will come from elsewhere, but you and yours will be destroyed." May the second half of this Biblical passage never find fulfillment!

The thoughts expressed by Zunser in his dispute with Paley attained poetic formulation in the song *A Missive from Mother Zion (A Brief fun der Mutter Zion)*, composed in 1892. To her children beyond the Atlantic, Mother Zion sought to send cheering news: her offspring were returning to her from various lands of exile; the Biblical tongue was again resounding through her hills and dales; the happy days of King Solomon were again in sight. Only her children in distant America failed to participate in their mother's rejoicing and rejuvenation. They were completely absorbed in forging ahead on the free continent. Alas, experience had demonstrated that increasing Jewish prosperity anywhere was always accompanied by increasing anti-semitism. Though New York had become the largest Jewish community in the world, and the Jews were justly proud of their contribution to its welfare, let them not be forever estranged from ancient Zion. Snow or rain might follow the present fair weather. It would be wise to maintain closer contact with Mother Zion.

Not until the turn of the century did Zunser overcome his fear that America too might be infected with anti-Jewish sentiments infiltrating from European countries where prejudice was rampant. But when year followed year and his pessimistic premonitions were not realized, he was glad to acknowledge that America had achieved the seemingly impossible: it had at last furnished a secure and free home for the eternally wandering exiles from Zion. He, therefore, called upon his coreligionists in America, in a pageant composed for the Fourth of July and performed in New York's Seward Park, to celebrate the American Day of Independence as their second Passover.

Cast away the wanderer's staff! Lift your heads high! Sing the Song of the Fourth more lustily than others! The hearts that pined so long in darkness are more jubilant in the sunlight. See in the Fourth the end of your lamenting! After the years of tyranny and travail, this resplendent day is yours!

The bard of Eastern Europe, who in his mid-fifties had ventured across the ocean in search of a free and dignified existence for himself and his family, had attained the goal of his longing. He had become an integral part of the new cultural and political environment.

CHAPTER XVIII

Last Years

YIDDISH poetry reached its full flowering in the generation before the First World War. Both in Eastern Europe and in the United States lyricists arose who could compose with an elegance of diction, a creative intensity, and an imaginative sweep far beyond the reach of the aging Zunser. The younger writers were, however, conscious of their debt to the Nestor of Yiddish poetry and referred to him as their pioneer and inspirer. He himself felt the urge to compose ebbing away. Although his songs continued to be sung, especially by the older generation, and although his booklets continued to be reprinted both in Vilna and in New York, he himself made no attempt in the twentieth century to enhance his literary reputation.

The hard task of earning a living for his large family occupied all his time and energy. His printing shop was kept open until nine o'clock in the evening. Officers of lodges and fraternal societies, which were being organized by the immigrants in ever increasing numbers, came to him with their leaflets and projected constitutions, often at the end of their workday, and he undertook not merely the printing but also the editing and the proofreading. He assumed responsibility even for the accuracy of the texts of scholarly works and Yiddish treatises. Although he enjoyed this work, he found its manual aspects more and more difficult. Large sheets of paper had to be cut to the required size for visiting cards, handbills, or pamphlets. The seventy-year-old poet still had to bear down on the cutting-machine.

Zunser insisted on working long after his children had grown up and were ready to care for their parents. He recognized that this attitude was old-fashioned, but still he clung to it. In an unpublished poem, *The Correct Way (Der rikhtiger Veg)*, he agreed that the law of nature which required parents to provide for young children also imposed an obligation upon grown-up children to provide for aged parents. He saw this law followed by Americans far more than by Europeans, and he praised it as the correct way of life. He himself, however, preferred to follow another law to his dying day, a law which was no less in vogue in America and which was originally proclaimed by God to Adam, namely, that a man should earn his bread by the work of his hands and the sweat of his brow.

Hutchins Hapgood, who visited Zunser in 1902, portrayed him sitting in his printing office, wearing a small, black cap or *Yarmulke* on his head. "He is a man of about seventy years of age with kind little eyes, a gray beard, and spare, short figure." *

Hapgood and other visitors were especially impressed by his hospitality. About the dining-table in the modest home of the Zunsers would gather not only the members of the family, but also Yiddish writers, musicians, and simpler folk. They would discuss art, politics, and religion, far into the night, sipping hot tea served by Feigel Zunser, Russian style, in tall glasses with lemon and preserves. Feigel's culinary skill earned for her a remarkable reputation in this circle; and people who dropped in at almost any hour of the day or evening knew they would be invited to partake of her delicacies. During these informal gatherings, her husband would often sing his old songs, accompanied on the violin by his son Philip. Sometimes, the entire family and the visitors would join in the choruses, and then the

* Hutchins Hapgood, *The Spirit of the Ghetto*, New York, 1902, pp. 91–98. [In 1902 Zunser was actually in his middle sixties.]

conversation would revert to the happy and tragic incidents in the Old Country that inspired the original texts.

Hutchins Hapgood, a keen observer, witnessed such a scene and set down his impression in these words:

> As the old man read in a chanting tone, he swayed gently backwards and forwards, unconscious of his visitors, absorbed in the rhythm and feeling of the song. There was great sweetness and tenderness in his eyes, facility and spontaneity in the metre, and simple pathos and philosophy in the meaning of what he said. He was apparently not conscious of the possession of unusual power. Famous as he is, there was no sense of it in his bearing. He is absolutely of the people, childlike and simple. . . . Along with the simplicity of old age, he has the maturity and aloofness of it. The feeling for his position as an individual, if he ever had it, has gone, and left the mind and heart interested only in God, race, and impersonal beauty. . . . As he chanted his poems, he seemed to gather up into himself the dignity and pathos of his serious and suffering race, but as one who had gone beyond the suffering and lived only with the eternities. His wife and children bent over him as he recited, and their bodies kept time with his rhythm.

In 1904, eleven years after the opening of the printing shop, silence was beginning to gather about the unassuming poet, as more vigorous voices championed the causes of Zionism, Socialism, and universal enlightenment, for which he had once run great risks in Russia. It was then that the poet Morris Rosenfeld, on the initiative of Shomer, wrote an essay in one of the Yiddish dailies, calling the attention of the Jewish public to the fact that the legendary Zunser was aging, half-forgotten in their midst. The publication of this article evoked an immediate response from other organs of opinion. *The Jewish World* commenced the daily republication of the old, popular poems. Other papers, not to be outdone, printed feature articles and called upon the Jewish leaders to do something tangible for the poet.

At the Educational Alliance, twenty-eight prominent figures
of New York Jewry formed a Jubilee Committee to commemo-
rate half a century of the bard's creative activity, which had
begun in 1855 towards the end of the reign of Czar Nicholas I.
Dr. David Blaustein of the Educational Alliance was chairman
of the committee, which included representatives of orthodox
and reform synagogues; Zionist leaders; editors; theatrical and
literary luminaries; educators; political leaders. The famous
actor and theatrical producer, Jacob P. Adler, told the group
that when he first came to the Jewish stage in his early days,
his repertoire consisted in the main of Zunser's songs.

With the sudden revival of interest in Zunser, Jacob Saphirstein, publisher of the *Jewish Morning Journal*, prevailed upon
him to release for publication his unfinished autobiography,
which he had written for his descendants and had not intended
for a larger audience. When the manuscript appeared in serial
form, however, the interest it aroused was so great that many
readers who had missed the opening chapters wrote to the editor
requesting that it be reprinted. The *Jewish Daily News* urged
an English translation for its English page. Simon Hirsdansky
undertook to translate an abridged form of the text, and, because of the demand of the editor for immediate copy, three
young men volunteered their help. They were Charles Zunser,
son of the bard; Charles Cowen, a young Zionist; and Morris
Raphael Cohen, a graduate student of philosophy, who was
later endeared to thousands of his own students during his
quarter-of-a-century as Professor of Philosophy at the College
of the City of New York. Their translation afterwards appeared
in Anglo-Jewish weeklies throughout the United States and
England, and also in book form under the title *A Jewish Bard*.

Zunser's autobiography is a cultural document of great
value. It mirrors a half-forgotten epoch in Jewish history, the
post-Napoleonic century, when Eastern European Jewry awoke
from its medieval sleep, rubbed its eyes, and set out for dimly
seen, glamorous vistas beyond the Atlantic and on the Eastern
shores of the Mediterranean. Zunser was aware of the symbolic

character of his own personal experiences when he wrote towards the conclusion of his narrative:

My world is nearing its end, my life is almost over, my personal history parallels the history of my people Israel: a little joy, a great deal of sorrow. But, when I look upon my Jewish brethren here in America, when I see how these former Russian slaves have evolved into giants, when I see their growth, their prosperity, their fruition under the benign sun of free America, when I watch them step out on the road of progress, education, art, and industry—tears of joy fill my eyes and together with our great prophet Isaiah I cry out: "For one brief moment have I left you but with great mercy will I gather you together. With wrath have I hidden my countenance from you for a moment, but with mercy everlasting will I enfold you, says the Lord, your Redeemer."

Early in 1905, the Zunser Jubilee Committee went to work with great enthusiasm. The anniversary celebration was held on March 30 at historic Cooper Union.

The large hall was packed to capacity. Just as Dr. Blaustein arose to open the program, the poet himself stepped on the stage, accompanied by his wife. As he took his seat in the easy chair that had been provided for him in the center of the platform, thunderous applause shook the building. Time and again he bowed his thanks, but his admirers literally shouted themselves hoarse.

When order was restored, Dr. Blaustein began:

We are here tonight to do honor to a man whose name has for fifty years been on the tongues of more than six million people. . . . Mr. Zunser has been rightly called the People's Poet. . . .

There are today Yiddish poets, Yiddish playwrights, Yiddish journalists. All say that they were shown the way by Mr. Zunser. . . .

This gathering tonight will encourage him to renewed effort. It is already giving him strength. We realize today, as perhaps never before, all that he has done for us.

Rabbi Samuel Shulman, of Temple Emanuel, the leading Reform Synagogue of New York, spoke next. "Mr. Zunser," he said, "has sung the joy and sorrow of the Jewish heart . . . with the simplicity of truth, the strength of sincerity, the warmth of the poet, and the austerity and sublimity of the thinker. . . . He has been a democratic poet in the best sense of the word."

After a recitation in Yiddish by Abraham Goldfaden, Cantor Abraham Minkowsky sang Zunser's most recent composition, *Elegy on the Death of Herzl*. The audience was deeply stirred, for its grief at the loss of the Zionist leader was still fresh. Masliansky, in one of his great orations, payed tribute both to the bard and to the Yiddish tongue in which he sang. Winchevsky and Rosenfeld, and the actors Jacob Adler and Maurice Moshkowitz paid their tributes, and a scroll was presented by Abraham Liessin and Aaron Grayzel in behalf of the Yiddish Literary Society. Then came the climax of the evening.

Zunser arose to express his appreciation of the love so lavishly showered upon him and was overcome by emotion as he peered into the faces of the hundreds of men and women who had also risen to their feet and who were cheering as if they would never grow weary. Near him on the stage was his wife, radiant with happiness. Before him, in the front row, were his children. Something akin to the old magic fire lit in his eyes. He was finally able to utter his first word and a hush fell upon the crowded hall. His former power to sway audiences, to move them by a glance and a gesture to exaltation and to tears, returned to him. Improvising new words to his famous melody *Shivas Zion*, he expressed in verse his astonishment at the warmth of the reception and his gratification at the sight of people coming en masse to reward a singer, upon whom the sun was setting, for the labors of his early creative years in Russia.

A quarter of a century later, Harold Debrest recalled in the *Jewish Tribune* of December 13, 1929, the impression produced upon news reporters of all creeds at Cooper Union as Zunser sang the songs that had gladdened the hearts of three generations. "Among our neighbors at the Press table in front of the platform were the representatives of every newspaper in Gotham, Jewish and secular. The men and women in the crowded auditorium were laughing and weeping. . . . The young lady on our right, who had been jotting down her impressions, turned to us and tearfully requested that we translate the words. A Gentile reporter from one of the metropolitan dailies, she was carried away by the human intensity of the touching spectacle. Our newly found, valued acquaintance later became a leader in the woman's suffrage movement and the wife of Edward Bjorkman, one of the foremost translators of Norwegian classics in this country."

The evening came to an end with the playing of a potpourri of Zunser's famous melodies by an orchestra under the direction of Barodkin, flutist of the Metropolitan Opera House. Barodkin's father, who had been a *Klezmer* or musician at Minsk, had often accompanied the Badchen Eliakum at weddings in the 1870's and 1880's. As the audience recognized each melody, it bust into applause and joined in, singing and humming.

The Zunser Jubilee of 1905 was the brilliant finale of a long career. Although the bard received invitations from many communities, far and near, that wished to pay him homage, he accepted only one in near-by Philadelphia. He continued to spend his days in his printing shop, still working hard, glad to be able to pay his bills on time and to have a few dollars to turn over to his wife for her household expenses.

On festive occasions, sons and daughters, sons-in-law and daughters-in-law, and an ever increasing number of grandchildren came together for a brief visit and filled his home with gaiety and laughter.

Sadie, who remained with her mother until a year after her father's death, when she married George Hyman of Washington, an ardent admirer of Zunser's and a prominent building contractor, described a typical gathering of the Zunser clan in the paternal home:

> Each little one was as welcome and received as warm a greeting as though he or she were an important visitor. What happy occasions they were! Father would improvise songs for the little children, anecdotes were related, puns and bons mots exchanged and all the members of the family joined in singing some of father's songs and other popular folksongs. When the hour grew late, each member of the family gathered up his own little brood, and after an exchange of greetings and goodbyes, reluctantly took leave of the remaining group.

In the summer of 1907 the aging couple spent several weeks in the Catskills. The beautiful landscape, the pure air, the scent of flowers filled Eliakum with enthusiasm. The following summer he wrote from Colchester, in the hills of Connecticut, to his son Charles: "This is a veritable Garden of Eden."

By 1911 his eyesight began to fail and he was reluctant to leave the bench in front of his shop and the remaining friends with whom he could share common memories.

By 1913 he began to have premonitions of his approaching end. The recollections of his daughter Sadie, still unpublished, are well worth quoting:

> Sitting in Seward Park one evening in early September, 1913, where a crowd always congregated to hear him, and, in fact, gathered in advance, knowing his habit of coming there on warm, summer evenings, he suddenly turned to Mother and said: "Enough! I've had enough!" When both reached home, he handed her his walking stick,which he had come to use on account of his failing eyesight, also his keys, his pocketknife, and prepared for bed. There he stayed for two weeks, refusing food and medicine. He did not wish to recover. Mother nursed him faithfully. On Monday, September 22, after it had been raining hard all morning, he passed away quietly at one o'clock. The rain stopped sud-

denly, the sun broke through and shone into the dark, back room of the small flat, where he had spent his last years. He had, shortly before, made several remarks which showed his desire to pass on to us, whom he was leaving behind, the thoughts that coursed through his mind. For example, "Where am I? I am no longer here, but not yet there." In his last hours, he called for Joseph Barondess, who had charge of a fund that had been collected for the purpose of getting out an edition of his poems. He asked, "With how much am I going to my grave?" When told the amount, about $1,500, he said: "I want that given to my wife, my Feigel." He was ready to let his life's work sink into oblivion in order to give his wife some measure of security. Such was his devotion to her, such was his humility in appraising the value of his own creative work. Later, more than this amount was used by his widow to publish the three volumes of his *Collected Works*.

The funeral took place on September 24. Thousands of Jews crowded the streets from early morning. Hundreds followed the mournful procession, which paused at the headquarters of the Hebrew Immigrant and Sheltering Society. The poet's body was taken into the assembly room for solemn services. Barondess spoke first. Then Masliansky:

> Zunser lived through three eras. He swam in the same river of blood, in which millions of Jews are drowning. He experienced their pain and he always had a word of comfort for his unfortunate brothers. He quickened their tortured hearts with poetic messages of better days ahead.

Dr. Max Girsdansky and Moritz Winchevsky paid their tributes. The funeral procession continued to Williamsburg Bridge and on to Brooklyn's Washington Cemetery. Reserves of two police precincts had to be called out because of the constantly augmented crowds.

The bard was laid to rest near his friends Abraham Goldfaden and David Blaustein. On his tombstone was inscribed a stanza from his *Elegy on Levanda* and a Yiddish verse by

M. Ginsburg which read: "O Passerby, pause in reverence. Here, muted in the dust, lies the faithful voice of his people."

In the following weeks, the Educational Alliance arranged a memorial meeting at which Barondess presided. Its leading participants included Professor Israel Friedlaender, Professor Richard Gottheil, Louis E. Miller, Bernard G. Richards, Jacob Saphirstein, Jesse Isidor Straus, Morris D. Waldman, Judge Samuel Greenbaum, and Abraham Cahan.

Long before his death in the New World, however, Zunser had become a legend in the Old World, where millions of Jews still suffered the agonies to which he had given utterance, and sang his songs of Zion—of ultimate triumph in a land of their own. In answer to their yearning to see and to hear the kind Eliakum, of whom their fathers spoke and whose lullabies their mothers chanted, itinerant pseudo-Zunsers arose in various parts of the Czarist realm. The Yiddish press kept before their interested readers the image of the revered pioneer of modern literature in the tongue of the common man. The colonists of Biro-Bidjan on the banks of the Amur sang his songs of the dignity of labor. The Zionists in Palestine remembered with gratitude his agitation for the homecoming of the Jewish exiles to their ancient motherland. *Chalutzim* in Emek Israel and along the shores of Kinnereth intoned in the revived Hebrew his lyrics *Shivas Zion, Shoshana, Hamkharesheth.*

On the American continent, however, Zunser shared the fate of all his contemporaries whose medium of expression was Yiddish. He became the victim of a growing apathy towards Jewish cultural values. The new, Assimilationist generation that rose to dominance on the American scene between the two World Wars cultivated a negative attitude towards all manifestations of the Eastern European Jewish heritage. It closed its ears to the melodies that had brought tears to the eyes of its forebears. It denuded itself of the folklore and the folkcustoms that might have imparted warmth and beauty to life. It strove to efface all distinguishing characteristics that set it apart from its non-Jewish neighbors; and yet it did not arrest the growth of anti-semitism. It resembled in this respect that generation of Russian Jewry whose tragic awakening Zunser had so poignantly depicted. It resembled also the generation of German Jewry that dreamed of complete immersion in the vaunted *Kultur* of the *Herrenvolk* and that found itself confronted with the nightmare of Hitlerism.

A third Jewish generation is now coming to the fore, a generation reared on American soil. These young American Jews, while risking their lives on far-flung battlefields in behalf of American ideals, came in contact with fellow Jews in various parts of the globe, and learned more clearly to recognize their task as American Jews: to enrich America with Jewish insight into eternal problems, with Jewish wisdom painfully distilled from millennia of historic experience, even as descendants of other immigrants are contributing their cultural gifts to America on the basis of their historic experiences; at the same time as Jews to retain and to strengthen existing links with Zion, the cradle of the Jewish religion and of the Jewish ethnic fellowship.

This was also the final dream of Eliakum Zunser: cultural cross-fertilization of Jews and non-Jews on American soil; integration of Jews as Jews into the American community; renewal of spiritual bonds with Zion and with the children of Israel of all lands of the Diaspora. When this dream ripens to fulfillment, the songs of Zunser may have renewed meaning for American Jews, and the People's Bard will take his rightful place among the progenitors of the contemporary Jewish renaissance.

INDEX